The Other New York

SUNY series, An American Region:
Studies in the Hudson Valley

Thomas S. Wermuth, editor

The Other New York

The American Revolution beyond New York City, 1763–1787

EDITED BY

Joseph S. Tiedemann
and
Eugene R. Fingerhut

State University of New York Press

Published by
State University of New York Press, Albany

© 2005 State University of New York

For information, address State University of New York Press,
90 State Street, Suite 700, Albany, NY 12207

Production by Diane Ganeles
Marketing by Anne M. Valentine

Library of Congress Cataloging-in-Publication Data
The other New York : the American Revolution beyond New York City, 1763-1787 / edited by
Eugene R. Fingerhut and Joseph S. Tiedemann.
    p. cm. — (SUNY series, an American region)
  Includes bibliographical references and index.
  ISBN 0-7914-6371-0 (alk. paper)—ISBN 0-7914-6372-9 (pbk.: alk. paper)
1. New York (State)—History—Revolution, 1775-1783. 2. New York (State)—History—
Colonial period, ca. 1600–1775. 3. New York Region—History, Military—18th century. 4.
New York (State)—History, Local. 5. New York (State)—History—Revolution, 1775–1783—
Social aspects. 6. United States—History—Revolution, 1775–1783—Social aspects. I.
Fingerhut, Eugene R. II. Tiedemann, Joseph S. III. Series.
E263 .N6087 2005
974.7'03—dc22

                                                 2004007225

To
Lyn and Barbara

Contents

Contents

Part III: The Revolution on the Frontier

Illustrations

Illustration

Acknowledgments

We began this project after we had read *Beyond Philadelphia: The American Revolution in the Pennsylvania Hinterland* (1998). Our first thought was to bemoan the fact that there was no such work for New York State. Our second thought was that we should tackle the problem ourselves. New York historians were in the same quandary as were Pennsylvania historians; we knew so much more about the capitol city than we did about the rest of the state. So our first acknowledgment goes to John B. Frantz and Bill Pencak and the other historians who were engaged in the Pennsylvania project. We also owe a very special thank you to Bill for his encouragement and for reading and commenting upon the entire manuscript. The dinners we all enjoyed together while Bill was doing research at the Huntington Library in San Marino, California, were delightful too.

We wish to extend our thanks as well to the authors who contributed chapters to *The Other New York*. They all cooperated fully in the endeavor and made our task of editing a very pleasant one. It was our pleasure to work not only with senior historians in the field but also with younger scholars who are sharing their dissertation research with us. Our hope is that historians of Revolutionary New York will now share a greater sense of community, and that we will all collaborate with one another in the future on new projects.

We are grateful to Vincent Mazzuccelli, Professor Emeritus in the Geography Department of California State University, Los Angeles. Dr. Mazzuccelli prepared the three maps for this volume in the old fashioned manner of hands-on noncomputerized cartography. We also thank Kenyon Chan, former Dean of the Bellarmine College of Liberal Arts, Loyola Marymount University, for graciously covering the cost of producing them.

We also express our deep appreciation to our own families. To our wives, Lyn Fingerhut and Barbara Tiedemann, for amiably sacrificing family time. To Terry, Keith, Mindy, Gady, Shiri, Talia, Karin, Steve, Zachary, and Haley for being there. To Scott, Erika, Michael, Colleen, Hannah, and Emma Tiedemann, who bring constant joy and who good-naturedly and unfailingly put the study of history in the proper perspective.

Introduction

Studies of the Revolution in the northern colonies typically emphasize the demonstrations, crowd actions, and political intrigues that took place in the leading port cities, especially Boston, Newport, Philadelphia, and New York City.[1] These studies have imparted an urban ambiance to the historical literature and have rendered the rural areas as little more than appendages to these colonial cities. Some of this emphasis is justifiable. Colonial officials governed from the port cities, which were usually also provincial capitals and the nexuses between Britain and British North America. Moreover, the imperial policies promoted by the Grenville administration (1763–1765) and the Townshend Program (1767) more immediately affected the economies of, and political power within, these cities than of the farming areas, thereby inciting a greater public reaction in the urban centers than in the countryside.

This urban focus, nonetheless, obscures an essential element of the story and is thus not entirely accurate. At least 93 percent of the entire American colonial population lived in rural areas, and the Revolution could neither have been waged nor won without their steadfast support.[2] For example, farmers sent food and other supplies to Boston, when it labored under the hardships caused by the so-called Intolerable Acts (1774), especially the Boston Port Act. American farmers also fed both Continental and state troops throughout the military conflict.

Much of the manufacturing performed in large commercial enterprises during the colonial period was carried out in rural areas. For example, the colonial iron industry was situated in rural areas, close to the iron and coal pits and the forests required for production. These country forges and the associated settlements, where the workers lived, constituted laboring villages, not unlike later lumber and mining camps—artificial towns in the countryside. It was a forge in a valley near Philadelphia that provided so many buildings and facilities that George Washington used it for his encampment at Valley Forge, Pennsylvania, in the winter of 1777 to 1778. The ironworks of William Alexander (or Lord Stirling) in rural Orange County, New York, produced vital war equipment.[3]

1

Table 1
New York Population–1771

COUNTIES	TOTAL POPULATION	WHITES MALES Under 16	WHITES MALES 16–60	WHITES MALES Over 60	WHITES FEMALES Under 16	WHITES FEMALES Over 16	TOTAL WHITES	BLACKS MALES Under 16	BLACKS MALES 16–60	BLACKS MALES Over 60	BLACKS FEMALES Under 16	BLACKS FEMALES Over 16	TOTAL BLACKS
Albany*	42,706	9,740	9,822	1,136	9,086	9,045	38,829	876	1,100	250	671	980	3,877
Cumberland+	3,947	1,071	1,002	59	941	862	3,935	0	6	1	3	2	12
Dutchess	22,404	5,721	4,687	384	5,413	4,839	21,044	299	417	34	282	328	1,360
Glouchester	722	178	185	8	193	151	715	2	4	0	1	0	7
Kings	3,623	548	644	76	513	680	2,461	297	287	22	261	295	1,162
New York	21,863	3,720	5,083	280	3,779	5,864	18,726	568	890	42	552	1,085	3,137
Orange	10,092	2,651	2,297	167	2,191	2,124	9,430	162	184	22	120	174	662
Queens	10,980	1,253	2,083	950	2,126	2,332	8,744	374	511	271	546	534	2,236
Richmond	2,847	616	438	96	508	595	2,253	177	152	22	106	137	594
Ulster	13,950	2,835	3,023	262	2,601	3,275	11,996	518	516	57	422	441	1,954
Westchester	21,745	3,813	5,204	549	3,483	5,266	18,315	793	916	68	766	887	3,430
TOTALS	168,007	34,877	37,302	4,314	33,492	38,139	148,124	4,416	5,372	848	4,050	5,197	19,883

*Includes Tryon and Charlotte counties, which were created from Albany just before the beginning of the Revolution

+Includes part of the land claimed by New York that later became Vermont.

From Evarts B. Greene and Virginia D. Harrington

American Population Before the Federal Census of 1790 (New York: Columbia University Press, 1932), 102–104

Table 2
New York Population–1786

COUNTIES	TOTAL POPULATION	WHITES MALES			FEMALES		TOTALS	SLAVES		TOTALS	INDIAN
		Under 16	16-60	Over 60	Under 16	Over 16	Whites	Males	Females	Slaves	Taxed
Albany	72,360	17,703	15,866	1,364	16,644	16,093	67,670	2,335	2,355	4,690	
Dutchess	32,636	8,209	6,973	628	7,700	7,481	30,991	830	815	1,645	
Kings	3,986	542	776	66	519	766	2,669	695	622	1,317	
Montgomery*	15,057	3,564	3,487	342	3,844	3,415	14,652	217	188	405	
New York	23,614	4,360	5,742	399	4,260	6,746	21,507	896	1,207	2,103	4
Orange	14,062	3,382	3,182	247	3,206	3,187	13,204	442	416	858	
Queens	13,084	2,441	2,717	295	2,308	3,140	10,901	1,160	1,023	2,183	
Richmond	3,152	616	622	43	540	638	2,459	369	324	693	
Suffolk	13,793	2,917	3,141	334	2,700	3,633	12,725	567	501	1,068	8
Ulster	22,143	4,971	4,792	464	4,381	4,865	19,473	1,353	1,309	2,662	
Washington+	4,456	1,130	1,152	58	1,118	983	4,441	8	7	15	
Westchester	20,554	4,972	4,477	491	4,546	4,818	19,304	649	601	1,250	
Totals	238,897	54,807	52,927	4,731	51,766	55,765	219,996	9,521	9,368	18,889	12

*Formerly Tryon County.

+ Formerly Charlotte County.

From Evarts B. Greene and Virginia D. Harrington
American Population Before the Federal Census of 1790
(New York: Columbia University Press, 1932), 102–104

Most of the Patriot soldiers, who used this equipment, also came from the countryside. Farmers rather than urban dwellers filled the armies that won American independence. Rural communities also politically dominated the new states. In those colonies, where the British army controlled the key ports and stifled urban revolutionary activity, rural people nurtured and sustained the struggle. The New England states were the exception, for the British evacuated that area early in the war, and urban political leaders could thus continue vigorously to support the Revolution. However, during the period that the British occupied Newport (December 1776–October 1779), the burden of keeping the Revolution alive fell on the people in the more rural areas of Rhode Island. Of course, in the colonies to the south of New York, rural Americans (along with some urban refugees from British-occupied cities) played key roles in creating the new states.

The contribution of rural New York to the Revolution has long been underestimated. From 1776 until 1783 the British occupied New York City and ruled it under martial law. Here, the military commander-in-chief maintained his headquarters. Here, too, was located the capital of what remained of the royal province of New York.[4] And from here, raiding parties scoured the middle states, searching for supplies and military victory. Meanwhile, rural political leaders, in concert with politicians from Albany and other small towns of the Hudson and Mohawk Valleys, began fashioning the new State of New York and its republican government. George Clinton, the state's first governor, came from the village of Little Britain on the west bank of the Hudson, near Newburgh. Melancton Smith, a prominent state politician during and after the war, came from Dutchess County. Abraham Yates, who served with John Jay on the committee that drafted the New York State Constitution of 1777, hailed from Albany. Of course, Whig members of the Livingston family retreated at the outbreak of the war to their upstate properties, where they become leaders of the new state.[5]

Although New York's rural areas may have played a key role in the Revolution, they did not cause the conflagration. Instead, they were reacting (albeit hesitantly) to decisions made in Great Britain. The Great War for Empire (1754–1763)—also known as the Seven Years' War and the French and Indian War—persuaded the British government to reevaluate the role and place of its colonies within the empire.[6] Wartime experiences, especially smuggling between its North American colonists and the enemy, led British officials to conclude that they must enhance their authority over the empire and rationalize the quilt of regulations that had been patched together over the past century.[7] They also thought they needed to reduce the debt that had mushroomed during the war, for the government's creditors were writing memorials demanding their due. Some of these petitioners also sat in Parliament, where they listened sympathetically to their own appeals.[8]

Even before the conflict had ended, the government had already embarked on its program to remake the empire. The Revenue Act of 1762 authorized the Crown to use the navy in peacetime to enforce the acts of trade and navigation. The pace of reform quickened in April 1763, when the Grenville ministry assumed power. It issued directives implementing the Revenue Act and demanding that colonial governors comply fully with their lawful responsibilities or face dismissal. The cabinet also increased the number of naval vessels stationed in North America.[9]

In October the king issued the Proclamation of 1763, which forbade colonists from settling west of the Appalachian Mountains. At first, all colonials believed that this prohibition injured their economic prospects by restricting their ability to acquire land, but over time loopholes enabled investors and settlers to ignore the line and to move beyond the mountains. However, the proclamation included another important provision. Land that the crown controlled and for which no land grants had been made was to be allotted to veterans of the war. Pursuant to this provision many former soldiers settled in northern New York and were eventually indifferent to the Revolutionary cause.[10]

The Revenue (or Sugar) Act of April 1764 sought to help pay for the British troops stationed in America, supposedly to protect the colonies from attack, but also to keep the colonists in check. The act cut the duty on foreign molasses in half in the belief that the lower rate would inhibit smuggling. The act also boosted the duty on foreign sugar; banned the importation of foreign rum into the colonies; doubled the duties on foreign products that were shipped from England to the colonies; set new or higher taxes on non-British coffee, indigo, pimento, textiles, and wines imported into the colonies; and extended the list of enumerated goods that colonists could ship only within the empire. The act also authorized creation of a new vice-admiralty court in Halifax, Nova Scotia, that was to have concurrent jurisdiction with the vice-admiralty courts, which were already operating in America, but which were notoriously lax. At a prosecutor's discretion, any colonial maritime or civil case falling within the jurisdiction of a vice-admiralty court could now be filed at the new site. Removing the trial to a different court, the cabinet hoped, would improve the chance of conviction, enhance compliance with the act, and increase revenues.[11]

The Currency Act also became law that April, because the ministry feared that provincial legislatures might allow American debtors to pay the sterling debts owed to British creditors in depreciated colonial paper currency. The act forbade colonial governments to issue paper money as legal tender. It also prohibited these governments from delaying the redemption date for existing paper issues. No colonial governor could sign a paper-money bill that did not have a clause suspending its operation until the Privy Council approved it. The act infuriated many colonists, because they had long used paper money successfully;

their imbalance of trade with Britain had relentlessly drained species from the colonies and made the use of paper money essential.[12]

The Quartering Act of March 1765 required that colonial governments supply and house British troops sent into their provinces. Supposedly, these troops were present to protect the empire from attacks by a revived French military or by aggrieved Native Americans. But colonists argued that the act was really taxation without representation, for Parliament was alleging that it could compel provincial assemblies to allocate money for specific purposes. Urban Americans claimed, too, that these troops were being kept in or near the major cities along the Atlantic coast to enforce the government's postwar policies and to intimidate their residents. The presence of these troops on American soil inescapably became a sore point. Not only did British Americans oppose standing armies in peacetime, they also clashed physically with the redcoats. In 1766 British troops were used to crush land riots in the Hudson Valley. In 1770 the "Battle of Golden Hill" in New York City pitted British regulars against neighborhood civilians.[13]

Focused upon the intended outcome of its legislative agenda and heedless of the negative (although predictable) consequences of its actions, Parliament also passed the Stamp Act (March 1765), the first direct tax Britain ever levied on its North American colonies. The measure taxed most printed material, including newspapers, broadsides, pamphlets, and many commercial and legal documents. The tax was to be paid in sterling and used to support the army stationed in America. Infractions of the law could be tried, at the prosecutor's discretion, in either the juryless vice-admiralty courts or the local common law courts. The tax antagonized many crucial economic constituencies in New York. Merchants were incensed, because the need for stamps on commercial documents would increase costs and complicate business transactions. The requirement that the tax be paid in specie threatened (following the Currency Act) to kill the very commerce upon which the measure aimed to raise revenue. Land speculators were vexed by the new taxes that were now to be levied on their deals. Lawyers were upset, for stamps would have to be affixed to court documents. Printers were appalled, because the statute inflated the cost of what they printed, threatened to undermine freedom of the press, and could wreck their business.[14] Dissenting clergymen feared that baptisms, marriages, and funeral services would not be performed, for the certifying documents would be taxed. The Stamp Act managed to offend all the major leadership groups of colonial New York.

More than self-interest was involved. As early as 1752, before the Great War, William Livingston had argued: "It is a standing Maxim of *English Liberty*, 'that no Man shall be taxed, but with his own Consent.'"[15] This argument was repeated in rebuttal to the postwar British imperial policies. One New York writer neatly summarized the American constitutional position: "Since we are agreed in the *Right* of the Colonies, *to be taxed only by their own Consent given by their*

Representatives; It follows, that if they are not so represented in Parliament, [then] they have not given, nor can they possibly give their Consent to be there taxed, consequently . . . such a Tax must be arbitrary illegal and oppressive." A second New Yorker, "Freeman," avowed that it was "not the Tax itself," but "the unconstitutional Manner of imposing it, that is the great Subject of Uneasyness to the Colonies. Whatever Justice there may be in their bearing a proportional Charge of the War, they apprehend, that Manner of levying the Money upon them, *without their own Consent*, by which they are deprived of one of the most valuable Rights of British Subjects, *never can be right*." A third, "A.B.C.," insisted that Americans could be "taxed only by our Legal constitutional Representatives."[16]

The parliamentary acts outlined above burdened urban New Yorkers more than their rural counterparts, who, for the most part, did not own the ships or the cargoes that were subject to stricter commercial regulations. Often they traded by barter or in commodities rather than in currency. They rarely saw the redcoats who were usually barracked in urban or frontier areas. Even the Stamp Act impinged more on urban than on rural New York. As a result, it was New York City and Albany that reacted first and most vigorously to the stamp tax. Neither city garnered much support from its rural neighbors. The intensity and violence of the rioting in New York City (November 1765), however, helped persuade the British government to repeal the tax in March 1766.[17]

Rioting was not new to British North America.[18] Colonial protestors had used rural and urban crowd actions throughout the eighteenth century to obtain redress from unpopular laws, proclamations, and practices. Notable were the New Jersey land riots (1740s); the Paxton Boys riots in Pennsylvania (1763); the tenant riots in Dutchess County, New York (1741, 1766); the Regulator Movements in South Carolina (1767–1769) and North Carolina (1768–1771); and the riots involving New England and New York settlers on the western slopes of the Green Mountains (1770s). The new British imperial regulations of the 1760s provoked disturbances, especially in urban areas, where the new policies had the greatest impact. None of the participants aimed to overthrow the British Empire or realized that a revolution was in the offing, but most historians consider the disturbances that took place in the decade before the Battle of Lexington to be critical steps leading to the American Revolution.

Although the ministry had backed down and repealed the Stamp Act, the government's general policy remained the same. Immediately after the repeal, Parliament passed the Declaratory Act, which proclaimed its supremacy over the colonies "in all cases whatsoever."[19] The continued need for revenue led George Townshend, the Chancellor of the Exchequer, to persuade Parliament in 1767 to pass the Townshend Act, which levied duties on glass, lead, paint, paper, and tea imported into the colonies. The proceeds were to be spent both for colonial defense and for defraying the cost of government and the administration of justice in America. A companion measure created an American Board of Customs at Boston that had power over all colonial customs officials and that reported to the British Treasury Board. The colonists responded with a boycott of British goods, and Parliament again backed down, this time by repealing in April 1770 all the Townshend duties except the one on tea, which was to remain in effect as a symbol of parliamentary sovereignty. New Yorkers consequently lifted their boycott against all items except tea, and relations with the mother country improved.[20]

The next crisis finally did involve rural areas in the protest movement. In 1773 Parliament enacted the Tea Act, mainly because the East India Company faced bankruptcy. To regain financial solvency, the company needed to sell the vast amounts of tea overflowing its warehouses. The Tea Act remitted all British duties on tea exported to the colonies and now allowed the company to sell directly to consignees there, instead of at public auction in Britain. Company tea would thus be cheap, even less expensive than the tea British Americans smuggled into the colonies to avoid paying the Townshend duty. The ministry gave scant consideration to how colonists would react to a law that overturned established patterns of trade, that ruined businesses by granting the East India Company a monopoly in America, and that would set a precedent for Parliament's creating similar monopolies over other commodities on the American market. It also reopened the question of whether Parliament could tax the colonies. Many Americans considered the Boston Tea Party (December 1773) and the corresponding events that prevented the marketing of tea in other cities, including New York, to be virtuous resistance to a program that would harm all Americans.[21]

Parliament responded to the Boston Tea Party with the Coercive (or Intolerable) Acts, which aimed to punish Massachusetts for its insubordination and to intimidate colonists elsewhere from following that province's lead. But the altering of Massachusetts's charter, tampering with the administration of justice in the province, and closing the port of Boston, only awakened colonists through-out America, in both urban and rural areas, to the imperial dangers that menaced them. If Parliament could unilaterally change Massachusetts's charter and mis-treat that colony, it could do the same to them.[22] Some rural and urban communi-ties sent food and money to support Boston in its crisis. This was the first time that many agrarian areas became active in the protest movement. Most of the colonies also agreed to send representatives to Philadelphia in September 1774 for what became the First Continental Congress. In October, Congress adopted the Continental Association, which called for the cessation of all British imports begin-ning on December 1, 1774, and for an embargo on all exports to Britain, Ireland, and the British West Indies from September 1, 1775. Most important, Congress called for the creation of committees in every town, city, and county to enforce the Association and to punish violators. In time, these extralegal bodies would become the de facto governing bodies in each colony.[23] When the North ministry and Gen. Thomas Gage responded with military force against the protesters in Massachusetts and shed American blood at Lexington and Concord (April 1775), both urban and rural Americans rose to meet the challenge.[24] It was now almost inevitable that only a clash of arms could settle the conflict.

While these imperial crises were unfolding in the 1760s and 1770s, rural New York was also plagued by its own (sometimes violent) controversies that were unrelated to the quarrel with Britain. But these disputes often influenced how residents responded to the Revolution. They pitted one group against another and so created antagonists and allies. Many of the people who opposed each other before the war were to do so during the war. Many who were allies in the prewar years were to remain so when fighting commenced. Therefore, by considering these earlier controversies we may perceive clues to wartime allegiances.

During the French and Indian War (1754–1763), northern New York, from Albany to Canada, was a wilderness. To settle the region and to safeguard the fertile Hudson Valley from fresh, armed incursions, the British government encouraged new communities in the region. Throughout the 1760s and 1770s veterans of the French and Indian War and immigrants from the British Isles settled in what was to be Charlotte County, which was situated along the east side of the Hudson River, immediately north of Rensselaer and along the shores of Lakes George and Champlain. These settlers established their homes and farms under land patents New York had granted them. There they encountered and clashed with land-hungry settlers from New England, who had moved west from the Connecticut Valley with land patents issued by New Hampshire. Dozens of Yankees, led by Ethan Allen, engaged in many small-scale battles along the western slopes of the Green Mountains in a campaign that aimed to drive the Yorkers out of the region. These hostilities engendered so much enmity between these settlers that their prewar animosity powerfully shaped their wartime allegiance. It is little wonder that early in the Revolution, when Green Mountain Yankees became enthusiastic rebels, the veterans who had fought for their crown against the French stayed neutral or became Loyalist. Moreover, given that the Allen family was religiously liberal and inclined toward deism, it is not surprising that the staunch Presbyterian immigrants from Ulster and Scotland were loath to champion the Revolution.[25]

Long Island, too, was plagued by such controversies. In the town of Jamaica, Anglicans and Presbyterians fought, sometimes violently, for control of the local church, parsonage, and minister's salary. In nearby Hempstead, residents in the northern part of town fought for autonomy against residents of south Hempstead, who opposed separation. In the Revolution, the Patriots found support among Jamaica Presbyterians and residents of north Hempstead; the Crown, among their enemies.[26]

In the western part of the colony, along the Mohawk River, ethnic and religious groups were enmeshed in conflict in the 1770s. Since the early 1700s,

German Palatines from the Rhine Valley and Lutherans had been settling not only in Pennsylvania but also in New York's Mohawk Valley. These ardent Protestants were soon forced to share this frontier region with their traditional enemy, Catholics. In 1773 and 1774 Sir William Johnson located settlers and tenants on extensive land grants that the crown had awarded him for his work with Native Americans and for his leadership role in the wars against the French. Many of these settlers belonged to the Roman Catholic McDonnell clan from the Highlands of Scotland. They created flourishing settlements north of the Mohawk around Johnson Hall, where an Irish priest ministered to them. Most Johnson tenants became Loyalists, and so too did many other Scots, who came to British North America. However, most of the Germans became revolutionaries and in 1777 contributed to the American military victory at Oriskany by preventing Col. Barry St. Leger from reinforcing Gen. John Burgoyne.[27]

The rural residents of Dutchess and Westchester Counties and of the eastern part of Albany County also experienced in the prewar period considerable violence that was not directly connected to British imperialism. In this region several New York landlords, including members of the Livingston family, forcefully confronted many of their tenants, who had migrated from New England, over such issues as political power, land rights, fees, and other manorial and estate policies. The very fact that these people were fighting over strictly local issues clearly demonstrates that the British government was not the only, or even the primary, source of discontent in rural New York. However, during the war these antagonisms continued, with many Livingstons becoming Whigs, and many of their tenants becoming Tories.

Conflicts emerged elsewhere. Notably, by the end of the Great War for Empire, the ethnic makeup of Albany, the province's most populous county, had begun to change. As a consequence, its economy, culture, and lifestyle were also evolving. In 1756 Albany County had only 17,424 residents. However, a short fifteen years later, its population had increased by almost 250 percent to 42,706 people. Almost all of the newcomers were Britons, and their presence altered the demographics of the county and the distribution of political power. For generations the Dutch had dominated the Albany County courts; but in the 1760s the British newcomers challenged the Dutch for control over jury and judicial decisions. The new inhabitants also made English, not Dutch, the primary language in the area.

In the town of Albany, enmity between the established Dutch mercantile families and the new British commercial interests grew significantly, especially over Canadian and Native American commerce. Britain's victory in the French and Indian Wars had dramatically affected Albany's Dutch traders. The continent now belonged to Great Britain, and the Dutch could no longer profit by smuggling goods between French Canada and Albany. To offset the loss of this lucrative trade, some Dutch and French Canadian traders formed commercial

alliances that sent emissaries as far west as Detroit to develop trading connections with Native Americans. However, British merchants, who believed that
the wealth of the West was theirs by right of conquest, strenuously countered
these efforts. Indicative of the eventual success of British mercantile interests
was the rising power and stature of Sir William Johnson, his Loyalist family,
and his supporters in American Indian affairs. Such commercial competition
also demonstrated that British imperialism in the years after 1763 was not the
only issue that pitted New Yorkers against one another.[28]

Not nearly as dynamic was Richmond, the county with the colony's smallest population. Isolated from the state and nearer to New Jersey, its less than
3,000 residents were politically dominated for most of the eighteenth century
by a few leading families led by the Billopps. The county's docile villages and
farms socially and politically slept their way into the revolutionary period. Staten
Islanders deliberately held themselves aloof from the emerging conflict and
remained overwhelmingly loyal, when the British army and navy occupied the
county in 1776. However, late in the conflict some Staten Islanders began to
chafe under martial law and the military's seizure of produce and services, so
that by war's end most residents accepted the conversion to statehood as less
onerous than continued British domination.

Despite the many and often violent divisions that plagued rural New York
in the colonial period, the Revolution created fresh challenges and demanded
that the Patriots move simultaneously on several fronts. They had to support the
war effort by mounting military initiatives to keep the British from moving south
from Canada and north from New York City; to create a new political entity, a
state with a constitution and a functioning government; to maintain an economy
capable of feeding the people of the new state and supplying its soldiers in the
field; and to ferret out Loyalists and to watch over residents who opposed the
new government. Their success in all these endeavors not only helped bring victory over Great Britain but also aided in the transformation of New Yorkers from
colonial subjects to republican citizens.

The Whigs saw the Loyalists as an unremitting menace. One of the first
actions of the new provisional government was to destroy the power of the
Loyalist Johnson family and its cohorts, because their power in the Mohawk
Valley threatened the security of Albany and much of northern New York. Many
of the Johnsons and their allies consequently fled to Upper Canada (present
Ontario) rather than remain under the control of the nascent revolutionaries.

Meanwhile, the residents of rural Long Island (about 18 percent of the
state's population) had to endure the harsh British occupation of their communities, martial law, the nearly constant demands that the British army made for
supplies, the harassment of local residents by British officers and soldiers, and
raids from across the Long Island Sound. Although their plight was in many
ways different from that of rural New Yorkers living in areas controlled by the

Whigs, the war was transforming them, too, from provincial New Yorkers into citizens of the new republic. British oppression had convinced both neutrals and Loyalists, who did not evacuate the state, that they were American, not British, and that their future belonged in New York.[29]

Before the Revolution most white New Yorkers, who protested against Great Britain because their rights were being trampled and their status was being reduced to servitude and slavery, did not think about the rights of the 19,883 African American New Yorkers, most of whom were slaves. Nevertheless, over time, the rhetoric of the Revolution did have an effect upon how European Americans thought and acted concerning slavery. The number of slaves declined in New York State from 21,193 in 1790, to 15,017 in 1810, 75 in 1830; and 0 in 1850.[30]

Once the war was won, the people of New York had to rebuild their society, their economy, and their political system. Despite the long years of war, the state's population had increased by 42 percent (from 168,007 to 238,897 residents) between 1771 and 1786. Moreover, the areas of New York that the British had occupied from 1776 to 1783 had to be reintegrated into the state. New York's war-torn economy had to be rebuilt. Patriots had to determine how to handle defeated Loyalists who still remained in New York and how to dispose of the property of those who had departed the state. Residents also had to demonstrate that republicanism was a workable form of government. During and after the war, state offices that had not existed in the colony or that had been filled by appointment, were now filled by election. This opened the political system to ambitious men who had previously been kept out of office. The political needs of the new state thus encouraged political participation and furthered the creation of a democratic republic. Because the postwar challenges were eventually met does not mean that the road was not daunting, that the tests were not severe, or that failure was not a real possibility.

In sum, the American Revolution created crises and challenges for rural New York. Yet, by doing so (and as the chapters that follow will demonstrate), it allowed rural New Yorkers to emerge as citizens and leaders of the new State of New York. Although historians of Revolutionary America have typically focused their attention upon New York City, rural New York was just as important in the birth of the new state. This book consequently considers the revolutionary experiences of the people who lived not in New York City but in what we have termed *The Other New York*.[31]

Notes

1. See, for example, Carl Bridenbaugh, *Cities in Revolt, Urban Life in America, 1743–1773* (New York, 1955); Benjamin W. Labaree, *The Boston Tea Party* (New York, 1964); Hiller B. Zobel, *The Boston Massacre* (New York, 1970); Richard Allen Ryerson, *The Revolution Is Now Begun: The Radical Committees of Philadelphia, 1765–1776* (Philadelphia, 1978); Gary B. Nash, *The Urban Crucible: Social Change, Political*

Consciousness, and the Origins of the American Revolution (Cambridge, Mass., 1979); Elaine Forman Crane, *A Dependent People: Newport, Rhode Island in the Revolutionary Era* (New York, 1985); and Joseph S. Tiedemann, *Reluctant Revolutionaries: New York City and the Road to Independence* (Ithaca, 1997).

2. In 1771, 87% of New York's population (or 146,144 people) lived in what we have termed *The Other New York*. In 1786 approximately 90% (or 215,283) did so. See Evarts B. Greene and Virginia D. Harrington, *American Population before the Census of 1790* (New York, 1932), 102–104.

3. "Lord Sterling's Hibernia Furnace [1767–79]," New Jersey Historical Society, *Proceedings* 71 (1953): 174–86. See also George H. Danforth, "The Rebel Earl" (Ph.D. diss.: Columbia University, 1955) and Cathy Matson, *Merchants and Empire: Trading in Colonial New York* (Baltimore, 1998), 259–60.

4. Despite New York City's political prominence, both Albany and Dutchess counties had larger populations in 1771, and Westchester County had almost as many people. Greene and Harrington, *American Population*, 102–104.

5. For Gov. George Clinton, see Ernest W. Spaulding, *His Excellency George Clinton, Critic of the Constitution* (New York, 1938); and John P. Kaminski, *George Clinton: Yeoman Politician of the New Republic* (Madison, Wis., 1993). For Melancton Smith, see Robin Brooks, "Melancton Smith, New York Anti-Federalist, 1744–1798" (Ph.D. diss., University of Rochester, 1964). Abraham Yates is considered in Stephen Bielinski, *Abraham Yates, Jr. and the New Political Order in Revolutionary New York* (Albany, 1975). The standard and still classic biography of Robert R. Livingston is George Dangerfield, *Chancellor Robert R. Livingston of New York, 1746–1813* (New York, 1960).

6. Tiedemann, *Reluctant Revolutionaries*, especially pp. 7–9; and Fred Anderson, *Crucible of War: The Seven Years' War and the Fate of Empire in British North America, 1754–1766* (New York, 2000), especially pp. 557–59.

7. Thomas C. Barrow, "Background to the Grenville Program, 1757–1763," *William and Mary Quarterly*, 3rd ser., 22 (1965): 93–104; Jack M. Sosin, *Agents and Merchants: British Colonial Policy and the Origins of the American Revolution, 1763–1775* (Lincoln, Nebr., 1965), 90.

8. Jack P. Greene, "The Seven Years' War," in Peter Marshall and Glyn Williams, eds., *The British-Atlantic Empire before the American Revolution* (London, 1980), 98; Lawrence Henry Gipson, *Triumphant Empire: Thunder-Clouds in the West*, vol. 10 of his *The British Empire before the American Revolution*, 15 vols. (New York, 1936–1970), 182.

9. Greene, "Seven Years' War," 90, 94; Gipson, *Triumphant Empire*, 202–207; Sosin, *Agents and Merchants*, 39; and Bernhard Knollenberg, *Origins of the American Revolution, 1759–1766* (New York, 1960), 134–35.

10. For this issue, see Eugene R. Fingerhut, "Assimilation of Immigrants on the Frontier of New York, 1764–1776" (Ph.D. diss., Columbia University, 1962)

11. Gipson, *Triumphant Empire*, 228–31; Knollenberg, *Origins of the American Revolution*, 166–68.

12. Jack P. Greene and Richard M. Jellison, "The Currency Act of 1764 in Imperial Colonial Relations, 1764–1776," *William and Mary Quarterly*, 3rd ser., 18 (1961): 485–518; Jack M. Sosin, "Imperial Regulation of Colonial Paper Money, 1764–1773," *Pennsylvania Magazine of History and Biography* 88 (1964): 174–98.

13. Sosin, *Agents and Merchants*, 34–36; John Shy, *Toward Lexington: The Role of the British Army in the Coming of the American Revolution* (Princeton, 1965), 178–90; and Tiedemann, *Reluctant Revolutionaries*, 108–12, 147–49.

14. Tiedemann, *Reluctant Revolutionaries*, 68.

15. William Livingston et al., *The Independent Reflector or Weekly Essays on Sundry Important Subjects More Particularly Adapted to the Province of New York*, ed. Milton M. Klein (Cambridge, Mass., 1963), 62.

16. *New York Gazette, or, Weekly Post Boy*, May 16, June 13, July 11, 1765.

17. Tiedemann, *Reluctant Revolutionaries*, 83–88, 97.

18. For a discussion of crowd actions in Europe and America, see George Rudé, *The Crowd in History: A Study of Popular Disturbances in France and England, 1730–1848* (New York, 1964); William A. Pencak, ed., *Riot and Revelry in Early America* (University Park, Pa., 2002); Paul Gilje, *The Road to Mobocracy: Popular Disorder in New York City, 1763–1784* (Chapel Hill, N.C., 1987); Pauline Maier, *From Resistance to Revolution: Colonial Radicals and the Development of American Opposition to Britain* (New York, 1972).

19. Edmund S. Morgan and Helen M. Morgan, *The Stamp Act Crisis: Prologue to Revolution*, rev. ed. (New York, 1963), 347–48.

20. Thomas C. Barrow, *Trade and Empire: The British Customs Service in Colonial America, 1660–1775* (Cambridge, Mass., 1967), 226; Robert Middlekauff, *The Glorious Cause: The American Revolution, 1763–1789* (New York, 1982), 146–52; and Tiedemann, *Reluctant Revolutionaries*, 121–24, 153–54.

21. Tiedemann, *Reluctant Revolutionaries*, 175–83.

22. For these acts, see Merril Jensen, ed., *American Colonial Documents to 1776* (London, 1955), 779–85.

23. Jensen, ed., *American Colonial Documents to 1776*, 813–16.

24. Tiedemann, *Reluctant Revolutionaries*, 220–25.

25. There is no adequate survey of the Vermont-New York controversy in this period. See Dixon Ryan Fox, *Yankees and Yorkers* (New York, 1940). For the Vermont side of the issue, see Frederick F. VanDeWater, *The Reluctant Republic: Vermont 1724–1791* (New York, 1941). For an account of the controversy that considers the Ulster Irish immi-

grants in this series of running skirmishes, see Fingerhut, "Assimilation of Immigrants on the Frontier of New York, 1764–1776."

26. Joseph S. Tiedemann, "Communities in the Midst of the American Revolution: Queens County, New York, 1774–1775," *Journal of Social History* 18 (1984): 57–78.

27. The role of the Johnson family is considered in Arthur Pound and Richard E. Day, *Johnson of the Mohawks* (New York, 1970). See also the republication of a biography by James Thomas Flexner, *Lord of the Mohawks: A Biography of Sir William Johnson* (Boston, 1979). The Loyalist-Indian-British campaigns east from Niagara to the Mohawk Valley are surveyed in Howard Swiggett, *War out of Niagara: Walter Butler and the Tory Rangers* (New York, 1932); and the biography of the Mohawk leader, by Isabel T. Kelsay, *Joseph Brant, 1734–1807: Man of Two Worlds* (Syracuse, 1984). The prewar problems of the Johnson family's immigrant tenants may be surveyed in Fingerhut, "Assimilation of Immigrants on the Frontier of New York, 1764–1776."

28. The problems of Albany merchants are briefly surveyed in David A. Armour, "Merchants of Albany, New York, 1686–1760" (Ph.D. diss., Northwestern University, 1965.)

29. Joseph S. Tiedemann, "Patriots by Default: Queens County, New York, and the British Army, 1776–1783," *William and Mary Quarterly*, 3rd ser., 43 (1986): 35–63.

30. Greene and Harrington, *American Population*, 102–104.

31. For New York politics during and after the war, see Jackson Turner Main, *The Sovereign States, 1775–1783* (New York, 1973); Edward Countryman, *The American Revolution and Political Society in New York, 1760–1790* (Baltimore, 1981); and Edward Countryman, "From Revolution to Statehood (1776–1825)," in Milton M. Klein, *The Empire State: A History of New York* (Ithaca, 2001), 229–304.

Part I

The Revolution
in Downstate New York

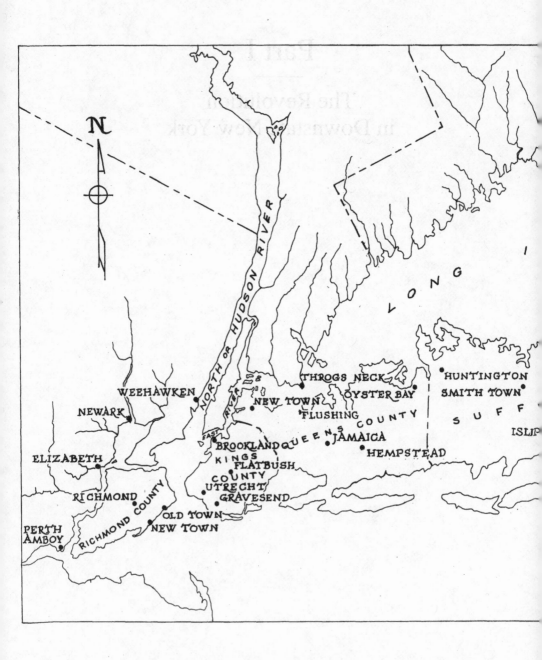

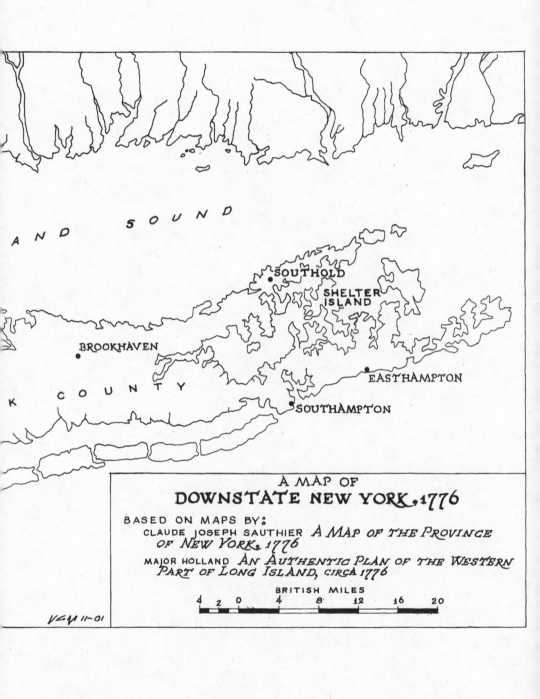

A N D   S O U N D

· SOUTHOLD

SHELTER
ISLAND

· BROOKHAVEN

K   C O U N T Y

· EASTHAMPTON

· SOUTHAMPTON

A MAP OF
DOWNSTATE NEW YORK, 1776
BASED ON MAPS BY:
CLAUDE JOSEPH SAUTHIER *A MAP OF THE PROVINCE*
OF NEW YORK, 1776

MAJOR HOLLAND *AN AUTHENTIC PLAN OF THE WESTERN*
PART OF LONG ISLAND, CIRCA 1776

BRITISH MILES

4 2 0   4   8   12   16   20

VGM 11-01

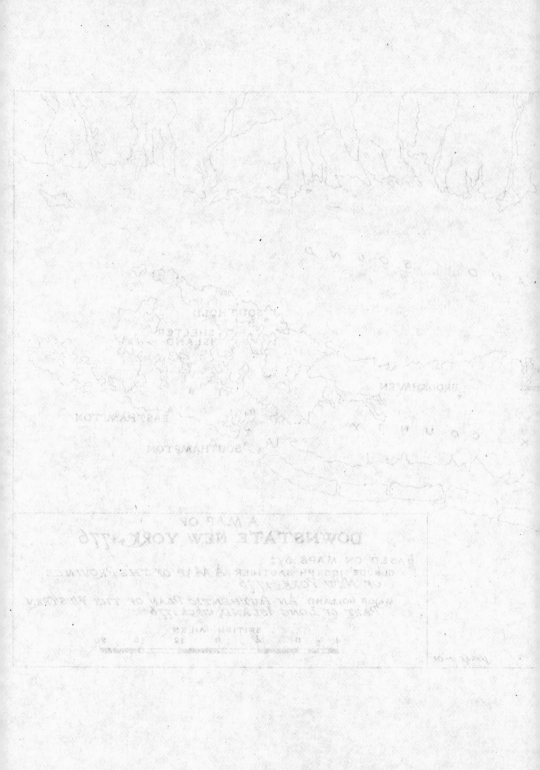

1

Kings County

Edwin G. Burrows

In the first half of the eighteenth century, despite its proximity to Manhattan, Kings County grew more slowly than any other in the province. Between 1698 and 1771, its population rose from 2,017 to 3,623 (an 80 percent increase); during the same period, the population of New York County, just across the East River, climbed from 4,937 to 21,863 (a 343 percent increase), while that of the entire colony jumped from 18,067 to 163,348 (an 804 percent increase).[1] Not that Kings County was an undesirable place to put down roots: its original Native American inhabitants had been driven out or marginalized, and by all accounts the western end of Long Island (then often called Nassau Island) was as fertile as it was beautiful. Visitors never failed to marvel at its abundant wildlife, dense forests, bountiful orchards, fat cattle, and sweeping fields of wheat, corn, and tobacco—"the richest spot, in the opinion of New-Yorkers, of all America," wrote the Rev. Andrew Burnaby.[2]

Why would the richest spot in New York, let alone all America, have captured so small a share of the burgeoning provincial population? The answer turns on two circumstances, both of which bear directly on how the people of Kings County would experience and remember the Revolution.

First, the vast majority of its white inhabitants were fourth- or fifth-generation descendants of the Dutch and Walloon colonists who colonized New Netherland in the middle of the previous century and stubbornly resisted Anglicization after the English conquest of 1664. They spoke and wrote in Dutch, and they insisted on Dutch mates for their sons and daughters; many could boast of working the same land that had belonged to their grandfathers and should in the fullness of time belong to their own grandchildren. They relied on the Reformed Church rather than English courts for the resolution of disputes, and they clung to the Roman-Dutch legal tradition, which among other

21

things allowed married women to use their maiden names and control their own property. Thus, although Kings County itself was an institution of English local government (set up when the entire province was "shired" in 1683), its small rural communities remained so determinedly Dutch—so insulated from the economic and social forces reshaping British North America in the eighteenth century—that it is no wonder prospective settlers tended to look elsewhere.[3]

But Kings County presented a second and arguably even more formidable obstacle to newcomers: the growing dependence of its Dutch farmers on African slave labor. Between 1698 and 1771, the number of slaves in the county rose from 296 to 1,162—an increase of 866 as against an increase of only 740 in the number of whites. On the eve of the Revolution, one out of every three residents was in bondage, a greater proportion than any other county north of the Mason-Dixon line, and slaves represented a significant share of the wealth of the Rapeljes, Van Brunts, Cowenhovens, Leffertses, Sudayms, Lotts, Wyckoffs, Remsens, and other prominent families. It is the breadth of slave ownership that commands attention, however. Nearly 60 percent of the county's white families owned one or more slaves, relying on them to perform a wide variety of tasks: cooking and cleaning, tending crops and livestock, hauling agricultural produce to mills and markets, maintaining fences, building roads. The result, as a pair of observant Hessians discovered in 1776, was that Kings County offered few if any opportunities for a poor white man to make a living. "Near every dwelling-house negroes (their slaves) are settled, who cultivate the most fertile land, pasture the cattle, and do all the menial work," observed Major Baurmeister. Whites, added Chaplain Waldeck, "cannot earn anything with fieldwork or other handwork in this area, since the landed gentleman has his work done by his own Negroes." Besides, as the county's servile population grew, so had the urgency of vigilance. Disorderly, disobedient, and runaway slaves became a more and more familiar feature of local affairs, and all whites, whether they owned slaves or not, were expected to aid and abet the racial regime.[4]

These two circumstances—Dutch clannishness and resistance to assimilation, plus the intensifying exploitation of slave labor—not only help explain why the population of Kings County failed to keep pace with the rest of the province, but also why the bulk of its white landowners took a dim view of Whig resistance to Britain's colonial policy after the end of the Seven Years' War. True, their forebears had rejoiced when Admiral Cornelis Evertsen drove the English out of New York in 1673, then despaired when the Netherlands gave it back; true, too, they had cheered Jacob Leisler's revolt, neither forgetting nor forgiving his brutal execution in 1691. Since then, however, they had been left pretty much to their own devices—and indeed flourished under the umbrella of imperial commercial regulations, which encouraged New York City merchants to funnel more and more of the county's grain and cattle into the lucrative West Indian trade. No less important, the provincial political establishment had steadfastly supported the power of white masters over their black chattel, crushing slave rebellions without mercy and tightening the colony's slave code, until the color line became absolute and immutable. Even the most Anglophobic Dutchman could see that nothing good would come from meddling with the status quo, least of all in the cause of liberty.[5]

Just how few Kings County residents sympathized with the Whigs became clear over the summer of 1774, when a countywide meeting was called to elect delegates to the first Continental Congress and only two men appeared.[6] Shortly thereafter, Congress warned the inhabitants of America to prepare for war, announced a boycott of British goods, and urged every town and county in America to form an association to enforce the boycott. This time Kings County did not respond at all. In fact, the first significant countywide political event—after a decade of turmoil elsewhere in America—apparently did not occur until mid-April 1775, when twenty-one delegates from all of the towns except Flatlands converged on the County Hall in Flatbush. Their task was to pick delegates to the Provincial Convention that would assemble a week later in New York City for the purpose of choosing representatives to the second Continental Congress. Judging by what happened elsewhere, the unprecedented interest in the Flatbush meeting probably reflected a widespread Tory assumption that if they could not stop Congress from meeting, the next best thing would be to control it.[7]

But no sooner had the New York Convention concluded its business than reports began to arrive of the clash at Lexington and Concord. Buoyed by public outrage, Whigs in the city immediately called for the formation of a Provincial Congress to stiffen and coordinate resistance. On May 20 the "Magistrates and Freeholders" of the village of Brooklyn gathered to denounce "the unjust plunder and inhuman carnage committed on the property and persons of our brethren in Massachusetts." They then chose two delegates to the Provincial Congress and resolved "to observe all warrantable acts, associations and orders, as said Congress shall direct." At a second meeting in Flatbush on May 22, deputies from the other towns added another half-dozen names to the county's delegation.[8]

Kings County Whigs nonetheless remained a distinct minority and very much on the defensive. During the summer and fall of 1775, while the Provincial Congress cautiously began to assume the powers and responsibilities of government, the county's Tories drew additional strength from an influx of refugees fleeing the turmoil in New York City. Flatbush alone played host to such luminaries as Mayor David Mathews, Gov. William Tryon, Chief Justice Daniel Horsmanden, and William Axtell, a member of the Governor's Council whose rural seat, Melrose Hall, stood just north of the village on the road to Brooklyn. (Flatbush Tories also took comfort from the presence of the Rev. Johannes Rubel, an outspoken supporter of the Crown who shared the pulpit of the Flatbush Church with the Rev. Ulpianus van Sinderen, an equally outspoken Whig.) As one American officer reported from Red Hook the following June, "most of the country towns" in the neighborhood were crawling with Tories from the city. "It is almost incredible how many of these vermin there are." In October, when the Provincial Congress drew up a Defense or General Association (not to be confused with the Continental Association) and prepared to seize the weapons of those "inimicals" and "equivocals" who refused to sign, and when the Continental Congress then ordered the arrest of anyone who might endanger "the safety of the colonies," Tories prepared for armed conflict.[9]

Whites throughout the region had in the meantime become alarmed by rumors of renewed discontent among their slaves. In August 1775, worried that nothing cooled patriotic ardor like the prospect of servile insurrection, the Provincial Congress ordered that if a local militia unit were called away to deal with a British invasion, its commanding officer should leave a detachment behind "to guard against the insurrection of slaves, or if judged more expedient and safe, may take the slaves or part of them with him and employ them in carrying baggage, dragging cannon or the like."[10] Then, in late November, came word that Governor Dunmore of Virginia had offered freedom to any slave who deserted a rebel master and enlisted with His Majesty's forces. Whigs everywhere cried foul, and six months later the Declaration of Independence would complain that the Crown "has excited domestic insurrections amongst us." Kings County slave owners now had more than enough reason to conclude that they stood on the brink of the abyss. Support for the Patriots, such as it was, boiled away almost overnight, and by the end of November, the county evidently did not even hold public elections for delegates to the Second Provincial Congress. The few men who eventually served were probably dispatched by local Whig committees and attended only intermittently. After May 1776, they stopped altogether.[11]

II

It was against this background of mounting racial tensions and receding Whig resolve that Kings County endured two invasions—by the Americans in the spring and summer of 1776, and then by the British, who drove the Americans out at the end of the summer and held on for the next seven years. What made the county a prime target for both armies was the understanding that New York City could not be defended against an enemy who held Brooklyn Heights overlooking the harbor and was thus able to interdict shipping on the East River. For His Majesty's forces, securing Kings County, and indeed all of Long Island, was also a logistical imperative, because without access to the county's bountiful farms, herds, and forests, a prolonged occupation of New York would be extremely difficult. As General Charles Lee advised Washington in February 1776, "should the enemy take possession of New York, when Long Island is in our hands, they will find it almost impossible to subsist."[12]

The American invasion began at the end of February 1776, when Washington sent Lee to prepare the city's defenses, and Lee deployed a regiment of 600 Connecticut volunteers to fortify Brooklyn Heights. The Provincial Congress suggested, with a touch of exasperation, that the Kings County deputies might want to attend its sessions, so they could help arrange suitable lodgings for the Connecticut men in Brooklyn. The deputies consented to appear, and after making inquiries, advised Congress that it would be necessary to billet the soldiers in private houses, for which the inhabitants would charge 7s. per week for officers and 1s. 4d. per week for privates. Not unreasonable rates, perhaps, but not exactly a memorable display of patriotism, either—which probably explains why Congress then "recommended" that local residents also supply all timber for the project. "The known zeal of the inhabitants of Kings County to promote the public cause," Congress added dryly, "we doubt not will stimulate them to promote the necessary work." Once it became definite that the British were on the way, however, the gloves came off. In mid-March Congress simply ordered the people of Brooklyn to help on the fortifications by "turning out for service at least one-half their male population (negroes included) every day, with spades, hoes, and pickaxes," until they finished the job.[13]

Construction of the Brooklyn works continued on through the spring and summer of 1776 under a succession of commanders designated by Washington—General William Alexander (Lord Stirling), who replaced General Lee in early March, then General Nathanael Greene, who replaced Stirling in April, and finally General John Sullivan, who took over from Greene in mid-August. When finally completed, the American defenses in the county consisted of three elements: first, a pair of harbor batteries at Fort Stirling on Columbia Heights and Fort Defiance on Red Hook, which in conjunction with batteries on Governors Island and Manhattan were intended to prevent British warships from approaching New York; second, a chain of redoubts, trenches, and palisades along the shore of New York Bay between Gowanus and Wallabout, situated to thwart an attack on the harbor batteries by land; and third, an outer line of posts on the roads cutting through the Heights of Guan or Gowanus, a thickly wooded ridge, forty to ninety feet high, that split Kings County from southwest to northeast about two miles outside the inner line. In addition to these fixed positions, a company of Pennsylvania riflemen patrolled the shore above and below the Narrows to stop "disaffected" locals from communicating with British warships in the harbor, evidently a regular occurrence that underscored how little support the American cause enjoyed in the county.[14]

Meanwhile, at the end of June, the much-anticipated British invasion had begun with the arrival off Staten Island of more than a hundred vessels and nine thousand regulars under the command of General William Howe and his brother, Admiral Richard Howe. Generals Henry Clinton and Lord Charles Cornwallis, having failed to capture Charleston, South Carolina, appeared a month later with eight regiments of veterans. Only days behind them came a convoy of twenty-two ships bearing additional regiments from England and Scotland. Finally, in mid-August, still another fleet arrived with eight or nine thousand Hessian mercenaries under General Philip von Heister. In all, the Howe brothers now had at their disposal two men-of-war and two dozen frigates mounting a combined twelve hundred cannon, plus four hundred transports, thirty-two thousand troops in twenty-seven regiments, and thirteen thousand seamen. It was the greatest concentration of military and naval power ever assembled in the colonies and the largest British expeditionary force in history to date, marshaling better than 40 percent of all men and ships on active duty in the Royal Navy.

Washington, by contrast, had no proper navy, and the forces at his disposal in and around New York—which by the most generous accounting numbered over thirty-five thousand men and officers—were a hodge-podge of inexperienced militia and Continental levies without adequate equipment or training. Often entire units broke camp and went home on a moment's notice. Worse, dysentery and "putrid fever" (a term used for both typhus and typhoid fever) ran through the camps in July and August, laying up as many as one-third of the men at a time. If Washington had twenty-three thousand troops left and fit for duty by mid-August, he was lucky.[15]

While they waited for the hammer to fall, Washington and the provincial government continued to grapple with widespread apathy, even defiance, in Kings County.[16] The county's regiment dwindled alarmingly, as disaffected militiamen went over to the British on Staten Island or simply dropped out of sight, "skulking" in the marshes and thickets around Jamaica Bay; provincial authorities eventually did the prudent thing and moved the regiment within the lines at Brooklyn, where the men who remained could be kept under tighter discipline.[17] Militia from Queens and Suffolk had in the meantime begun the gargantuan task of stripping local farms of livestock, hay, grain, and anything else that might be useful to the enemy; what could not be carried off was burned. This necessary but inevitably unpopular policy bred more disaffection, and the Provincial Congress, now calling itself the State Convention, soon got wind of allegations "that the inhabitants of Kings county have determined not to oppose the enemy." On August 19 the Convention angrily responded by dispatching a committee to investigate. Should the rumors prove true, Continental troops from the Brooklyn defenses would be sent to disarm and arrest troublemakers, seize or destroy their crops, and if necessary *"lay the whole county waste."*[18]

Before that order could be carried out, however, General Howe made his move. At daybreak on Thursday, August 22, 1776, a swarm of British transports crossed the narrows from Staten Island to Gravesend Bay, disgorging 15,500 redcoats and Hessians along with forty pieces of artillery on the beach below Denyse's Ferry in New Utrecht. Marching inland, the men appeared "as merry as in a Holiday, and regaled themselves with the fine apples, which hung every where upon the Trees in great abundance." Wisely, the Pennsylvania riflemen on shore patrol nearby offered no opposition, but fell back through the village of New Utrecht toward Flatbush, burning stacks of hay and shooting cattle as they went. By late afternoon, the British were spread out along a broad arc, about eight miles long, that ran east from New Utrecht, where Howe established his headquarters, through Gravesend, east to Flatlands. General Cornwallis led an advance column up from Gravesend to occupy Flatbush, whose residents displayed some uncertainly as to whether their indifference to the American cause would matter to His Majesty's soldiers. "The whole village was in commotion," one resident recalled many years later. "Women and children were running hither and thither. Men on horseback were riding about in all directions." As the family watched nervously, "our faithful old negro man, Caesar" loaded the wagon with their most prized possessions—"the great Dutch Bible with its huge brass clasps and brass corners" and "the old Dutch clock," as well as assorted furniture and articles of clothing. Instead of fleeing, Dominie Rubel welcomed the British with open arms and led His Majesty's soldiers to the extensive wine collection of David Clarkson, one of the village's few Whigs.[19]

Washington quickly sent reinforcements from New York to strengthen the forward posts on the Gowanus Heights, which under General Sullivan's management had become increasingly important to the American defenses. On Friday the 23rd, the Americans skirmished with the Hessians on the outskirts of Flatbush, drove them back into the village, and then withdrew. Several private houses and other buildings were burned, according to Sullivan, and "one of our gunners threw a shell into Mr. Axtell's house where a number of officers were at dinner."[20] More impromptu skirmishing flared around Flatbush over the weekend. The Americans gave as good as they got, but Washington began to hear complaints that his soldiers were looting the homes of friend and foe alike—the kind of "licentious and disorderly behavior," he grumbled, that one would expect of a mob, not a well-regulated army.[21]

With instructions to improve discipline, Washington abruptly shifted the overall command on Long Island from Sullivan to General Israel Putnam of Connecticut, a crusty but popular old veteran of the fighting in the Seven Years' War and on Bunker Hill. On Monday, August 26, Washington fed Putnam additional regiments from New York City, bringing the size of the American force in Kings County to around nine thousand officers and men. About three thousand were deployed to block the country roads that wound around and through the Gowanus Heights to Brooklyn. Of these, approximately eight hundred men from Maryland, Delaware, Pennsylvania, and New York covered the Gowanus Road, which ran along the shore on the right or west end of the American lines. Further east, near the American center, a somewhat larger body of troops from New Jersey, Connecticut, and Rhode Island, supported by a battery of field pieces, occupied the Flatbush Pass, a wide notch, where the road from Flatbush ran up to Brooklyn. The remainder, a mix of Continental regulars and Connecticut militia, held the Bedford Pass, the point at which the road from Bedford came down to join the Flatbush Road just above Flatbush village. Opposing them were almost twenty thousand redcoats, Hessians, and Tories, including hundreds of newly emancipated blacks from New York and other colonies. It was a strange scene indeed—British, German, and African soldiers massing in Dutch fields and villages, while boys from New England, New Jersey, Pennsylvania, and Maryland, led by a Virginia tobacco planter, waited on the hills to give them battle.[22]

The Americans did not wait for long. General Clinton had discovered— maybe when reconnoitering the American positions, maybe from one of the many Kings County Tories who attached themselves to the British army—that Washington or his subordinates had neglected to guard a fourth opening in the Gowanus Heights. This was the Jamaica Pass, four miles east of Brooklyn on the far left of the American lines, where the Jamaica Road, running east from Bedford, wound through a deep ravine on its way to Queens County and eastern Long Island. Clinton persuaded Howe to let him attack the pass in strength. Just after sundown on Monday the 26th, he and Cornwallis led ten thousand regulars in a two-mile-long column out of Flatlands toward New Lots in the east. With them went two companies of Long Island Tories under Colonel Oliver De Lancey and several Tory scouts from Flatbush. To deceive any watching Americans, they moved quietly and left their campfires burning. At New Lots they turned north to Jamaica and at about 3:00 a.m. on the 27th slipped through the Jamaica Pass without opposition. They then wheeled west toward the village of Bedford, where they arrived around 8:30 a.m. and fired a signal gun to alert the rest of the army.

Two smaller forces now swung into action. In the center of the American line, five thousand blue-coated Hessians charged into the Flatbush Pass. Realizing from the signal gun that the enemy had somehow snuck around behind them, the Americans and their commander, General Sullivan, fell back along the road to Brooklyn—only to discover Howe's light infantry pounding down the Jamaica Road from Bedford. Hundreds of Americans sprinted into the woods and fields in a desperate attempt to reach safety behind the lines in Brooklyn Heights, joined as they ran by the men who had been defending the nearby Bedford Pass. Those who failed to get away and attempted to surrender were slaughtered by the oncoming Hessians. "The greater part of the riflemen were pierced with the bayonet to trees," gloated a German officer, while a British officer observed that "it was a fine sight to see with what alacrity they dispatched the Rebels with their bayonets after we had surrounded them so they could not resist." Sullivan himself was taken in a cornfield near what is now Battle Pass in Prospect Park. By late morning the fighting in this part of the battlefield was done.[23]

At Gowanus, on the far right of the American line, Maj. Gen. James Grant had meanwhile led seven thousand redcoats and two companies of Long Island Tories against the defenders commanded by General Stirling. Stirling's men fought gamely to keep control of the high ground (now "Battle Hill" in Green-Wood Cemetery), until the collapse of the American center at Flatbush made their position hopeless. Redcoats from Bedford were closing in behind them, while Hessians were crashing through the woods on their left. To give the rest of his force time to escape across the tidal flats along Gowanus Creek, Stirling counterattacked with a few hundred Maryland troops. Washington, observing Stirling advance from a small hill where Court Street now crosses Atlantic Avenue, reportedly cried out, "Good God! What brave fellows I must this day lose!" Survivors remembered the "confusion and horror" that followed, as the fleeing Americans tried desperately to cross eighty yards of muddy flats under a hail of British canister, grape, and chain. "Some of them were mired and crying to their fellows for God's sake to help them out; but every man was intent on his own safety and no assistance was rendered." After savage fighting on the Gowanus Road near the Cortelyou House (today called the "Old Stone House"), Stirling was captured. By 2:00 p.m. all but a handful of the Marylanders had been taken prisoner or killed. Thanks to them, however, hundreds of their countrymen managed to wade or swim to safety in Brooklyn Heights.[24]

Had Howe kept up the pursuit, he might well have driven Washington's demoralized forces off the Heights and into the East River. In only a few hours of fighting they had lost two or three hundred dead and approximately several times that number wounded, captured, or missing—among them three generals and scores of junior officers. The British and Hessians together reported only 63 dead and 314 wounded or missing.[25]

But despite pleas by Clinton, Cornwallis, and others to finish what they had begun, Howe stopped—deterred perhaps by the memory of British losses at Bunker Hill, by the hope that the rebels would give up without a struggle, or by the contrary winds and rain and tides that prevented his brother from moving up the fleet to provide cover. Whatever the reason, he allowed the Americans to remain unmolested on Brooklyn Heights for another two days. That was all the time Washington needed for one of the boldest strokes of the war. On the night of Thursday, August 29, under the very noses of the enemy, he quietly evacuated the entire army across the East River to New York. Six weeks later, the slow-moving Howe crossed the river in pursuit, seized the city, and proceeded to drive the Americans off Manhattan altogether.[26]

III

As the war moved elsewhere, the residents of Kings County began the grim work of repairing the damage inflicted on their homes and farms by both armies—fields littered with debris and rotting animal carcasses, orchards put to the ax for firewood and fortifications, yards full of smashed furniture, wells stuffed with garbage, houses used as stables.[27] They expected nonetheless that the restoration of royal authority would allow them to rebuild their lives in short order, and they took immediate steps to affirm their loyalty—sporting red badges on their hats and clothes, dispatching congratulations to His Majesty's victorious generals, and even changing the names of local landmarks (Brooklyn's Ferry House Tavern became the King's Head, a favorite rendezvous for local Tories, while a racecourse in Flatlands became Ascot Heath). In mid-November, four hundred men from every town converged on the Flatbush church to sign an oath of allegiance: "I do sincerely promise and swear, that I will be faithful and bear true allegiance to His Majesty, King George the Third, and that I will defend his crown and dignity, against all persons whatsoever. So help me God." In early December, several dozen men who had served in the Provincial Congress or on various local committees also signed a memorial to the royal governor, "rejecting and disclaiming all power of Congress and Committees, totally refusing obedience thereto, and revoking all proceedings under them whatsoever, as being . . . ruinous to the welfare and prosperity of this County."[28]

It was a short honeymoon. His Majesty's officers soon grew suspicious of the alacrity with which people throughout the colony lined up to profess their loyalty, openly ridiculing them as "red rags." As one disbelieving officer wrote to his English patron: "They swallow the Oaths of Allegiance to the King, & Congress, Alternately, with as much ease as your Lordship does poached Eggs."[29] For their part, the inhabitants quickly tired of the restrictions imposed on them by the British military. They needed passes for travel to and from New York and special certificates to bring goods out of the city. The prices of essential commodities were regulated by proclamation. Army quartermasters and barrack-masters commandeered horses, wagons, grain, hay, firewood, and even slaves as needed, leaving only IOU's that were almost impossible to redeem. Shortages became commonplace, and famine a distinct possibility, in what had once been hailed as among the richest agricultural regions in America. As Jeremiah Johnson later recalled: "The inhabitants of Brooklyn were often in great distress for want of food, as no grain or produce of any kind could be raised on this part of the Island, for the fences were all destroyed and the farms were all a great common over which the soldiers and animals roamed at will." Certainly no one had bargained on quartering all those soldiers in their homes—especially the Hessians, whose disorderly behavior and habits prompted local Dutch farmers to dub them the "Dirty Blues." Nor had anyone bargained on the venality of the county's erstwhile liberators. Over and over again, money intended to compensate the owners of property taken by the army found its way into the pockets of officers and other functionaries who had no visible means of support. William Axtell got into the act, collecting funds to raise a regiment of five hundred men in the county, recruiting only thirty rather unsavory characters from somewhere else, and keeping the balance of the money for himself. He named his so-called "regiment" the "Nassau Blues," but his disgusted Flatbush neighbors called them the "Nasty Blues."[30]

Adding to the county's woes was a sharp rise in crime and lawlessness directly attributable to the occupation. "We were constantly being plundered," declared one Flatbush matron, recalling experiences with predatory soldiers that formed the stuff of local memory for generations. That the Hessians figured prominently in these stories as well was, as Johnson explained, the consequence of "their cupidity and proneness to commit petty theft, and their readiness to appropriate every species of property which they could lay their hands upon." Almost as bad as the Hessians were the army's Tory guides and scouts—hard men from all over the colonies who fought mainly for personal gain and plundered with impunity; several companies of these ruffians camped out for five years on a farm in Bushwick, subjecting the residents of that unlucky town to five years of steady abuse and predation. Many army units were withdrawn from the island in 1778 to bolster the British offensive in the south, but conditions actually went from bad to worse because whaleboat raiders from New England— many of whom were Whig refugees from Long Island living along the Connecticut coast—seized the opportunity to step up their forays across Long Island Sound. Tories operating under the authority of the Board of Associated Loyalists then retaliated in kind, and the ensuing free-for-all rapidly degenerated into pointless revenge and brigandage from which no one was immune. As Judge Thomas Jones of Queens County described matters, it was common for the whaleboat men to strike even the south shore of the island, where they "frequently landed, robbed the inhabitants of their furniture, linen, wearing apparel, money, negroes, rum, wine, sugar, and salt; killed their cattle, hogs, sheep, and poultry; and burnt their hay, their oats, wheat, rye, and Indian corn." American raiders from New Jersey descended on New Utrecht and Flatbush twice in 1778, hunting for prominent Tories they could exchange for American prisoners of war but allegedly making off with silver and other valuables as well.[31]

But nothing proved more worrisome than the unsettling effect of the occupation on race relations. Once Howe's forces took New York City, it became a magnet for runaway slaves from all over the colonies, and whites on both sides of the lines grew fearful that they would soon have no slaves at all. Their fears mounted in 1779, when General Clinton (now commander-in-chief of His Majesty's forces), taking a leaf from Governor Dunmore's book, issued a proclamation offering sanctuary and employment to "every Negro who shall desert the Rebell Standdard." Besides drawing still more runaways to the city, Clinton's offer struck a resonant chord with the slaves of Tories as well. As the *New York Weekly Mercury* remarked the following year, "A desire of obtaining freedom unhappily reigns throughout the generality of slaves at present"—particularly disturbing news for nearby Kings County farmers, who were long accustomed to relying on their bondsmen to move goods back and forth from the city.

Even more unsettling was the fact that the British often seemed perversely oblivious to the anxieties and sensitivities of whites on both sides. William Cunningham, the sadistic Provost-Marshall, thought to intimidate American prisoners of war by strutting around accompanied by a "negro with a halter." British foragers employed black drivers ("chiefly . . . run-away negroes," Judge Jones wrote with disdain) to haul grain and wood taken from Tory farmers, blacks and whites mingled freely in local taverns and racecourses, and black units were from time to time billeted in and around villages where one out of every three or four residents was enslaved. At one point, Flatbush voters pleaded with the British to allow no more taverns in the town, because they led to excessive partying, especially among "our Negroes already sufficiently loose and licentious."

When trouble occurred, moreover, British officials often failed to support the customary prerogative of whites to discipline contrary or disobedient blacks. Military courts-martial were known to accept the testimony of blacks and acquit them of crimes, even when their accusers were white. Judge Jones recounted the story of how "a young gentleman of fortune" from Long Island was abused and insulted "in the grossest manner" by a black driver attached to a foraging party. After getting a well-deserved boot in the seat of the pants, "the black rascal" complained to a British officer, who hauled the young gentleman before a court-martial—"For what?" asked Jones incredulously. "For kicking a negro runaway, in the very act of committing a trespass upon his uncle's property." In 1869, drawing heavily on local tradition for his history of Brooklyn, Henry Stiles likewise observed that British officers "required the utmost condescension from the inhabitants, who were expected, while addressing them, to hold their hats under their arms: and should a farmer, in passing, neglect to doff his hat, he ran a strong risk of a good caning; although if he did it, the Briton rarely deigned to notice him or return his civility. As a natural consequence, insubordination arose among the slaves, who either ran away from or became less respectful to their masters." More than a few slaves, Stiles added, became the "willing aiding and abettors" of the bandits who infested the county during the war "and frequently guided them in their predatory expeditions." As the war drew to an end, slaves in Kings County and elsewhere around the state thus found themselves more feared and despised than ever—by Whigs, who believed they had become Tories, and by Tories, who believed they had become intractable.[32]

IV

In November 1783 Kings County whites celebrated Washington's return to New York with enthusiasm. Residents of Bushwick offered him "our sincere congratulations, on this glorious and ever memorable era of the sovereignty and independence of the United States of America," then treated themselves to an ox roast on the banks of the East River, just across from Manhattan—a day "spent in the greatest good humor, decency, and decorum." In New Utrecht and Flatbush, revelers fired cannon and raised liberty poles; in Flatbush, "the occasion was one of great joy and hilarity."[33] Although cynics might have recalled the county's equally enthusiastic reception of General Howe seven years earlier, there is no reason to assume that these sentiments were anything but genuine. Patriots driven out or silenced by the American defeat in 1776 could now speak their minds freely; influential Tories like Axtell and Mathews had fled, never to return; and except for the county's numerous slaves, the most troublesome of whom had probably run away or left with the British, residents of every political stripe must have been eager to put the long and onerous occupation behind them.[34]

Yet if they imagined that their lives would go on as before, they were in for another disappointment. An early signal of what lay in store came almost immediately after the war, when a pair of New York developers, Comfort and Joshua Sands, bought a farm previously confiscated from one of the county's most notorious Tories, John Rapalje. Lying along the East River between Brooklyn and Wallabout Bay, the 160-acre tract became the site of their "City of Olympia," which the brothers envisioned as a center for ship construction and repair. They built wharves, warehouses, and a ropewalk, chopped the property into lots, and sold the lots to several dozen Yankee artisans and their families from New London, Connecticut. The Sands's success inspired imitators like John Jackson, a shipbuilder who laid out Vinegar Hill, close by what would soon be the Brooklyn Navy Yard, and marketed the development to Irish refugees. In light of all this hustle and bustle, it comes as no surprise that the county's population began to grow at an unprecedented pace, climbing to 4,495 in 1790 (up 872 since 1771, a 24 percent increase in two decades) then to 5,740 in 1800 (a 28 percent jump in just a single decade). It also explains why the percentage of Dutch residents dropped below 60 percent, the lowest on record, and continued to decline. Land values in and around Brooklyn meanwhile rose steadily, boosted by New York City's spectacular growth over the same period—from 23,610 in 1786 to 60,515 in 1800—and by the city's continuing appetite for the output of Long Island farms.[35]

The pressure of these developments on the traditional order in Kings County was magnified, as burgeoning numbers of city dwellers acquired a taste for excursions to bucolic hamlets and shore resorts. Henry Wansey, who took "a pleasant rural ramble" through the county in 1794, observed that a Sunday afternoon in July or August might find three or four thousand Manhattan tourists strolling around what remained of Brooklyn's Revolutionary War fortifications, picking fruit in local orchards, or hiring "coachees" to Flatbush, New Utrecht, and Gravesend, where enterprising locals had opened seaside boarding houses and pleasure gardens. Near the Coney Island beach, one entrepreneur reportedly had plans for "a very handsome tea-drinking pleasure house, to accommodate parties who come hither from all the neighboring ports; he intends also to have bathing machines, and several species of entertainment. It seems parties are made here from thirty or forty miles distance, in the summer time." According to Moreau de St. Méry, an observant Frenchman who toured the United States in the mid-1790s, "many New Yorkers" had also taken to renting houses in and around Brooklyn Heights for the entire summer. "The men," he wrote, "go to New York in the morning, and return to Brooklyn after the Stock Exchange closes"—Wall Street commuters taking back the high ground that Washington had lost fewer than twenty years before.[36]

Yet the decisive blow to the county's old way of life would be the extinction of slavery. Despite numerous wartime runaways—and despite a 1784 state law manumitting the slaves of attainted Tories like William Axtell—the number of slaves in Kings County actually increased somewhat, from 1,317 in 1786, to 1,432 in 1790, then to 1,479 in 1800; a significant majority of white households still relied on slave labor, and the proportion of households with four or more slaves nearly quadrupled, from 12 percent in 1755 to 44 percent in 1800. Opposition to the institution was nonetheless building steadily outside the county. Antislavery Whigs failed to get a clause in the 1777 state constitution "recommending" abolition, but the Manumission Society (1785), Quakers, and other groups kept up the pressure. Ultimately, over the strenuous objections of legislators from Kings County, a gradual emancipation bill passed both houses of the state legislature in 1799. As one of the measure's supporters recalled, the Dutchmen "raved and swore by *dunder* and *blixen* that we were robbing them of their property. We told them that they had none and could hold none in human flesh . . . and we passed the law." Many owners hung on as long as they could—879 slaves still remained in Kings County as late as 1820—but the old order was doomed.[37]

Notes

My thanks to Donald Gerardi, Sara Gronim, Mike Wallace, and the editors for helpful readings of earlier versions of this essay.

1. Eighteenth-century Kings County comprised six towns (i.e., townships)—Bushwick, Brooklyn, Flatbush (the county seat), Flatlands, New Utrecht, and Gravesend. Within each were assorted hamlets or villages, one of which might bear the same name

as the town, e.g., Breuckelen or Brookland (now Brooklyn), Bushwick, Flat Bush, Flatlands, New Utrecht, Gravesend. The growth of Brooklyn village in the early decades of the nineteenth century prompted the legislature to incorporate it in 1816 and then, in 1834, to create the City of Brooklyn by combining what remained of the town with the former village, both of which ceased to exist. Over the next sixty years, the expanding city swallowed up the county's other towns and villages as well as the rival City of Williambsburgh, which had likewise engulfed the old town of Bushwick. When the City of Brooklyn annexed the town of Flatlands in 1896, "Brooklyn" and "Kings County" became synonymous—only two years, ironically, before both were absorbed into Greater New York City. For present purposes, I will adhere to eighteenth-century practice and apply "Brooklyn" only to the unincorporated village or town.

2. Ira Rosenwaike, *Population History of New York City* (Syracuse, 1972), 8, 12–13; *The Statistical History of the United States* (New York, 1976), 170–171; Bernard Mason, *The Road to Independence: The Revolutionary Movement in New York, 1773–1777* (Lexington, Ky., 1966), 94n.; Andrew Burnaby, *Travels through the Middle Settlements in North-America, in the Years 1759 and 1760* (London, 1775), 66–67. For a sampling of other views from the late seventeenth to the late eighteenth century, see Nicholas Cresswell, *The Journal of Nicholas Cresswell, 1774–1777* (New York, 1924), 231; Daniel Denton, *A Brief Description of New-York* (London, 1670), 3–6; Jaspar Dankers and Peter Sluyter, *Journal of a Voyage to New York and a Tour in Several of the American Colonies, 1679–80*, trans. Henry C. Murphy (Brooklyn, 1867), esp. 117–124; cf. Johann Dohla, *A Hessian Diary of the American Revolution*, trans. Bruce E. Burgoyne (Norman, Okla., 1990), 76–77; William Eddis, *Letters from America*, ed. Aubrey C. Land (Cambridge, Mass., 1969), 218; Ernst Kipping, *The Hessian View of America* (Monmouth Beach, N.J., 1971), 22 and passim; David John Jeremy, ed., *Henry Wansey and His American Journal: 1794* (Philadelphia, 1974), 130–131. Denton, *Brief Description*, 6, and Dankers and Sluyter, *Journal*, 124–133, describe the remnants of Native American peoples in the final decades of the seventeenth century. A few still lived on the fringes of white communities in Kings County until after the Revolution; according to tradition, the last of their number, Jim de Wilt (Jim the Wild Man), died in 1832. Henry R. Stiles, *A History of the City of Brooklyn*, 3 vols. (Brooklyn, 1867), 1: 232.

3. On the persistence of Dutch culture after the Conquest, see Joyce D. Goodfriend, *Before the Melting Pot: Society and Culture in Colonial New York City, 1664–1730* (Princeton, N.J., 1992); David Narrett, *Inheritance and Family Life in Colonial New York City* (Ithaca, 1992); Linda Briggs Biemer, *Women and Property in Colonial New York: The Transition From Dutch to English Law, 1643–1727* (Ann Arbor, Mich., 1983); Charles Gehring, "The Survival of the Dutch Language in New York and New Jersey," *De Halve Maen* 58 (October 1984), 7ff.; William McLaughlin, "Dutch Rural New York: Community, Economy, and Family in Colonial Flatbush" (Ph.D. diss., Columbia Univ., 1981). In 1698 the Dutch may have comprised 70 or 80 percent of the county's white residents. No doubt that figure declined somewhat before the Revolution, and it is probably significant that Dutch would be taught in the Flatbush schoolhouse until 1776, when a new rule mandated instruction in English instead. Gertrude Lefferts Vanderbilt, *Social History of Flatbush* (New York, 1881), 53; Rosenwaike, *Population History*, 12. One

village, Gravesend, remained predominately English; it was also the smallest in the county. For examples of sporadic Dutch violence against county sheriffs and judges, the hinges of English county government, see Douglas Greenberg, *Crime and Law Enforcement in the Colony of New York, 1691–1776* (Ithaca, 1974), 65–66, 111–112, 115, 181, and passim.

4. Henry P. Johnston, *The Campaign of 1776 Around New York and Brooklyn* (1878, repr. New York, 1971), 95–98; William E. Dornemann, trans., "A Diary Kept By Chaplain Waldeck During the Last American War: Part II," *Journal of the Johannes Schwalm Historical Association* 2 (n.d.), 41. Craig S. Wilder, *A Covenant with Color: Race and Social Power in Brooklyn* (New York, 2000), 21–41, neatly disposes of the perdurable local legend that slavery in Kings County was kinder and gentler than its southern counterpart—as in, e.g., Stiles, *Brooklyn*, 1: 232–233; Vanderbilt, *Social History of Flatbush*, esp. 249, 252, 259–263, and 267; Gabriel Furman, *Antiquities of Long Island*, ed. Frank Moore (New York, 1874), 222–223; Stephen M. Ostrander, *A History of the City of Brooklyn*, 2 vols. (Brooklyn, 1894), 1: 172–173; and John J. Snyder, *Tales of Old Flatbush* (Brooklyn, 1945), 176–177. Alexander Graydon, a captured American officer billeted on a Dutch farmer, recalled meals during which "a black boy, too, was generally in the room; not as a waiter, but as a kind of *enfant de maison*, who walked about, or took post in the chimney corner with his hat on, and occasionally joined in the conversation. It is probable, that but for us, he would have been placed at the table; and that it had been the custom before we came. Certain it is, that the idea of equality, was more fully and fairly acted upon in this house of a British subject than ever I have seen it practised by the most vehement declaimers for the rights of man among ourselves. It is but fair, however, to mention, that I have never been among our transcendent republicans of Virginia, and her dependencies." This well-known remark needs to be read with caution, however. Graydon, a prominent Federalist, was clearly deploying his memory of long-ago events to score points against the Jeffersonians—and in the process mistaking intimacy for equality. John S. Littell, ed., *Memoirs of His Own Time, With Reminiscences of the Men and Events of the Revolution by Alexander Graydon* (Philadelphia, 1846, rep. 1979), 248. See also Marc Linder and Lawrence S. Zacharias, *Of Cabbages and Kings County: Agriculture and the Formation of Modern Brooklyn* (Iowa City, Iowa, 1999), 79–88; Richard Moss, *Slavery on Long Island: A Study in Local Institutional and Early African-American Communal Life* (New York, 1993), 69–91; Graham Russell Hodges, *Root & Branch: African Americans in New York & East Jersey, 1613–1863* (Chapel Hill, N.C., 1999); Hodges and Alan Edward Brown, *"Pretends to Be Free": Runaway Slave Advertisements From Colonial and Revolutionary New York and New Jersey* (New York, 1994); Don Skemer, "New Evidence of Black Unrest in Colonial New York," *Journal of Long Island History* 12 (Fall 1975), 46–49; Robert J. Swan, "The Black Presence in Seventeenth-Century Brooklyn," *De Halve Maen* 63 (1990), 1–6; and Thomas J. Davis, "New York's Long Black Line: A Note on the Growing Slave Population, 1676–1790," in Wendell Tripp, ed., *Coming and Becoming: Pluralism in New York State History* (Cooperstown, N.Y., 1999), 79–97. The impact of slavery on white employment is treated in Edgar McManus, *A History of Negro Slavery in New York* (Syracuse, 1970), 47–49; Samuel McKee, *Labor in Colonial New York* (New York, 1935), 90–95; and Edwin G.

Burrows and Mike Wallace, *Gotham: A History of New York City to 1898* (New York, 1998), 126–129, 146–149, 159–166.

5. On the law of slavery in New Netherland and New York, see A. Leon Higginbotham, *In the Matter of Color: Race and the American Legal Process* (New York, 1978), 100–135. On Evertsen and Leisler, see Burrows and Wallace, *Gotham*, 77–102.

6. Carl Becker, *The History of Political Parties in the Province of New York, 1760–1776* (Madison, Wis., 1909), 139–140.

7. Onderdonk, *Revolutionary Incidents of Suffolk and Kings Counties* (1849; repr. Port Washington, N.Y., 1970), 113–114; Becker, *Political Parties*, 188; Mason, *Road to Independence*, 44–45.

8. Onderdonk, *Revolutionary Incidents of Suffolk and Kings*, 114–115; Peter Force, *American Archives*, Fourth Series, 6 vols. (Washington, D.C., 1837–1846), 2: 837–838.

9. Stiles, *Brooklyn*, 1: 248.; Thomas Jones, *History of New York during the Revolutionary War*, 2 vols. (New York, 1879), 1: 304–309.

10. O'Callaghan, *Documents Relative to the Colonial History of New York*, 15: 34; *Journals of the Provincial Congress, Provincial Convention, Committee of Safety, and Council of Safety of the State of New York*, 2 vols. (Albany, 1842), 1: 215; Hodges, *Root and Branch*, 136–137.

11. Mason, *Road to Independence*, 116–117; *Journals of the Provincial Congress*, 1: 572, 582. The impression of Whig inaction may owe something to the fact that many county and town records were allegedly spirited away after the war by prominent Tories like William Axtell and John Rapalje. Philip Klingle, "Kings County during the American Revolution," in Rita S. Miller, ed., *Brooklyn USA* (New York, 1979), 81n.; Thomas W. Field, *The Battle of Long Island* (Brooklyn, 1869), 12; Ostrander, *History of Brooklyn*, 1: 302; Stiles, *Brooklyn*, 1: 327. Also Judith Van Buskirk, "Crossing the Lines: African Americans in the New York City Region during the British Occupation, 1776–1783," *Pennsylvania History* 65 (1998), 78 and passim—the gist of which may now be found in her *Generous Enemies: Patriots and Loyalists in Revolutionary New York* (Philadelphia, 2002). On the uproar triggered by Dunmore's proclamation, see Sylvia R. Frey, *Water from the Rock: Black Resistance in a Revolutionary Age* (Princeton, N.J., 1991), esp. 63ff., and Moss, *Slavery on Long Island*, 143. The reaction of Kings County slaveowners to Dunmore's proclamation is a subject that bears further investigation, but the absence of widespread indignation suggests the decisive role of local circumstances— among them the influence of prominent Tories like Axtell and Mathews and the long tradition of British support for Dutch masters. Besides, Dunmore's proclamation applied only to the slaves of rebels, of whom there were already so few in the county that slaveowners there could believe they need not worry.

12. John J. Gallagher, *The Battle of Brooklyn, 1776* (New York, 1995), 81–83; Johnston, *Campaign of 1776*, 56n.

13. *Journals of the Provincial Congress*, 1: 308, 309, 332, 340–341; Stiles, *Brooklyn*, 1: 247; Onderdonk, *Revolutionary Incidents of Suffolk and Kings*, 115–117; Eric I.

Edwin G. Burrows

Manders, *The Battle of Long Island* (Monmouth Beach, N.J., 1978), 10; Johnston, *Campaign of 1776*, 65.

14. Onderdonk, *Revolutionary Incidents of Suffolk and Kings*, 117–120; Stiles, *Brooklyn*, 1: 249–252; Johnston, *Campaign of 1776*, 69–84; Thomas Strong, *History of the Town of Flatbush* (New York, 1842), 141; Edward H. Tatum Jr., ed., *The American Journal of Ambrose Serle* (San Marino, Calif., 1940), 60; Manders, *Battle of Long Island*, 15–16, 33–34; Gallagher, *Battle of Brooklyn*, 73–80.

15. Manders, *Battle of Long Island*, 28, 31; for more conservative estimates, see Gallagher, *Battle of Brooklyn*, 50, 58, 61, 66–67, which has an American force of 29,000 shrinking to 17,000 by mid-August, of whom only 13,500 were fit for combat.

16. Their uneasiness about preparing for battle amid a hostile population ripened in late June, when Mayor Mathews was arrested in his Flatbush home for aiding the so-called "Hickey Plot"—a rather hazy Tory scheme to prepare for the British invasion by gathering money and arms, corrupting Whig soldiers, and perhaps abducting Washington himself. Mayor Mathews was packed off to prison in Connecticut but escaped and made his way to London. Thomas J. Wertenbaker, *Father Knickerbocker Rebels: New York City during the Revolution* (New York, 1948), 82.

17. Manders, *Battle of Long Island*, 31–32, 59. The Kings County regiment belonged to the 1st New York Brigade. On paper it consisted of two troops of light horse and seven companies on foot, one raised from each township except Brooklyn, which supplied two. Exactly how many men this meant is unclear. Every white male resident between the ages of 16 and 60 could be called for militia duty, and one investigation turned up the names of 676 men qualified for service by age alone, fully 630 of whom defected to the British between August 1776 and August 1777. Klingle, "Kings County," 74–75; also Kenneth Scott, "Loyalists and 'Doubtful' Men of Kings County, 1777," *The New York Genealogical and Biographical Record* 105 (April 1974), 67–72. This is not inconsistent with Stiles's guess that only about 200 of the county militia fought on the American side in the Battle of Brooklyn, and that desertions immediately after the battle reduced that number to around 150. Stiles, *Brooklyn*, 1: 296. Cf. Thomas W. Field, *The Battle of Long Island* (Brooklyn, 1869), 137.

18. *Journals of the Provincial Congress*, 1: 567–568 (italics in original).

19. Manders, *Battle of Long Island*, 34–35; Gallagher, *Battle of Brooklyn*, 87–90; Johnston, *Campaign of 1776*, 139–145; Tatum, ed., *Journal of Serle*, 71–74; Vanderbilt, *Social History of Flatbush*, 370–372. Cf. Strong, *Flatbush*, 142–144; and "Dominie Rubel, Tory Preacher of Flatbush," in Joseph W. Halpern, ed., *Flatbush in the American Revolution* (Flatbush, N.Y., 1976), 22–24.

20. Onderdonk, *Revolutionary Incidents of Suffolk and Kings*, 125, 132–134; Stiles, *Brooklyn*, 1: 256–257; Manders, *Battle of Long Island*, 34–35; Gallagher, *Battle of Brooklyn*, 91; Tatum, ed., *Journal of Serle*, 74–75.

21. Manders, *Battle of Long Island*, 35–36; Gallagher, *Battle of Brooklyn*, 92–94; Stiles, *Brooklyn*, 1: 254–255, 296–297; Onderdonk, *Revolutionary Incidents of Suffolk*

and Kings, 156–157. On the skirmishing around Flatbush, see Dennis P. Ryan, *A Salute to Courage: The American Revolution as Seen Through Wartime Writings of Officers of the Continental Army and Navy* (New York, 1979), 37–39; and "The Diary of Col. Josiah Smith," in Frederick G. Mather, *The Refugees of 1776 from Long Island to Connecticut* (Albany, 1913), 1010–1011.

22. Manders, *Battle of Long Island*, 33–34, 61. Here, too, there is no agreement as to the numbers deployed in Brooklyn or along the outer perimeter. Manders appears to have made the most thorough examination of the available sources, but cf. Gallagher, *Battle of Brooklyn*, 60, 109; Stiles, *Brooklyn*, 1: 260; Johnston, *Campaign of 1776*, 145–160. A spy reported to General Greene that eight hundred blacks were under arms on Staten Island, including units of the Aetheopian Regiment brought up from Virginia after Dunmore was driven out. Force, *American Archives*, Fifth Series, 3 vols. (Washington, D.C., 1848–1853), 1: 486. In addition, the Tory companies raised by Colonel Oliver De Lancey in Kings and Queens counties are said to have included several score free blacks. Moss, *Slavery on Long Island*, 141.

23. Manders, *Battle of Long Island*, 39–41; Gallagher, *Battle of Brooklyn*, 97–122; George F. Scheer and Hugh F. Rankin, *Rebels and Redcoats* (Cleveland, 1957), 187–188; Onderdonk, *Revolutionary Incidents of Suffolk and Kings*, 138; Ryan, *Salute to Courage*, 39–41. Although most of the American dead were buried on the grounds of the Flatbush Reformed Dutch Church, area farmers were still turning up bones in their fields well into the next century.

24. Manders, *Battle of Long Island*, 43–46; Scheer and Rankin, *Rebels and Redcoats*, 189; John C. Dann, *Revolution Remembered: Eyewitness Accounts of the War of Independence* (Chicago, 1980), 50; Martin Joseph Plum, *Private Yankee Doodle*, ed. George F. Scheer (Boston, 1962), 26; Onderdonk, *Revolutionary Incidents of Suffolk and Kings*, 148.

25. Manders, *Battle of Long Island*, 62; Gallagher, *Battle of Brooklyn*, 135–137; Howard H. Peckham, *The Toll of Independence: Engagements and Battle Casualties of the American Revolution* (Chicago, 1974), 22; cf. Ryan, *Salute to Courage*, 42, in which a captain from Virginia reports "1000 men killed & taken this I can affirm for a truth as I had it from five or six Maryland officers that were in the action." General Howe, on the other hand, initially reported 3,300 Americans killed, wounded, or taken prisoner. Onderdonk, *Revolutionary Incidents of Suffolk and Kings*, 136.

26. Manders, *Battle of Long Island*, 46–49; Gallagher, *Battle of Brooklyn*, 138–164; Onderdonk, *Revolutionary Incidents of Suffolk and Kings*, 161–165; Stiles, *Brooklyn*, 1: 282–296.

27. Vanderbilt, *Social History of Flatbush*, 375–376, and passim; and Strong, *Flatbush*, 151–156; Stiles, *Brooklyn*, 2: 325. Strong, Stiles, and Vanderbilt made extensive use of the oral traditions preserved among townsfolk who had lived through the fighting and subsequent occupation; the Flatbush home of Vanderbilt's great-grandparents, Evert Hegeman and Seidtje Suydam, was one of three burned by the British, and its destruction became a staple of village lore. Cf. Joseph W. Halpern, "The British

Occupation of Flatbush," in Halpern, *Flatbush in the American Revolution*, 13–21. After the American defeat, several thousand patriots from Suffolk and Queens Counties fled across the Sound to Connecticut. Few if any Kings County patriots joined this exodus—partly because there were not many of them, and partly because their conspicuously Dutch culture and connections would not have been well-received in Yankee New England, which had supplied Queens and Suffolk with many of their original settlers and where Anglo-Dutch animosity had deep roots. Mather, *Refugees of 1776*, 187 and passim.

28. Klingle, "Kings County," 74–75, identifies only thirty-seven Kings County men, twenty from Brooklyn alone, who refused the oath, died in service with American forces, or went into exile. Onderdonk, *Revolutionary Incidents of Suffolk and Kings*, 167–171; Stiles, *Brooklyn*, 1: 297–299, 311–312; Gallagher, *Battle of Brooklyn*, 164; Mather, *Refugees of 1776*, 1050.

29. Marion Balderston and David Syrett, eds., *The Lost War: Letters from British Officers during the American Revolution* (New York, 1975), 131.

30. Stiles, *Brooklyn*, 1: 300–301, 326; 2: 360–363; Strong, *Flatbush*, 156; Moss, *Slavery on Long Island*, 143–144; and "Recollections of Johnson, Part 2," 28. No one chronicled official venality with greater outrage than Judge Thomas Jones, a solid Queens County Tory who came to believe that greed and peculation had fatally undermined the British war effort. His contempt for Axtell's shady dealings was boundless. See Jones, *History*, 1: 269, 331–340, 347, and passim. Between 1777 and 1782, the residents of Kings County were saddled with the additional burden of providing room and board for several hundred captured American officers sent out from New York City on parole. Larry G. Bowman, "Military Parolees on Long Island, 1777–1782," *Journal of Long Island History* 18 (Spring 1982), 21–29. Ironically, there were probably more parolees billeted in the county's villages and hamlets than there had been Whigs when the war broke out—which is probably what a Major Matthews had in mind when he reportedly complained in 1778 that "there were to many Damn'd Rebbels in Flatt-Bush." Margaret E. Irwin, "One Man's War of Independence," *America in Britain* 9 (1971), 15–19.

31. Onderdonk, *Revolutionary Incidents of Suffolk and Kings*, 178–182, 185, 186, 189, 190, and passim; Stiles, *Brooklyn*, 1: 318, 35–36; 2: 361–362; Strong, *Flatbush*, 159–162; Jones, *History*, 1: 265–269, 271, 302, 304–309; Thomas W. Field, ed., "Recollections of Incidents of the Revolution of the Colonies Occurring in Brooklyn, Collated from the Manuscripts and Conversations of General Jeremiah Johnson," *Journal of Long Island History* 12 (Spring 1976), 19; "Recollections of General Johnson: Part 2," *Journal of Long Island History* 13 (Fall 1976), 27; Vanderbilt, *Social History of Flatbush*, 322. Also Philip Ranlet, *The New York Loyalists* (Knoxville, Tenn., 1986), 84 and passim; Stephen Conway, "'The Great Mischief Complain'd of': Reflections on the Misconduct of British Soldiers in the Revolutionary War." *William and Mary Quarterly* 47 (July 1990), 381 and passim; Milton M. Klein, "Why Did the British Fail to Win the Hearts and Minds of New Yorkers?" *New York History* 64 (October 1983), 357–376. "So many thousands of these illegal and felonious acts were committed within the British lines during the war," Jones remarked bitterly, "that an enumeration of them would . . . fill a folio."

32. Stiles, *Brooklyn*, 1: 300, 303; Klingle, "Kings County," 79; Van Buskirk, "Crossing the Lines," 84–85, 92, as well as *Generous Enemies*, 147ff.; Jones, *History*, 1: 287–288, 334; 2: 84. Cf. Field, "Recollections of Johnson," 18–19, and Ostrander, *History of Brooklyn*, 1: 212; Moss, *Slavery on Long Island*, 92, 143, 144; Dennis Ryan, *Salute to Courage: The American Revolution as Seen Through the Wartime Writings of Officers of the Continental Army and Navy* (New York, 1979), 67–69. Also Wertenbaker, *Father Knickerbocker Rebels*, 247; Oscar T. Barck, *New York during the War for Independence, with Special Reference to the Period of British Occupation* (New York, 1931), 128, 133; Burrows and Wallace, *Gotham*, 245–261; Graham Hodges, *Root and Branch*, esp. 139–161. In 1777 Oliver De Lancey acknowledged heightened antiblack feeling among New York Tories by discharging "all Negroes Mullattoes and other Improper Persons" from his corps. At the same time, one rebel escapee from the infamous British prison ships anchored in Wallabout Bay would be warned by the Brooklyn farm wife who gave him shelter: "For God's sake, don't let that black woman of mine see you, for she is as big a devil as any of the King's folks and she will bring me out."

33. Stiles, *Brooklyn*, 1: 365–369; Strong, *Flatbush*, 171.

34. When the British evacuated New York in 1783, they took with them only a couple of dozen Long Island runaways; the number who simply vanished was almost certainly much larger. Moss, *Slavery on Long Island*, 140, 146.

35. Thomas L. Purvis, "The National Origins of New Yorkers in 1790," *New York History*, 67 (April 1986), 133–153; Rosenwaike, *Population History*, 18, 30–31; Eugene L. Armbruster, *The Olympia Settlement in Early Brooklyn, N.Y.* (n.p., 1912); Armbruster, *Broooklyn's Eastern District* (Brooklyn, 1942), esp. 1–4; Kenneth Roberts and Anna M. Roberts, eds., *Moreau de Saint-Méry's American Journey: 1793–1798* (New York, 1947), 170 ("The proximity of New York daily increases the value of property in Brooklyn as well as those elsewhere on Long Island."). Another symptom of change was the town's decision in May 1784 to build a "cage for the confinement of vagrants" near the ferry house. Sidney Pomerantz, *New York: An American City, 1783–1803* (New York, 1938), 263. New York City's postwar surge is described in Burrows and Wallace, *Gotham*, 265–287, 299–304, 333–352.

36. Pomerantz, *New York*, 500–501; Jeremy, ed., *Wansey and His American Journal*, 130–131, 134; Isaac Weld, *Travels Through the States of North America . . . in 1795, 1796, and 1797*, 2 vols. (London, 1807), 1: 267; Kenneth Roberts and Anna M. Roberts, eds., *Moreau de Saint-Méry's American Journey: 1793–1798* (New York, 1947) 170–173; cf. John A. Kouwenhoven, *The Columbia Historical Portrait of New York: An Essay in Graphic History* (New York, 1972), 99. Kenneth Jackson, *Crabgrass Frontier: The Suburbanization of the United States* (New York, 1985), 25–32, discusses Brooklyn's transformation into the nation's first "ferry suburb" in the early nineteenth century. By the 1830s, Flatbush too was being transformed, Thomas Strong boasting that "nearly all the houses which were standing during the Revolutionary War are removed." Strong's reference to the demise of the communal brewery soon after the war suggests, however, how quickly life even there began to change. Strong, *History of Flatbush*, 51–52, 176.

37. Shane White, *Somewhat More Independent: The End of Slavery in New York City, 1770–1810* (Athens, Ga., 1991); Higginbotham, *In the Matter of Color*, 135–148; Wilder, *Covenant with Color*, esp. 35–41; Moss, *Slavery on Long Island*, 72, 154–155; Burrows and Wallace, *Gotham*, 285–287, 347–349. After the adoption of gradual emancipation, Kings County slaveowners, like those elsewhere, began unloading their property down south. In 1802 Henry Murison of Flatbush sold Cato, his wife, and their four children to a buyer from Georgia. Moss, *Slavery on Long Island*, 157. Murison and others like him got their revenge, if that is the word for it, with the invention of a local tradition that they had been benevolent masters, beloved by their grateful and faithful servants even after slavery ended. Gertrude Lefferts Vanderbilt, for example, professed to remember elderly residents of Flatbush in the 1860s "who were always called 'old Mis'es' or 'old Master' in certain colored families." Vanderbilt, *Social History of Flatbush*, 266, and other sources identified in note 2 above. The last resident of the county to have experienced slavery firsthand seems to have been "Uncle Sammy" Anderson, once owned by the Lott family, who died in 1910 at the age of ninety-two. Snyder, *Tales of Old Flatbush*, 176–77.

2

Queens County

Joseph S. Tiedemann

Revolutionary Queens County constituted what is today the Borough of Queens and the adjacent County of Nassau. Situated on the western end of Long Island, it contained 410 square miles and was bordered on the north by the Long Island Sound, on the east by Suffolk County, on the south by the Atlantic Ocean, and on the west by Kings County and the East River. In 1776 the county contained five towns—Newtown, Flushing, Jamaica, Hempstead, and Oyster Bay—and had a population of about 11,000, most of whom were farmers. Because of the war, Hempstead was divided in 1784 into two towns, North Hempstead and South Hempstead.[1]

Economically, the county was divided by a line running from east to west. The last glacial advance had left in the northern part of the island a soil which was composed of clay, sand, and granite. Although this "glacial till" was stony, it was very fertile, and the farms in Newtown, Flushing, Hempstead's northern necks, and some Oyster Bay areas, were "wonderfully prolific." The soil in the south was sandy and had better drainage but was never as productive. As a result, in 1784, the per capita wealth of the inhabitants of Flushing was £546; North Hempstead, £488; Newtown, £426; Oyster Bay, £367; Jamaica, £277; and South Hempstead, £265. The sale of agricultural products to the nearby New York City market made quite a few county families wealthy. Prosperity, in turn, fostered slavery. In 1771, 20.4 percent of the population of 10,980 people was African American, most of whom were slaves. In 1786 slaves constituted 16.3 percent of the population of 13,084 individuals.[2]

Queens County was not in the vanguard of the American Revolution. Indeed, if the majority of its people had had their way, there would not have been a revolution in 1776. Still, the ordeal of county residents from 1763 to 1787

sheds light on vital aspects of the Revolution. This essay will examine why residents choose the sides they did, how the Loyalists were able in 1775 to out-
maneuver the Whigs in Queens, how the British occupation of the county from
1776 to 1783 did irreparable harm to the royal cause, and how residents in the
postwar period established a new political community based upon the principles of the Revolution.

Loyalties in Queens County

Despite the passions generated by the Tea Act (May 1774), the Boston Tea
Party (December 1774), and the Coercive Acts (March–May 1775), most county
residents refused to support either the Whig or Tory cause. Every adult male had
the opportunity—at least once in 1775—to declare himself a Patriot or Loyalist.[3]
Only a tiny minority, 12 percent, championed the American cause, and only in
Newtown did Whigs outnumber their opponents. The Loyalists, too, were a distinct minority, constituting only 26.8 percent of the population. A decisive majority, 60.3 percent, remained neutral and uncommitted. Moreover, neither
ideology nor the imperial crises in the years after 1763 determined whether a
person became a Patriot or Royalist. Instead, residents acted in response to specific local quarrels that had begun in the previous century and that now became
the basis for the Revolutionary divisions within Queens. These local disputes
served as a medium through which partisans acquired an appreciation of the
broader conflict swirling about them. The Revolution in Queens was thus a
small-scale civil war in the midst of an intercontinental, colonial struggle for
independence. Unlike neighboring Kings County, the institution of slavery was
not a key factor in determining allegiance in the struggle. Nor was economic
status an important reason.[4]

In western Queens—the towns of Jamaica, Newtown, and Flushing—
Patriots and Loyalists divided along religious lines. The quarrel had begun with
the establishment of the Anglican Church in Queens in 1693, and partisans now
saw the Revolution as the latest phase in that enduring dispute. Presbyterians
embraced Patriotism (and eventually Independence) as the path to the disestab-
lishment of the Church of England, and Anglicans proffered their political loyalty to the Crown to safeguard their church's privileged position. The protracted
nature of the struggle between these two denominations—an ordeal that had
lasted almost a century and that had included violence, forcible occupation of a
church, destruction of ecclesiastical property, and sporadic suits in provincial
courts—had politicized participants, provided them with a mind-set and vocab-
ulary attuned to conflict, and predisposed them to take sides in the Revolution.
Whereas 52 percent of the Presbyterians in western Queens became Whigs, 39
percent of the Anglicans became Tories. Despite the religious quarrel, or per-

haps because of it, neutrality remained a strong force in both churches: 37.1 percent of the Presbyterians and 48.7 percent of the Anglicans remained unaligned.[5]

Although 47.1 percent of the members of the Dutch Reformed Church in western Queens also became Loyalists, they were followers and not leaders in the cause. The Dutch were a foreign-speaking cultural minority that had sought since the British conquest of New York in 1664 to ensure their autonomy by sustaining friendly relations with the Anglican Church.[6] Tellingly, the Dutch held few leadership positions in the king's cause. 18.9 percent of all county Loyalists were Dutch Reformed, but only 3.6 percent of the Tory political and military leadership belonged to that denomination. Anglicans, who comprised 32 percent of all county Tories, provided 64.3 percent of the group's leadership.[7]

The situation in Flushing is also noteworthy for two reasons. First, the town's Presbyterians constituted only about 9 percent of those of known religion, and the Patriot cause, therefore, lacked the well-disposed group and the identifiable issues that are so crucial for nurturing a nascent political movement. Second, Quakers constituted the single largest denomination in town, and their pacifism set the tone in a community, where more than three-quarters of the residents remained neutral. The data for Flushing signify that without a local grievance serving as a symbol for the larger struggle, few county men readily comprehended or cared about what was at stake in the dispute between Britain and its North American colonies.[8]

In eastern Queens, the American Revolution split the town of Hempstead in half. Patriots dominated the northern part of town and joined the Whig cause to achieve home rule. The Royalists, who controlled south Hempstead, were anti-separatists who supported the status quo in town and empire. Again, a local dispute, which can in fact be traced back in the town records to the seventeenth century, was crucial in determining how partisans reacted to the Revolution.[9] In Oyster Bay, located between Hempstead and Suffolk County, there were fewer partisans than in most areas of Queens. Not only was the population quite small, but the town also lacked a history of dissension. Unaccustomed to squabbling over local issues, few people took up the cudgel for either the Whig or Tory faction.

The most notable fact about Queens County, however, is that a clear majority remained neutral in the Revolution. Most of these neutrals were also apolitical. They were more concerned about the soil, weather, and next crop than with arguing the merits of Britain's colonial policies or waging revolution. Their lives revolved around family, farm, and community. To be neutral was to champion the local and immediate world they knew best. In short, they preferred harmony and stability to partisanship, discord, or violent strife. Put another way, the bitter heritage of dissension predisposed a majority of county men to remain firmly on the sidelines. The very real possibility that their farms would become battlefields gave them further cause to espouse neutrality. So long as they were left in peace, they could probably have accepted a government that was either British

46   *Joseph S. Tiedemann*

or American. Indeed, the people of Queens had a history of increasing political apathy. Two studies have proven that popular participation in government had declined during the eighteenth century. By the 1770s town meetings had stopped voting on provincial issues, and even some matters of local administration had passed beyond their purview. Jamaica, for instance, which held an average of 4.87 town meetings per year before 1700, held only one per year between 1760 and 1776, and the agenda was typically confined to electing town officials.[10]

The Contest between Whigs and Loyalists

Because so many inhabitants were neutral and apolitical in 1775–1776, it is not astonishing that in the years following the French and Indian War residents had said little about the imperial crises that were causing so much turmoil in New York City. It was not until November 1774, when that city's Committee of Correspondence urged Queens County residents to endorse the Continental Congress and to establish committees of correspondence and observation, that county men found they could no longer ignore the political storm that would finally culminate in revolution.[11] The county's response was tepid. Only in Newtown could Whigs elect a committee that could be said to embody the will of townsmen. Committees were also formed in Jamaica and Flushing, but it was plain they did not represent the majority viewpoint, so they had scant influence.[12]

In March 1775, after the New York Assembly had repudiated the Continental Congress, New York City Whigs asked the five towns to choose deputies to a Provincial Congress that was to convene on April 20. The request was debated at the annual April town meetings. Newtown and Flushing each agreed to send a delegate, but the other three towns failed to do so. When New York City Whigs sent another circular, this time urging the election of delegates to a new Provincial Congress to meet on May 24, Whigs chose five delegates from the county at large. But Tories soon dissuaded two from serving. In September, the Provincial Congress ordered that anyone in Queens who had not signed the Continental Association was to be disarmed, but the Whigs backed down when Hempstead Tories threatened armed resistance. In November 1775, at an election held at Jamaica, the county voted 778 to 221 against representation in Congress. The next month county Loyalists issued a declaration that they had not "interrupt[ed] the Quiet of others," and "wish[ed] only to remain in peace." But if others trampled upon their rights as Englishmen, they would resist with force.[13] In sum, Lexington, Concord, and Bunker Hill had persuaded very few county inhabitants of the justice of the American cause or of the need to combat British imperialism.

The Whig failure and Loyalist triumph in Queens are striking, for the reverse was the more typical outcome. The tasks Whigs faced in Queens were straightforward. They had to win the allegiance of the people, especially the large number of neutral residents; to develop a viable organizational structure that was capable of nurturing their nascent cause; and to crush the Loyalists' will to resist. The Whigs clearly failed, and their defeat resulted partly because of their own mistakes, partly because of the ability of their adversaries, but most especially because of the situation in which they found themselves.

Whig propaganda stressed that Patriots championed liberty over the "tyrannical measures of the enemies of our country," who would "reduce it to slavery."[14] Such language plainly appealed to Presbyterians in western Queens and separatists in north Hempstead, because they both already felt abused. Of course, it failed to sway residents who belonged to the factions that had opposed these two groups for as long as anyone could remember. The Whigs' real problem was that their message did not persuade their neutral neighbors. Britain's alleged abuses, from the Stamp Act to the Coercive Acts, had in Queens (as in other rural areas) caused scarcely a protest. Imperial issues were too remote—economically, politically, and psychologically—for the county's neutral, apolitical majority to feel threatened. In truth, these people remained unconvinced even after the Declaration of Independence. A century of local conflicts had inured them to the partisan outbursts of their more contentious neighbors. As a result, patriots failed to shake the apolitical out of their apathy or to remake them into revolutionaries.

About 20 percent of the county's neutrals were Quakers, who abhorred the use of violence. Unlike some other pacifist religious sects, Friends did not hold a negative opinion of the state. Instead, Quakers were enjoined by their religious principles to obey civil government, except when its laws demanded that a Friend commit an immoral act. Overthrowing a secular government was the responsibility of God alone. As a result, Whig propaganda repelled, rather than attracted, Friends. Complicating matters for the Patriots was the fact that Quakers had a demonstrable influence on opinion in the county: the larger the percentage of Friends in a community, the larger was the proportion of neutrals, not only in the population as a whole, but also in the non-Quaker segment of it.[15]

Because Whig propaganda failed to convert the neutral, patriots had real difficulty setting up the organizational structure needed to advance their cause. Only in Newtown, where they outnumbered Tories, were they able to score any lasting successes. As a result, the New York Provincial Congress felt compelled to attempt coercion as a form of persuasion. On September 16, 1775, it ordered the disarming of every New Yorker who had not signed the Continental Association, but backed down in Queens, when local Tories began to arm themselves for battle. After the county voted in November at Jamaica not to send delegates to the Provincial Congress, and Tories issued their declaration in December threatening the Whigs with resistance, the Continental Congress ordered Col. Nathaniel Heard to march troops into Queens, to disarm Royalists, and to arrest prominent Tories. Although Heard made some progress, several of his troops mistreated inhabitants and had to be withdrawn before residents were even further alienated.[16]

Even though a military solution imposed from the outside risked remaking neutrals into Loyalists, George Washington authorized Gen. Charles Lee to enter Queens County to disarm the Royalists. Both men were convinced that most Long Islanders planned to join British forces the moment they landed in New York. However, Whig committeemen from Hempstead were soon denouncing the abusive behavior of those acting under Lee's authority.[17] The Continental Congress transferred Lee, but the continued recalcitrance of local Loyalists and the imminent arrival of the British soon impelled the Provincial Congress and the Continental Congress to station troops in Queens and to engage in frequent Tory hunting parties. The presence of Patriot military forces finally allowed county Whigs to establish a committee system and to wrest control of political affairs in the county. Coercion had effectively silenced the opposition, but it had not broken its will. In the end, the Whigs were never able to resolve their chief dilemma: How could the Loyalist military threat be crushed and an expected invasion repelled without forsaking the struggle to win the allegiance of neutral residents?[18]

The Whigs were not wholly responsible for their setback in Queens, for they were opposed by a motivated and disciplined group of local Tories, who were adept at propaganda and organization. Because Queens was so close to New York City, royal officials often maintained a residence in the county, and their presence emboldened local Loyalist leaders. Led by Lt. Gov. Cadwallader Colden and his son David, the group included George D. Ludlow, a New York Supreme Court justice; his brother Gabriel G. Ludlow, colonel of the Queens County militia; Thomas Jones, another Supreme Court justice; Capt. Richard Hewlett, an officer in the French and Indian War and second in command of the county militia; and Daniel Kissam, the county's representative in the Assembly. This capable group was able to stiffen the courage of local Loyalists and to exploit the opportunities offered them. For example, the group responded to Whig propaganda by arguing that a tyranny existed in the county, but avowed that it was a Whig and not a royal tyranny. To support this claim, they pointed to the abuses Patriot soldiers and committees had perpetrated in the county. Of course, Tories had a much easier task than the Whigs. The former needed only to persuade neutrals to remain uncommitted; Patriots had to convince them to embrace the American cause.[19]

The most significant Tory feat was the *Asia* affair. In response to requests made by New York's royal governor, William Tryon, to British military officials for assistance in protecting Crown supporters, Capt. George Vandeput of the *Asia* provided arms to county Loyalists. How many shipments were made is unknown, but there were probably more than one. In November 1775 Samuel

Nostran and Isaac Lossie advised the Provincial Congress that naval officers from the *Asia* had supplied Captain Hewlett with powder, ball, small arms, a cannon, and a gunner to work it. While those arms were being distributed, Loyalists were told that five thousand British regulars would soon land at Rockaway, on the county's south shore. Farmers even stopped marketing their cattle in expectation of a rise in prices once the British appeared. Then, on December 18, Vandeput wrote that he had, at Tryon's request, furnished county residents with "two Barrels of Powder, some Flints, and 300 Weight of Musket balls." Tryon also sent arms to Dow Ditmas for dispersal among Royalists living in western Queens. Ditmas also gave instructions about the preparations to be made in advance of a British landing.[20]

The distribution of war materials had a powerful effect. On several occasions Loyalists had threatened to do battle with the Whigs; British arms now made that threat credible. Although full-scale fighting never broke out, the Continental Congress and the Provincial Congress were compelled to divide their already inadequate forces and to commit more troops to Queens than they could spare. The activities of the Whig soldiers, in turn, antagonized county inhabitants, making it more difficult for Patriots to win their support. The weapons were also a key element in the psychological warfare Tories were waging in Queens, for the arms provided tangible evidence of Britain's resolve to retake New York. This equipment emboldened neutrals to oppose the patriot cause, knowing that the British army was about to snuff out the rebellion in New York. Nonetheless, even though the Loyalist strategy in Queens had convinced neutrals not to become Whigs, it had not converted them into Tories.

On July 14, 1776, Gen. William Howe, the commander-in-chief of the British army in America, and his brother, Adm. Richard Lord Howe, the naval commander, issued a proclamation announcing their appointment as peace commissioners with power to grant pardons to all who would renew their allegiance to the Crown. Posters to that effect immediately appeared throughout the county, informing neutrals that they did not have to fear British retribution after the Patriots were defeated. The message was obviously important, but so too was the act of communication itself, for the posters were a conspicuous reminder that Whig rule over Queens was tenuous at best.[21]

The ease of the Loyalist victory makes it appear as if it were inevitable. But if that were the case, why were Royalists unable to replicate this triumph throughout British North America? The truth is Queens County was in many ways unique. It not only had a solid core of Tory leaders prepared to exert themselves on the Crown's behalf; it also had groups, like the Anglicans in western Queens and the residents of south Hempstead, who were predisposed to become Loyalist and around whom a movement could be fashioned. Most important, because Queens was on an island, the British navy could readily arm, protect, and embolden these local Loyalists. The county was also adjacent to New York

City, and few doubted the British army would soon recapture the area. It consequently proved impossible for the Whigs to coerce the disaffected or to convert the neutral.

The British Occupation of Queens County

Following the British victory at the Battle of Long Island in August 1776, Queens County came under the military's control and would remain so until 1783. From the outset, military officials realized that the war had both military and political dimensions. To crush the rebellion, the British needed not only to defeat the enemy in the field but to pursue a policy of reconciliation and to cultivate support in areas that its forces occupied. Success in this noncombative phase could not substitute for military victory, but the British war effort stood to benefit greatly from the manpower and materiel civilians could provide. Military misconduct against civilians would only create enmity, hinder the effective prosecution of the war, and make postwar reconciliation more difficult.

As events in Queens County make clear, the British army ultimately failed to win the political struggle. By war's end the people of Queens had become, not loyal subjects, but Patriots—as much by British default as by personal choice. As a British officer correctly observed, "We planted an irrecoverable hatred wherever we went, which neither time nor measures will be able to eradicate. What then are we to expect from it, conciliation or submission?"[22] Indeed, by ordering troops into Queens, the British set in motion a chain of events that they could not control and that in the end defeated the very purpose for which military forces had been sent. Instead of destroying the Revolution, the British army became one of its agents.

The British advantages began to unravel the moment redcoats landed on Long Island. One British officer argued that "we should (whenever we get further into the country) give free liberty to the soldiers to ravage it at will, that these infatuated wretches may feel what a calamity war is." Another averred that "the old Hatred for Kings and the seeds of sedition are so thickly sown against them, that it must be thrash'd out of them." The outcome was inevitable. During the Battle of Long Island, crews from British transport ships interrupted their mission to plunder inhabitants. Soldiers, who did not understand how they could wage war when they could not tell Patriot from Loyalist, began abusing all as rebels. Maj. Gen. James Robertson, commandant of New York City from 1776 to 1778, confessed, "When I first landed I found in all the farms poultry and cows, and the farms stocked; when I passed afterwards I found nothing alive."[23]

The military's approach to reconciliation troubled residents in yet another way. They had expected the British to punish Whigs and reward Tories. But, as Thomas Jones has described, when Royalists pressed complaints against rebels who had harmed them, the British often maltreated the accuser and accused him of being a Whig.[24] Then, on November 30, 1776, the Howes issued a proclamation pardoning all who would submit to royal authority within sixty days. Even Whig leaders could receive free and full pardon, provoking Lord George Germain, the American secretary of state, to grumble that it would alienate Royalists to find that rebels who had caused so much misery were now on an equal footing with those who had persevered in their loyalty.[25]

If affairs had gotten off to a dismal start, the abuses the army committed over the next several years against private property and the demands the military made each year for supplies only exacerbated the discord. Queens County not only supplied its own residents, the expanding refugee population within its borders, and the soldiers quartered there, but it also helped to feed the civil and military population of New York City and to outfit the army for each campaign. Establishing efficient and equitable arrangements for procuring war materiel would have been a good first step toward wining residents' allegiance. Yet the collection of supplies was never efficiently organized, and the methods employed often exhibited a criminal disregard for citizens' rights.[26]

Commissary officials, for example, sometimes used intimidation to seize cattle without paying or at prices below those set by the commander-in-chief; yet the crown still paid full price. Little ingenuity was needed to falsify financial records to defraud the government. Ambrose Serle, Lord Howe's secretary, reported that commissary employees often forced inhabitants to sign blank receipts to secure payment for supplies taken by the army; if a farmer refused, he was not paid. Officials then made a profit by writing in inflated sums of money. Such practices wasted government funds and encouraged residents to view the British army as the enemy. The guilty officials do not even appear to have been very discrete in conducting their business. Sir George Rodney, a British naval officer, was so disgusted by the corruption at New York that he wrote the ministry in 1780, complaining "of a long train of leeches, who suck the blood of the State, and whose interest prompts them to promote the continuance of the war."[27]

The longer the war dragged on, the more aggravated British officers became about their inability to crush the rebellion. They vented their frustration on residents. Some of the misconduct, although degrading, was trivial: Civilians had to dismount and remove their hats when passing the abode of an army commander. Other actions were more serious. Typical was the action of an officer on a foraging party, who led fifty horses into an orchard where apples were piled for making cider. The farmer pleaded with the officer to use another field, where the pasture was better, but the request was denied, and the farmer was called a "damned old rebel." The loss amounted to two hundred pounds. Paul Amberman, a miller, sold flour to Maj. Richard Stockton, but when he applied for payment, Stockton took personal offense. The next day, after watching a fellow officer horsewhip Amberman, Stockton killed the miller with a sword. Court-martialed for murder, Stockton was found guilty. The British commander-in-chief then asked the miller's widow to sign a petition to pardon the convicted officer. Despite her refusal, he released the murderer.[28]

Army officers came from the British upper class and viewed colonists as social inferiors, greedy and ill-bred. They were "a Leveling, underbred, Artfull, Race of people that we Cannot Associate with them. Void of principle, their whole Conservation is turn'd on their Interest, and as to gratitude they have no such word in their dictionary and either cant or wont understand what it means."[29] Cooped up on Long Island, some officers sought to relieve their boredom and to prove their superiority by bullying helpless civilians. This happened so often civilians became alienated, and the entire officer corps shared responsibility by failing to punish offenders. Instead, officers too often overtly sanctioned misconduct by shielding those who broke military discipline.[30]

Daily experiences with the military caused county folk to protest that they were living under a tyranny and not a government of laws. Patrick Ferguson, a Loyalist officer, wrote in 1779 "that the People in general are become indifferent, if not averse, to a Government which in the place of the Liberty Prosperity safety and Plenty, under promise of which it involved them in this war has established a thorough Despotism." The fact that the British could not win the war only further enraged residents.[31]

Inhabitants had no legal recourse against the abuses they were being forced to endure, because the Howes had placed the county under martial law following the Battle of Long Island. At first, they refused to end martial law in the areas of New York they controlled, until military operations for 1776 had ceased, and they could reestablish royal authority over the whole province. However, once it became clear the war would last for at least another year, the Howes found other reasons to keep civil government dormant. In truth, they were responsible both for waging war and for securing peace, and the former clearly took precedence. Reviving civil government, they feared, would hinder the war's prosecution, jeopardize a quick triumph, and as a result possibly tarnish General Howe's reputation. Although the Howes paid lip service to the war's political dimension, they did not sufficiently appreciate that reconciliation was as essential an objective as military victory.[32]

Despite insisting on martial law, the Howes never established a uniform policy of implementation; it varied by time and place within occupied New York. In matters relating to the conduct of the war, Col. Archibald Hamilton, commander of the Queens County militia, had overall responsibility. Under him were not only the militia officers but also the local justices of the peace. The latter likewise had to obey the commissary, quartermaster, and barrackmaster departments. At the outset, justices at times called residents together to determine how the army's demands were to be met, but by 1779 decisions were typically being made at meetings of the justices and the militia officers, who then enforced what they had agreed upon.[33]

Inhabitants did what they could to preserve as many of their former liberties as possible. Most of the prewar governmental institutions, including town meetings and the county Board of Supervisors, were allowed to function, so long as they did not disrupt military operations. Although a civilian could not sue a British soldier, the Queens County Court of Common Pleas, according to Thomas Jones, continued to hear cases until 1779, and justices of the peace performed at least some of their customary responsibilities. Nonetheless, town and county officials had to accept that they had become British collaborators, who could be abused, ignored, or overruled at any time.[34]

As the war dragged on, especially after the defeat at Saratoga in October 1777, the ministry began to realize that it needed to pay more attention to the war's political dimension. In February 1778 the government established a new peace commission, headed by the Earl of Carlisle, in which three of the five members were civilians. The Carlisle Commission had power to revive civil government, yet it declined to do so in New York. Even though the commissioners realized the harm already done in the province to the British cause, the army insisted on continuing martial law. In July 1779 the ministry appointed Sir Henry Clinton, who had become American commander-in-chief in March 1778, the sole peace commissioner. Although the ministry instructed him to restore civil government in New York, Clinton found one reason after another to evade doing so. At one point, he explained that "to open the Courts of Civil Law would increase the Confusion, and be productive of many other bad Consequences." Although he did not explicitly say so, he feared that if martial law were ended, New Yorkers would at once begin bringing civil suits for redress of grievances against military officers. In sum, to save the army from its misdeeds, Clinton was prepared to risk losing the political struggle for the minds and hearts of the people.[35]

In March 1780 the ministry appointed Maj. Gen. James Robertson governor of New York. Clinton and Robertson then commenced arguing about whether civil government should be restored.[36] Finally, in July 1780, with Clinton's approbation, Robertson appointed George Duncan Ludlow superintendent of the newly created Court of Police on Long Island. The superintendent had power "to hear and determine peace and good order"; all officials on Long Island were to assist and obey him. Ludlow's power even exceeded that of Col. Archibald Hamilton, the county militia commander. He issued orders on such varied matters as road and fence repairs, the weight and quality of bread, and the time for harvesting. In its judicial capacity his office combined the functions of police, judge, and jury.[37] Robertson extolled the Court of Police as a partial restoration of civil government, but it was merely martial law under a different guise. Ludlow became known as "the little tyrant of the island." When prominent local

Loyalists begged him to reopen the courts, he refused, arguing that doing so "would be inconvenient, prejudicial, and injurious to the king's service."[38]

Ludlow not only protected dishonest army officials, he made it possible for the Court of Police to participate in the corruption. For example, for a fee Ludlow began issuing letters of recommendation that allowed individuals within British lines to engage in trade with New England, an activity prohibited by law. The Court of Police also took charge of the property of absentee rebels, allegedly to assist distressed Tory refugees. During the two years and eleven months that the Court was in existence, the Court collected £7,660. The refugees got £300, and Ludlow and his assistants took the rest to pay their salaries. Ludlow, for example, collected £1,825 for working one day a month for thirty-five months.[39]

When the Court of Police was created, the people of Queens seem generally to have viewed it as a step toward the reinstitution of civil government, but Ludlow's tactics (and the British defeat at Yorktown in October 1781) fired disaffection afresh. After 1781 Queens County elected fewer Royalists to office each year. In the end, seven hard years of military misrule by an army that could not win the war on the battlefield had alienated county residents and readied them for independence. Loyalists as well as neutrals had come to realize that they were not British, but that Britain was the enemy. As Thomas Jones, a county resident, plainly explained it: "Deprived of their property at the caprice of the military, their lives and liberty under the same arbitrary power, law, justice, and equity denied them, the civil authority abolished, and the courts of justice shut up. Such were the steps taken by the military to 'conciliate' the affections of his Majesty's deluded subjects, to 'reclaim' the disaffected, and bring in the rebellious."[40]

The Aftermath

The British army's failure in Queens County and its defeat on the battlefield did not end the Revolution in Queens County. If the victorious Whigs treated county residents the way the British had, inhabitants might well have become an estranged, disruptive force in the postwar period, a fifth column dedicated to reunion with the mother country. New York Whigs consequently needed to reintegrate residents into the political life of the state. Although some historians have stressed how harshly New York State treated the Loyalists,[41] the evidence for Queens does not support that contention.

Reintegration did not mean that every county Royalist could or would become a citizen of the new state. Some Loyalists, especially those who had actively resisted the Patriot cause, or who could not accept the triumph of the Whigs, or who refused to live under a republican form of government, voluntarily left the new state and went into exile. The Whigs forced other Tories into exile by threatening them with violence, lawsuits, or prosecution for treason.

The Loyalists in this group were usually those who had made themselves especially obnoxious, who had collaborated with the British, or who might become
a threat to the new government. Many refugees suffered greatly and so did their
families and friends who remained behind. However, only about 5 to 6 percent
of the prewar population of Queens became refugees. The vast majority of residents remained to make their peace with the new state government.[42]

The state did enact some very harsh anti-Tory legislation.[43] This hostility
was in part the result of the bitter, protracted civil war that had so recently divided
New York, but the laws also expressed the Patriots' need for psychic reassur-
ance that their efforts had not been in vain and that they could secure in peace
what they had won in war. However, once the state had made explicit the kind
of peace that the more vengeful would impose if Loyalists refused to accept the
new political order, other Patriots successfully advocated leniency in the
enforcement of this legislation. Seen in this light, New York's anti-Tory legislation was a warning rather than the harsh punishment of a former enemy.

The Forfeiture Act of 1779 ipso facto attainted six prominent county inhabitants, and grand juries indicted about fifty more under this law. The state clearly
could not permit Tory leaders to remain after the peace settlement, for if these
leaders mobilized county Loyalists in postwar elections, as they had done before
the war, the Revolution's success would be imperiled. However, the state government did not attempt after the war systematically to indict Tories under this
law. Moreover, many indicted county residents appeared before the New York
Supreme Court when it opened in October 1783 at Albany. They "were treated
with the utmost hospitality and good humor by the worthy citizens of that community." After they pleaded not guilty and no one appeared to testify against them,
the charges were dismissed. If an individual failed to appear, his property was subject to forfeiture; but few county residents suffered this fate. Probably only twelve
county men had their property confiscated under the Forfeiture Act.[44]

In May 1784 the state legislature also passed "An Act for raising £100,000
within the several counties therein mentioned," which levied a tax on areas of
the state within British lines during the war.[45] The counties involved could
rightly argue that the levy was vindictive. Queens County's share of the burden
came to £14,000. Nonetheless, payment of the tax did not cause dire economic
hardship.

Another anti-Royalist enactment, the Voting Act of May 1784, threatened
county inhabitants with disfranchisement. However, the act's enforcement was
left to inspectors of elections who were to allow "any person" to vote who "by
fear of compulsion" had committed any of the acts listed in the law as a cause
of disfranchisement and who otherwise had been "a friend to freedom and independence." Disqualification thus depended on an inspector's interpretation of
the law and his willingness to enforce it. Because no poll list for the period has
survived, historians cannot determine exactly how many people were denied the

vote. However, in postwar elections for important town offices in Queens County, the percentage of officeholders who had been Tories before the war is as follows: 1783, 4.9 percent; 1784, 12.1 percent; 1785, 12.7 percent; 1786, 21.1 percent; and 1787, 23.6 percent. Notably, the 1783 and 1784 elections, in which the lowest percentages of Loyalists were chosen for office, were held before the law's passage. Time mellowed the anti-Loyalist sentiment in spite of the law. Indeed, the *New York Packet* reported in February 1786 that South Hempstead, "that most obnoxious part of the county" and the leading Royalist stronghold within Queens, had cast 127 of the county's 359 votes in the 1785 elections for the New York Assembly. In sum, the paper's call for legislation to deal with this "peculiar situation" and the remarkable number of former Loyalists who held town office make it clear that few residents were disfranchised because of the Voting Act of 1784.[46]

A Loyalist could also be sued under the Trespass Act for having occupied or destroyed the property of a Patriot refugee. But few residents could sue under this act, for few had fled Queens after the Battle of Long Island and had remained within American lines for the entire war. Those who did often had no one to sue, for the defendant was often a property-less Tory refugee who had resided in Queens during the war, but who had left in 1783 with the British. The act was amended in 1784 to make it easier for refugee Whigs to recover damages, but the changes in the law had little impact in Queens.[47] Although the courts attached the farms of a few Loyalists, one local historian's assessment of these cases remains valid: "The suits against the Tories (under the Trespass Act) for damages done the Whigs did not amount to much. Able lawyers, disagreeing jurors, certioraries, and the law's delay were obstacles in the way of indemnity."[48]

In sum, the evidence available regarding the enforcement of anti-Loyalist legislation indicates that the situation in postwar Queens was not as burdensome for Loyalists as some historians have supposed. A few Royalists did pay dearly for their actions and beliefs, but the important point is that most county Tories escaped legal persecution. Certainly some unofficial harassment may have taken place, but little evidence of it remains. The difficult ordeal residents as a group had endured during the British occupation perhaps convinced most Patriots of the wisdom of forgetting the past. That Tories had outnumbered Whigs by two to one may also have dissuaded Patriots from making an issue of past differences.

The rapid reestablishment of civil government in Queens in 1783, in particular, exemplified the state's conciliatory attitude and determination to reunite all under the banner of Independence. County Patriots had met in April 1783 to arrange for the orderly transfer of Queens County from the British army to New York State, for "inhabitants were under great apprehensions" about the possibility of violence in the interval between the British evacuation and the arrival of American troops. The meeting requested Gov. George Clinton's assistance and reminded him that county residents were "entitled to a voice with our fellow citizens of the State in the approaching election."[49] Their trust in Clinton was not misplaced, and the call for their political rights was not mistaken. The *Independent New York Gazette* reported on December 1, 1783, that "the mode of taking possession of their City in Tuesday last, evinced such inviolable regard to order and discipline, as Tyranny could never have enforced; and which nothing but an . . . exhaulted sense of the extraordinary worth of the great Offices . . . they have the honor to attend, natural prompted the troops and inhabitants so rigidly to observe." A county man noted rather succinctly, "One day the British patrolled the streets, next day the American soldiers."[50] By the time Governor Clinton called the legislature into session, civil government had already replaced martial law in what had been British-occupied New York. The five towns in Queens had already held meetings on the previous December 22, elected local officials, and resumed their usual responsibilities. Elections had also been held in December to select county representatives to the state Assembly. This immediate and earnest participation in the political life of the new state, in turn, betokened the county's genuine acceptance of the Revolution and republican government.

Notes

1. Portions of this article were previously published in the following journals and are used here with permission: "Communities in the Midst of the American Revolution: Queens County, New York, 1774–1775," *Journal of Social History* 18 (1984): 57–78 (herein cited as *JSH*); "A Revolution Foiled: Queens County, New York, 1775–1776," *Journal of American History* 75 (1988): 417–444 (herein cited as *JAH*); "Patriots by Default: Queens County, New York, and the British Army, 1776–1783," *William and Mary Quarterly*, 3rd ser., 43 (1986): 35–63 (herein cited as *WMQ*); "Loyalists and Conflict Resolution in Post-Revolutionary New York: Queens County as a Test Case," *New York History* 68 (1987): 27–43 (herein cited as *NYH*).

2. Myron L. Fuller, *The Geology of Long Island, New York*, United States Department of the Interior, United States Geological Survey, Professional Paper 82 (Washington, D.C., 1914), 22, 114–116, 158–176; Benjamin F. Thompson, *History of Long Island from Its Discovery and Settlement to the Present Time*, 3 vol. (New York, 1918), 1:11–13; Henry Onderdonk Jr., comp., "Copy of the Rate List of Jamaica for the £100,000 rate (1784 and 1788)" (Brooklyn, 1940), Typewritten, Manuscript File, Long Island Historical Society [LIHS], Brooklyn, New York; Henry Onderdonk Jr., comp., "Tax Bill for Raising £2466.12.0 in the Township of Flushing (1784–1788)" (Brooklyn, 1940), Typewritten, Manuscript File, LIHS; Henry Onderdonk Jr., comp., "Copy of the Tax List for Raising £3524.18 within the Township of Oyster Bay" (Brooklyn, 1940), Typewritten, Manuscript File, LIHS; Henry Onderdonk Jr., comp., "Tax Lists of Oyster Bay, Hempstead, North Hempstead, Flushing, Jamaica, and Newtown, 1784," MS, LIHS; Arthur Soper Wardwell, comp., "Annotated Hempstead, North Hempstead, and South Hempstead Tax Lists," (Brooklyn, 1940), Typewritten, Manuscript File, LIHS; "Newtown, Queens County Tax List [1784]," MS, New-York Historical Society, New York City.

3. The statistical material presented throughout this article and the definitions of Whigs, Tories, and Neutrals are based upon Tiedemann, "Response to Revolution: Queens County, New York, during the Era of the American Revolution" (Ph.D. diss., The City University of New York, 1977). Only adult males are included in the statistical data because of the impossibility of collecting such information on Queens County females. The interpretative framework for this section can be found in Tiedemann, "Communities in Revolution," *JSH* 18 (1984): 57–78.

4. Anne M. Ousterhout, *A State Divided: Opposition in Pennsylvania to the American Revolution* (Westport, Conn., 1987), 3, makes a similar argument for Pennsylvania: "The conditions in which people lived, their prewar friendships and enmities, their local problems and contentions usually determined their responses to the quarrel with Great Britain."

5. John Webb Pratt, *Religion, Politics, and Diversity: The Church-State Theme in New York History* (Ithaca, N.Y., 1967), 40–42; Horatio Ladd, *The Origin and History of Grace Church, Jamaica, New York* (New York, 1914), 68–77; George Winans, *First Presbyterian Church of Jamaica, New York* (Jamaica, N.Y.), 22–29; and Jean B. Peyer, "Jamaica, Long Island, 1656–1776: A Study of the Roots of American Urbanism" (Ph.D. diss., The City University of New York, 1974).

6. Nelson R. Burr, "The Episcopal Church and the Dutch in Colonial New York and New Jersey: 1664–1784," *Historical Magazine of the Protestant Episcopal Church* 19 (1950): 90–111 (herein cited as *HMPEC*).

7. Dutch Patriots were strong enough in 1775 in the two Whig strongholds, north Hempstead and Jamaica, to replace the pro-British Domine Hermanus Boelen with the pro-American Dominie Solomon Froeligh. James Tanis, "The Dutch Reformed Church and the American Revolution—II," *De Halve Maen* 52 (Fall 1977): 2–3.

8. Joseph S. Tiedemann, "Queens County, New York Quakers in the American Revolution: Loyalists or Neutrals?" *HMPEC* 50 (1983): 215–228.

9. For the sectional disputes in Hempstead, see Benjamin D. Hicks, ed., *Records of the Town of North and South Hempstead, Long Island, New York*, 8 vols. (Jamaica, N.Y., 1896–1904), 1:305, 378, 382–383, 384, 386, 419, 2:16–17, 24, 100–101, 264, 277, 3:73–75.

10. Peyer, "Jamaica," 47–51, 62, 81–84, 112; Jessica Kross, *The Evolution of an American Town: Newtown, New York, 1642–1775* (Philadelphia, 1983), 68–70, 140–141, 198.

11. Peter Force, ed. *American Archives . . . A Documentary History of . . . the North American Colonies*, 4th Ser., 6 vols. (Washington, D.C., 1843–1853), 1:328.

12. Tiedemann, "Communities in Revolution," *JSH* 18 (1984): 57.

13. Ibid., 57–58; Force, ed. *American Archives*, 4th Ser., 3:1389–1392.

14. "A Freeman of Newtown," *New York Journal*, Mar. 9, 1775.

15. Tiedemann, "Queens County, New York Quakers," *HMPEC* 50 (1983): 222.

16. *Journals of the Provincial Congress, Provincial Convention, Committee of Safety and Council of Safety of the State of New York, 1775–1776-1777,* 2 vols. (Albany, 1842), 1:58, 289–300, 2:125; *Journals of the Continental Congress,* 34 vols., ed. Worthington C. Ford, et al. (Washington, D. C., 1904–1937), 4:114, 150.

17. *Collections of the New York Historical Society,* 4 (1871): 234–237, 350–352; Force, ed. *American Archives,* 4th Ser., 5:75; *Journals of the Provincial Congress* 1:354, 355.

18. Tiedemann, "Revolution Foiled," *JAH* 75 (1988): 430–432.

19. Ibid., 435–438.

20. Bernice Schultz Marshall, *Colonial Hempstead: Long Island Life under the Dutch and English* (Port Washington, N.Y., 1962), 274–276; *Journals of the Provincial Congress* 1:215; Vandeput to Parker, Dec. 18, 1775, C.O. 5/123, Public Record Office (Library of Congress microfilm); Memorial of Dow Ditmas, n.d., A.O. 13/24, Public Record Office (Library of Congress microfilm).

21. *Journals of the Provincial Congress* 1:558, 561–562, 572, 2:287.

22. Charles Stuart to Lord Bute, Sept. 16, 1778, in E. Stuart-Wortley, ed., *A Prime Minister and His Son . . .* (London, 1925), 132.

23. Lord Rawdon to [Earl of Huntington], Sept. 23, 1776, in Francis Bickley, ed., *Report on the Manuscripts of the Late Reginald Rawdon Hastings, Esq., of the Manor House, Ashby de la Zouch,* vol. 3 (Historical Manuscripts Commission, *Twentieth Report* [London, 1934]): 185; William Bamford, "Bamford's Diary: The Revolutionary Diary of a British Officer," *Maryland Historical Magazine* 28 (1933): 13, *The Detail and Conduct of the American War under Generals Gage, Howe, Burgoyne, and Vice Admiral Lord Howe: With a Very Full and Correct State of the Whole of the Evidence as Given before a Committee of the House of Common. . . ,* 3rd ed. (London, 1780), 119.

24. Thomas Jones, *History of New York during the Revolutionary War and of the Leading Events in Other Colonies at the Period,* 2 vols., ed. Edward Floyd De Lancey (New York, 1879), 1:111, 114, 127, 2: 27, 116, 144–145, 160–161.

25. Proclamation by the Peace Commissioners, Nov. 30, 1776, C.O. 5/177. Germain to William Knox, Dec. 31, 1776, *The Manuscripts of Miss M. Eyre Matcham; Capt. H. V. Knox . . .* (Historical Manuscripts Commission, *Report on Manuscripts in Various Collections,* vol. 6 [Dublin, 1909]): 128.

26. For this aspect of the war, see R. Arthur Bowler, *Logistics and the Failure of the British Army in America, 1775–1783* (Princeton, N.J., 1975), 41–91.

27. Edward H. Tatum Jr., ed., *The American Journal of Ambrose Serle, Secretary to Lord Howe, 1776–1778* (San Marino, Calif., 1940), 77; George Rodney to Germain, Dec. 22, 1780, *Report on the Manuscripts of Mrs. Stopford-Sackville, of Drayton House,*

Northamptonshire, vol. 2 (Historical Manuscripts Commission, *Fifteenth Report* [London, 1910]), 191.

28. Jones, *History,* ed. De Lancey, 2:87–88, 92–93; Henry Onderdonk Jr., ed., "Correspondence of Major John Kissam Illustrating the Revolutionary History of Queens County . . . ," 13, Brooklyn Historical Society, Brooklyn, N.Y.; and Milton M. Klein and Ronald W. Howard, eds., *The Twilight of British Rule in Revolutionary America: The New York Letter Book of General James Robertson, 1780–1783* (Cooperstown, N.Y., 1983), 103, n. 21.

29. Letter from Capt. John Bowater, Apr. 4, 1777, in Marion Balderstron and David Syrett, The *Lost War: Letters from British Officers during the American Revolution* (New York, 1975), 122.

30. European soldiers considered such behavior to be a part of esprit de corps; see André Corvisier, *Armies and Societies in Europe, 1494–1789,* trans. Abigail T. Siddall (Bloomington, Ind., 1979), 179.

31. Patrick Ferguson to Sir Henry Clinton, Nov. 22, 1779, Clinton Papers, William L. Clements Library, Ann Arbor, Mich.

32. Troyer Steele Anderson, *The Command of the Howe Brothers during the American Revolution* (New York, 1936), 92–95; Ira D. Gruber, *The Howe Brothers and the American Revolution* (Chapel Hill, N.C., 1972), 52.

33. Jones, *History,* ed. De Lancey, 2:128–133; Resolutions for the Captains of Militia and Justices of the Peace in Queens County, November 27, 1779, Documents Collection, Nassau County Museum Collection, Long Island Studies Institute at Hofstra University, Hempstead, New York.

34. Tiedemann, "Patriots by Default," *WMQ,* 3rd ser., 43 (1986): 53–54; Jones, *History,* ed. De Lancey, 2: 119

35. Instructions to Commissioners, April 12, 1778, C.O. 5/180; for the commission's activities in America, see *The Manuscripts of the Earl of Carlisle, Preserved at Castle Howard* (Historical Manuscripts Commission, *Fifteenth Report* Appendix, 6 [London, 1897]): 322–429. Clinton to Germain, June 2, 1780, Clinton Papers.

36. Tiedemann, "Patriots by Default," *WMQ,* 3rd ser., 43 (1986): 57–58.

37. *Royal Gazette,* July 15, 1780.

38. Jones, *History,* ed. De Lancey, 2: 12, 23, 24.

39. Tiedemann, "Patriots by Default," *WMQ,* 3rd ser., 43 (1986): 60–62.

40. Jones, *History,* ed. De Lancey, 2: 72.

41. See, for example, Edward Countryman, *A People in Revolution: The American Revolution and Political Society in New York, 1783–1789* (Baltimore, 1981), 325.

42. For how I reached this conclusion, see Tiedemann, "Loyalists and Conflict Resolution," *NYH* 68 (1987): 32–34.

43. These acts can be surveyed in *Laws of the Legislature of the State of New York in Force against the Loyalists and Affecting the Trade of Great Britain* (London, 1786).

44. *Laws,* 3rd session, chapter 38; *Royal Gazette*, Oct. 29, 1783; and Henry Onderdonk Jr., ed., *Documents and Letters Intended to Illustrate the Revolutionary Incidents of Queens County* (New York, 1846), 258.

45. *Laws,* 7th session, chapter 58.

46. *Laws,* 7th session, chapter 66; *New York Packet*, Feb. 20, 1786.

47. *Laws,* 6th session, chapter 31; *Laws,* 7th session, chapter 54.

48. Henry Onderdonk Jr., ed., *Documents and Letters Intended to Illustrate the Revolutionary Incidents of Queens County. Second Series* (Hempstead, N.Y., 1884), 65.

49. An Address of the Inhabitants of Queens County to His Excellency George Clinton and His Reply, *Independent New York Gazette*, Dec. 13, 1783.

50. *Independent New York Gazette*, Dec. 1, 13, 1783; Onderdonk, ed. *Documents*, 253–254.

3

Suffolk County

John G. Staudt

Just days before the Continental Congress declared independence in July 1776, the British army landed on Staten Island in New York harbor. When General Washington heard the grim news, he wrote from his headquarters in New York City: "The Time is now near at hand which must probably determine, whether Americans are to be, Freemen, or Slaves; whether they are to have any property they can call their own; whether their Houses, Farms, are to be pillaged and destroyed, and they consigned to a State of Wretchedness."[1]

Less than two months later, Suffolk County, Long Island, New York, endured the "State of Wretchedness." British forces occupied the county in late August, and for seven years soldiers plundered, pillaged, and terrorized the civilian population. American partisans, who behaved more like pirates than Patriots, conducted raids across the Long Island Sound from Connecticut and compounded the war's viciousness by looting and killing Loyalists and Patriots alike. Meanwhile, those who fled to the mainland suffered greatly as wartime refugees.

By the time the British evacuated Long Island in November 1783, the brutality of the occupation had destroyed hundreds of farms, ruined the countryside, and left what remained of local society in disarray. Although the refugees returned, and together with those who bore the brunt of the British occupation rebuilt their communities, Suffolk County changed significantly as a result of the war. The Revolution's liberalizing spirit and the traumatic experience of military occupation together altered local political, religious, and social institutions forever. The study of Suffolk County provides an excellent example of how the Revolution transformed colonial America into a modern republic. It exposes the "tragic force" of the war—the pain and suffering residents endured during the agonizing birth of the nation.[2]

63

Revolutionary Suffolk County encompassed the eastern two-thirds of Long Island, covering approximately twelve hundred square miles. It was approximately ninety miles in length, thirty-four miles at its widest point, and it contained over six hundred miles of coastline. It consisted of eight townships, including from west to east, Huntington, Smithtown, Islip, Brookhaven, Southold, Southampton, Easthampton, and Shelter Island. Queens County bordered it on the west, the Long Island Sound on the north, and the Atlantic Ocean on the south.

In 1776 the majority of Suffolk's more than thirteen thousand inhabitants were white yeomen farmers who could trace their family roots back to New England, especially Connecticut.[3] Approximately fifteen hundred slaves, about 11 percent of the population, and a few hundred Native Americans, many of whom were servants, also inhabited the county. According to local census records, several of Suffolk's most prominent families owned the largest number of slaves. In 1776 the families of William Nicoll from Islip, Thomas Tredwell of Smithtown, and Nathaniel Woodhull, William Floyd, and his cousin Richard, all of Brookhaven, each owned a dozen or more slaves, but no one in the county owned more than fifteen. Most local slave owners, however, were less prominent residents who owned on average only one or two slaves per household. Despite the fact that the majority of Suffolk's inhabitants did not own slaves, there was little opposition towards slavery during the colonial period and, according to one historian, enslaved blacks and Native Americans were "held by colonists of all social and economic strata."[4]

Colonial Suffolk consisted of stratified, parochial communities, in which a few prominent families dominated local elective and appointive political offices. In Huntington, a mere five families controlled the position of town supervisor between 1694 and 1776.[5] In Smithtown the Smith family dominated local government. In 1763 the Smiths held twelve out of nineteen town offices. In Brookhaven, Daniel Smith, a relative of the Smithtown Smiths, was town clerk for almost forty years (1738–1775).[6] Some individuals were plural officeholders (i.e., simultaneously holding two or more offices). In 1749 Huntington trustee, Eliphalet Wickes held six different positions including town clerk, treasurer, and constable. In Brookhaven Richard Floyd served as supervisor (1742–1762) and president of the town trustees (1747–1762). On Shelter Island Nicoll Havens served as the town clerk (1759–1777) and town supervisor (1770–1777). Similar patterns appeared on the county level. William Nicoll, Nicoll Havens's cousin, was elected county clerk for twenty-six years (1750–1776). Other county officials were royal appointees. Brookhaven's town supervisor, Richard Floyd, was appointed a Suffolk County judge for almost twenty years (1752–1771). Dr. George Muirson, of Brookhaven, was appointed county sheriff for twenty-five years (1748–1773); the longest tenure of any Suffolk County sheriff.

The Presbyterian Church dictated local religious affairs and limited the toleration allowed to new denominations in Suffolk County.[7] Town churches were maintained through the assistance of local taxes, and religious matters were closely connected to civic affairs.[8] Ministers were often selected at town meetings, while local taxes and the granting of common lands for parsonages helped support their wages. Pastors retained their positions for extended periods and maintained a significant influence over public opinion.[9] The only non-Presbyterian parishes to appear in Suffolk's "puritan domain" before the Revolution were the Anglican Churches established in Brookhaven and Huntington. These two congregations languished, however, and after 1773 were without regular ministers.[10]

For most of the eighteenth century, the burdens of government and taxes were light, and residents readily conformed to Suffolk's deferential society. Even as colonial protests occurred elsewhere in the colonies between 1763 and 1774, Suffolk inhabitants remained aloof and more concerned with agricultural pursuits and the weather than with political strife. Following Parliament's passage of the Coercive or Intolerable Acts in 1774, however, residents quickly grew apprehensive that the British government was plotting to extinguish colonial rights. In the summer of 1774, town committees passed resolves condemning Parliament's heavy-handed policies.[11] Within a year, revolutionary committees had seized control of local government, elected delegates to the Continental and Provincial congresses, and effectively enforced the Continental Association. In Suffolk County "the great majority of inhabitants" supported the committees, and over 90 percent of those eligible signed the Association.[12]

Local Presbyterian ministers, such as Huntington's Ebenezer Prime, Setauket's Benjamin Tallmadge, and East Hampton's Samuel Buell were all born and educated in New England. As a result they maintained close ties with friends and colleagues across the Sound. Before the British occupation of Long Island these men helped sway public opinion in favor of colonial resistance. From their pulpits in Suffolk County, local ministers extolled the actions of the Continental and Provincial congresses and the righteousness of the American cause. In 1776 Charles Inglis, the Anglican rector of Trinity Church in New York City, wrote that he knew of no Presbyterian minister on Long Island "who did not, by preaching and every effort in their power, promote all the measures of Congress, however extravagant."[13]

Despite Suffolk's stance as a "county of Revolutionary consensus," a small, steadfast faction of inhabitants remained loyal to the Crown.[14] Foremost among the county's leading Loyalists were Brookhaven residents Dr. George Muirson; Col. Richard Floyd, and his brother Maj. Benjamin Floyd; and Southold's town supervisor Parker Wickham. These men came from privileged families, owned huge tracts of land, and were royal placemen. In the town of Brookhaven, four of the seven trustees and the town supervisor, Benjamin Floyd, were avowed

Loyalists. In March 1775 these men sent a petition to a New York newspaper declaring their support for the Crown. Later that summer the Brookhaven committee wrote to the Provincial Congress that six men in town were being carefully guarded, as "they have declared they will furnish the [British] men-of-war and cutters with provisions." The following year, Congress put two Brookhaven men, including a former member of the town's committee of safety, into "safe custody" for "taking up arms and corresponding with the British ships, and promoting discord among the inhabitants and seducing many to forsake the cause of their country."

Several factors probably explain why Loyalism was more prevalent there than elsewhere in the county. First, a number of the town's political leaders were Loyalists and may have used their offices to confound local colonial resistance. In a letter of apology written to Congress in June 1775, the Brookhaven Committee explained that the reason the town had "come so late into Congressional measures" was "not for want of patriotick spirit" but rather "from want of better information." Second, Gen. David Wooster, a Continental Army officer stationed in Suffolk from 1775 to 1776, complained in August 1775 to Connecticut's Gov. Jonathan Trumbull about Brookhaven's Anglican preacher, James Lyon: "Parson Lyons" was: "the mainspring of all the Tories on that part of Long Island. He has considerable money at interest in different hands among his neighbours, which gives him an ascendancy over them, and he has been indefatigable, both by writing and preaching, and in every other way, to gain proselytes; and by his connexions with those in other parts of the country, who are inimical to the cause we are embarked in, he will be able to do great mischief." Although Brookhaven Patriots eventually checked the Royalist efforts of "Parson Lyons" and other Tories, prominent Loyalists such as Col. Richard Floyd, who later commanded Suffolk's Loyalist militia during the British occupation, regained limited power after America's defeat at the Battle of Long Island.[15]

In general, Patriots did not purge local officeholders before the British occupation. Because an overwhelming majority of residents, including the members of the political and religious oligarchy, supported the Revolution, the men who led the county in the decade before the war remained the leaders between 1774 and 1776. In East Hampton, the longtime supervisor and town clerk, Burnet Miller (1746–1776), became the town's committee chairman, a delegate to the Provincial Congress, and a member of the New York Assembly. Suffolk County's treasurer, Col. Josiah Smith of Brookhaven (1764–1776), commanded the Suffolk militia in the Battle of Brooklyn. Nathaniel Woodhull, also of Brookhaven, was a member of the colonial Assembly before becoming president of the Provincial Congress and a general in the Suffolk and Queens Counties militias. Before the Revolution, the Havens family dominated local government on Shelter Island.[16] During the war, at least eight family members served as officers in the Continental Army or as captains on privateers.

As the military involvement of local Patriot leaders suggests, the defense of the county was a priority from the outset. In the late fall of 1775, after the Provincial Congress and the Suffolk militia failed to disarm Queens County Loyalists, Suffolk Patriots grew anxious. In December of that year, the Huntington Committee asked Congress to send additional men into Queens to subdue the Loyalists, who were supposedly "making interest with [their] slaves and other servants." Although Suffolk County could not subdue its pro-British neighbors to the west, its own revolutionary zeal increased, as a British military invasion became more imminent. By 1776 there were approximately two thousand men, over 70 percent of those eligible, under arms. In January 1776 the Provincial Congress sent over one thousand pounds of gunpowder to the Huntington Committee and other military supplies to Suffolk's local committees. In July 1776 three companies of Continental troops were sent to supplement the local militia and help protect Long Island's east end from British predatory raids.[17]

Despite these considerable efforts, the Suffolk militia was no match for the redcoats. On August 22, 1776, Gen. William Howe and fifteen thousand soldiers landed on the southern tip of Brooklyn at Gravesend Bay. Five days later Howe won a decisive victory at the Battle of Brooklyn and subsequently occupied New York City and all of Long Island.[18] Over five hundred Suffolk County troops, under the command of Col. Josiah Smith of Brookhaven, took part in that battle and then went home to remove their families and as much property as possible to safety in Connecticut. On August 29 other elements of the Suffolk militia attempted to rally in Smithtown; however, fearing their forces insufficient to oppose the enemy, the officers told their men to go home. Before the end of September, the British army had occupied Suffolk County and the rest of Long Island.[19] In November the British compelled the local committees to revoke "all their proceedings under the Congress," dissolve "their unlawful associations," and submit "to the King, His laws and Gov't."[20]

The number of British and Loyalist troops in Suffolk varied for the rest of the war. At times only a company or so of men and a handful of officers patrolled each town. At other times, such as in 1779, in response to an expected Franco-American assault, twenty-five hundred British and Loyalist soldiers were stationed throughout the county, and a fleet of British ships patrolled the Long Island Sound.[21] The British army also pressed members of the defunct Suffolk County militia into military service. Most men were reluctant to serve but had little choice, for the British threatened to "detach" or draft men into the militia. The British distrusted the loyalty of these men, however, and put them to work as laborers, drivers, and sentries.[22]

At the onset of the British occupation of Suffolk County, the army closed all civil courts and established martial law.[23] As a result, the military abused the citizenry.[24] One of the greatest burdens the British placed on residents was the seizure of their property. In September 1776 orders were issued to residents that they must support the army by driving "all the fat cattle and sheep in Suffolk Co . . . down to Jamaica [Queens County] . . . for the refreshment of the King's Troops." The British also demanded that all farmers turn over grain, straw, and all of their hay to the army. If residents refused to assist the army, Gen. William Erskine, the commander of the British troops in Suffolk County, threatened to "lay waste the property of the disobedient as persons unworthy of His Majesty's clemency."[25]

In addition to supplying the army with fresh provisions, residents were compelled to support the army's transportation needs, including horses, drivers, saddles, wagons, and stables. The British also commandeered pastures and farm fields for the grazing of their livestock. In addition, the army's appetite for wood was insatiable. Timber was needed not only for the construction of barracks but also as fuel for cooking and heating. Thousands of Loyalists seeking refuge in British-occupied New York served as woodcutters who readily denuded Suffolk's public and private woodlands. Wherever the supply of trees ran low, soldiers tore down churches and fences. In one season alone, Loyalist troops stationed in Huntington, under the command of Col. Benjamin Thompson, burned over 5,830 wooden rails, fourteen loads of timber, and three hundred ninety feet of boards.[26]

Housing was also in great demand. If there was insufficient space indoors, the soldiers set up tents and built huts or barracks on local pastures and meadows. Most often, however, officers and soldiers lodged either in local taverns and inns or in private homes. According to historian, Silas Wood, who lived in Huntington during the British occupation, the officers generally seized the best rooms and "compelled [owners] to furnish blankets and fuel for the soldiers, and hay and grain for their horses . . . and seized without ceremony, and without any compensation . . . whatever they desired to gratify their wants or wishes."[27]

Occasionally, a few officers would give receipts for commandeered goods. Most of the time, however, soldiers acting with or without orders took whatever they needed (or wanted) without providing receipts. Even when receipts were issued, they were almost worthless, because the holders were rarely compensated. For example, Smithtown innkeeper Epenetus Smith was left at war's end with receipts worth almost £600 for food, drinks, livestock, grain, hay, blankets, saddles, farm tools, and other goods and services. One particularly contemptible British officer, Banastre Tarleton, ran up a tab at Smith's for over £250. Smith's accounts and those of other Smithtown residents were recorded in a town ledger at the end of the war. The account book includes the names of fifty-four inhabitants whose claims came close to £4,000. The first page of the ledger stated that "however large this amount may seem, certainly know it falls greatly short of ye real value, with which his Majesties Officers & Army have been supplied from time to time." Huntington residents produced three town ledgers at the end of the war with claims in excess of over £21,383.[28]

Unlike Epenetus Smith and his neighbors who bore the brunt of British tyranny, approximately five thousand Long Islanders, the majority from Suffolk, fled to Connecticut and upstate New York.[29] The state and local governments in Connecticut greatly assisted the removal of refugees by commissioning ship captains to carry residents and as much property as possible across the Long Island Sound. Despite Connecticut's attempt to accommodate the refugees, the situation of displaced Long Islanders was "most pitiful." Many Patriot refugees evacuated Suffolk rather quickly and arrived in Connecticut with few provisions and little money.[30] Many grew so impoverished that they risked returning to Long Island to remove, sell, or lease whatever property they could. By war's end scores of refugees had petitioned the Connecticut General Assembly requesting permission to go back to Suffolk County either temporarily or permanently. For some, though, returning home was impossible, because the British had confiscated and redistributed their property.

Many Suffolk refugees participated in American whaleboat raids conducted from Connecticut against British and Loyalist targets on Long Island.[31] Rebel sympathizers who remained in Suffolk often assisted and sometimes even participated in the raids. In December 1777 the British caught Zephaniah Platt of Smithtown concealing in his barn two whaleboats used by rebel raiders. The boats were destroyed, Platt was arrested, and his livestock confiscated.[32] In March 1779 *Rivington's New-York Gazetteer* printed a "Caution to Travellers," warning that American bandits were ambushing Loyalists and robbing homes in Smithtown. The marauders also "harbored and supplied with provisions and intelligence" other American insurgents who frequently made incursions into Suffolk from Connecticut. *Rivington's* added that the "unfortunate Loyalists" in Smithtown "are greatly exposed to the savage cruelty of these assassins," because British sympathizers were so "few in number." This statement is true for other towns in Suffolk as well. In Huntington, in 1779, Gen. Oliver De Lancey threatened to deport and confiscate the property of anyone attacking or assisting in an attack on "his majesty's true and faithful subjects."[33]

In 1776 and in 1778, the British attempted to compel the allegiance of residents by forcing all males between the ages of sixteen and sixty who were capable of bearing arms to take a loyalty oath to the king. Anyone who refused was threatened with banishment and the confiscation of his property.[34] Despite such efforts to secure local allegiances, residents clandestinely continued to impede British operations. In 1778 a group of Long Islanders, mainly from Setauket, developed a sophisticated intelligence organization known as the Culper or Setauket Spy Ring that provided information to Washington.[35] As the war dragged on, residents openly defied British authority by disobeying direct orders to assist the army. In August 1779, 210 members of the Huntington Loyalist militia refused to obey orders from General De Lancey to work on fortifications in Brooklyn. The men eventually acquiesced to De Lancey's demands, but only after he threatened to deport them and confiscate their property. In July 1781 the British officially reprimanded the Huntington militia once again, this time for not helping to repel an attack on Ft. Franklin in nearby Lloyd's Neck.[36]

Suffolk inhabitants opposed British military rule in subtle ways as well. Although many Patriots had fled and continued their resistance from the mainland, remaining residents continued to hold town meetings, elect local officials, and enact ordinances. The minutes of several towns' wartime meetings reveal that despite the British occupation and martial law, residents did not reject their prewar leaders.[37] In East Hampton for example, trustee and former committee chairman, John Chatfield, served as the town clerk (1777–1784); Ezekiel Mulford, a former captain in the Patriot Suffolk militia, was elected town supervisor (1780–1785). Nevertheless, as historian Myron Luke has argued, it is obvious that despite the determined effort of inhabitants to "maintain the appearance of orderly government . . . in large measure they were at the mercy of whatever restrictions or decrees the British military wished to impose upon them."[38]

In fact, the defiant attitude of many residents led British officers to adopt a hardline approach in dealing with civilians.[39] At various times during the war, Col. John Graves Simcoe confiscated goods from Huntington residents without providing receipts, stating he did so "on account of their rebellious principles, and absolute disobedience of the general orders." In 1779 Simcoe also laid an eighty pound fine on the residents of Smithtown, after bandits operating in the area attacked and robbed his messenger.[40] Later that same year, Sir Henry Clinton, commander-in-chief of the British forces in North America, increased the number of troops on Long Island. Clinton also warned Adm. Marriot Arbuthnot that if his fleet lost control of the Long Island Sound "a detachment of French and New England troops will be passed immediately over to Long Island, where they will be joined by most of the people at the east end of it, who are generally disaffected."[41]

Although military oppression touched every aspect of life in wartime Suffolk, few institutions suffered as severe a fate as the Presbyterian Church. Presbyterian ministers, many of whom were born and trained in New England, were staunch promoters of American resistance. The resistance of the eight Suffolk County ministers to Britain's repressive colonial policies stemmed from their close ties to New England and the long-standing animosity between Presbyterians and the Church of England. During the war Rev. Samuel Buell of East Hampton corresponded with American officials. Rev. John Storrs, pastor at Southold, became a refugee and served as a chaplain in the Continental army. Meanwhile, the son of Brookhaven's pastor Benjamin Tallmadge, Maj. Benjamin Tallmadge, served as the chief of Washington's secret service. In addition, several Long Island ministers had sons who joined the American forces. As a result of the zealous Presbyterian support of the Revolution, the British desecrated or destroyed many local churches and meetinghouses, including those in Huntington and Smithtown. In Huntington, British officers devastated the home of Rev. Ebenezer Prime, whom they referred to as "the old rebel Prime," by destroying his library, breaking up his furniture, and vandalizing the rest of his property, including his stables. Rev. Joshua Hart of Smithtown was imprisoned in New York City. In addition, the Presbytery of Suffolk was prohibited from meeting during the war, and most religious services, except those of the two county Anglican Churches, were forbidden.[42]

Col. Benjamin Thompson, a Loyalist officer from New Hampshire, committed one of the more unnecessarily callous acts of the war. Thompson commanded the Loyalist unit, the King's American Dragoons, during their occupation of Huntington in the winter of 1782 to 1783. Despite the fact that the preliminary peace treaty had already been signed, Thompson ordered the construction of a fort, named Fort Golgatha, on top of the local Presbyterian church's burial grounds. He compelled residents to level mounds, knock down tombstones, and construct the fort on the graves of their ancestors. To obtain the wood needed for the project, Thompson's dragoons tore down the Presbyterian Church, stripped barns of their boards, knocked over rail fences, and cut down local orchards.[43] We will probably never know why Thompson took such actions. It is possible that he built the fort on top of the burying hill to discourage marauders who were still conducting raids from Connecticut. The ruthlessness of his actions, however, suggests that he was seeking retribution against Huntington's Presbyterian rebels for Britain's defeat in the war.

Unfortunately, as the war dragged on into its last years, the brutality of British actions was often matched by the viciousness of American raiders. By 1780 legitimate whaleboat warfare had, with a few exceptions, deteriorated into pillaging expeditions. Rebel looters from Connecticut and Loyalist marauders from Queens County indiscriminately robbed and killed Suffolk inhabitants.[44] These predatory attacks helped supply and support the illicit trade and black market operations that extended from the Thames River in Connecticut to the Shrewsbury River in New Jersey. According to historian Frederick Mather, "the center of the traffic was the Long Island Sound, and the chief actors [were] the whale-boat men."[45] The British army's failure to stop the rebels from attacking at will only encouraged further disdain for British authority, and by 1782 residents began to take the law into their own hands. In September a number of Southampton men took seven bandits by surprise. The group caught the plunderers on the beach and in the ensuing struggle killed two, wounded two others, and captured the rest. In August 1783 Huntington inhabitants formed a home guard of eight men who were responsible for sounding an alarm in case of marauders.[46] The British apparently did not interfere with the "vigilantes." The end of the war was drawing near, and the hostilities between imperial and rebel forces were at an end. Furthermore, the soldiers had had enough. In March 1783, soon after building Fort Golgatha, British troops in Huntington set fire to their barracks as a sign of their dissatisfaction with their service in America.[47] Eight months later, the British evacuated New York, and the Suffolk refugees returned home to find their churches destroyed, homes damaged, fields ruined, woodlands denuded, slaves missing, and livestock gone.[48]

Before the Revolution, Elias Pelletreau ran a successful silversmith business in Southampton. During the war, the British had converted his shop into a storehouse, and Pelletreau became a refugee in Connecticut. His account book records the following notation upon his return in early 1784: "Memorandum Sent by Cap _____ [paper torn] for Damages done by the British Troops—Negroman 300 pounds—for the Destruction of our Buildings by the Commesaries & fences & wood taken by the wagoners 200 pounds, 2 tuns of hay at 8 pounds pr Ton 16 pounds sum. Total 516 pounds March 26 1784."[49]

Pelletreau's business eventually recovered, but others were less fortunate. The British occupation had disrupted the livelihood of many inhabitants and the economic life of Suffolk as a whole. The amount of property damage was incalculable, and although there were no significant changes in land-holding patterns, changes in land ownership did occur. Because of their active support of the British, four Suffolk County men, Richard Floyd, George Muirson, Parker Wickham, and Henry Lloyd II, were named in the New York Act of Attainder in 1779. As the British evacuated New York, these men became Loyalist refugees, and the state seized and sold their property to seven purchasers for a total of £11,424 sterling. Benjamin Tallmadge, Caleb Brewster, and Nathaniel Norton, all of whom served in the Continental army, were among the purchasers of the Loyalist property. The other purchasers were John Lloyd II (an active Patriot and nephew of Henry Lloyd II), Joseph Brewster (a signer of the Continental Association in 1775), Benjamin Floyd (brother of Richard Floyd), and Mills Philps, a Suffolk farmer.[50]

At the same time as the Loyalist refugees fled from Long Island, Patriot refugees returned to find their property in ruins. The British had commandeered their homes for military purposes or leased them to Tories who neglected or abused their fields and left their tools in great decay. As a result, a number of refugee families were destitute and could not afford to keep their homes. Several farms, including six in Huntington, were auctioned off in 1785.[51] Even those refugees who were wealthy enough to recover and retain their farms had to overcome tremendous hardship. John Foster, a successful prewar ship owner in Sag Harbor and a member of the Provincial Congress, arrived home to find his ship, house, barn, outbuildings, books, and papers all destroyed. Henry Scudder, a committeeman, militia officer, American spy, and whaleboat raider returned to Huntington to find his woodlands cut down, his fences and outbuildings burned, and his cattle driven off. Continental Congressman William Floyd came home after burying his wife Hannah, who had died as a refugee in Middletown, Connecticut, in May 1781. Maj. Thomas Wickes, a prominent Huntington committeeman and member of the New York Assembly, suffered the loss of his wife and four of his five children in Connecticut during the war.[52]

As historian Gordon Wood has argued, the Revolution "shook up traditional hierarchies, cut people loose from customary ties . . . and brought authority of all sorts into question. To be sure, there was no immediate collapse of the social order . . . but everywhere there were alterations in the way people related to one another." Generally, the traumatic experience of the war altered traditional notions of power and authority in Suffolk County. The most discernible changes were an increase in the turnover of public officials and a decline in plural office holding. In the first decade following the war, the popularly elected Huntington town supervisor changed hands eight times; more times than during the entire colonial era.[53] On Shelter Island, in the two decades leading up to the Revolution, only three men had held the supervisor position. In the same span of time in the postwar years, seven different men were elected supervisor, and the office changed hands nine times from 1783 to 1799.[54] Similar alterations occurred on the county level as well. During the colonial era, the Floyd's of St. George's Manor (Richard Floyd I–IV) constituted a dynasty, as successive royal governors appointed each of them county judge and colonel of the militia. In the first twenty years after the war, three men served as county judge, the longest single tenure being ten years. After the Revolution, state law altered the amount of time that any one person could remain in certain offices. For example, before the Revolution, Dr. George Muirson had served as county sheriff for twenty-six years. After the war, an individual could serve as sheriff for no more than four consecutive years.

In the decades following the war, those Patriots who had contributed most to the war effort dominated elective and appointive local, state, and national offices in Suffolk County. William Floyd, Richard Floyd's cousin, had served as Brookhaven's revolutionary committee's chairman, an officer in the Patriot militia, a member of the Continental Congress, and signer of the Declaration of Independence. In the postwar period he was elected to the United States House of Representatives, the New York State Senate, and was a candidate for lieutenant governor in 1795. Southold's Ezra L'Hommedieu had been a member of the following revolutionary organizations: the Committee of Suffolk County, the New York Committee of Safety, all four Provincial Congresses, the New York Assembly, and the Continental Congress. Following the war, he was elected to the New York Senate and served on the New York Council of Appointment and as a Regent of the University. Smithtown's Thomas Tredwell served in the militia, on the town committee, in all four Provincial Congresses, on the New York Committee of Safety, and in the state assembly. After the war, he served as Surrogate of Suffolk County, a member of the Ratifying Convention in 1788, and was elected to the state senate and the United States Congress.

As with politics, the Revolution also caused significant transformations in religious life. During the war the British army had desecrated and destroyed many Presbyterian Churches. In 1784 several of the churches were rebuilt. Nevertheless, the war had altered the traditional relationship between religion and civil government, and Presbyterianism suffered a decline in membership and the loss of its privileged status. Before the Revolution, taxes paid for the construction of local churches. In the "new order," however, funds were raised by private donations. In addition, a state law passed in 1784 formally separated church and state in New York and allowed religious societies to incorporate and elect trustees for the administration of their "temporalities." Evidence indicates that New York State Senator Ezra L'Hommedieu from Southold helped write the legislation. The Southold Church was the first on Long Island, and among the first in New York, to take advantage of this law by incorporating itself as the "First Church, Congregation or Society in Southold" in June 1784. This law allowed new religious groups, such as the Methodist and Baptist Churches, to flourish. As early as the 1790s, union meeting halls appeared in Suffolk County, where members of different sects, such as Presbyterians, Congregationalists, Methodists, and Baptists could, according to prearranged schedules, worship. Historian Robert Cray argues that although new sects had to compete against established Presbyterian churches, they managed to "attract listeners and eventually followers during the early decades of the nineteenth century." The Methodist Church was particularly successful in gaining new members and by 1845 was the largest religious denomination in Suffolk.[55]

In addition to changes in politics and religion, the Revolution altered local attitudes towards slavery. Before the Revolution local manumissions were rare, and most residents recognized slavery as just another "form of debasement" in a largely deferential society.[56] Having just suffered dearly in a struggle to secure their own civil rights, a number of white residents questioned the justice of denying slaves their civil rights. As a result, some slaveholders began to manumit their slaves as early as 1784. In accordance with his will, Huntington and Suffolk County committeeman Dr. Gilbert Potter released his slave Mark in August 1786. Smithtown's Patriot leader Thomas Tredwell released his twenty-six-year-old slave Charles in 1788. In April 1789 Silas Powel of Huntington, an active Patriot during the war, bought a slave named James for eight pounds with the intention to "keep him for five Months in service and then let him go free." In order to ensure that masters were not just relieving themselves of aged or decrepit slaves, the Huntington town board examined and certified the health of slaves before their release. If a slave was deemed a public charge, masters were compelled to pay the town, which would then see to the slave's upkeep.[57]

Manumissions were spurred on by the outspokenness of local emancipa-
tionists. For example, in 1788, Constitutional Convention delegate Thomas
Tredwell voted against ratification in part, because the document failed immediately to end the slave trade. As Tredwell stated, the slave trade "was a stain to
the commerce of any civilized nation," which had "already blackened half the
plains of America with a race of wretches made so by our cruel policy and
avarice, and which appears to me to be already repugnant to every principle of
humanity, morality, religion and good policy."[58] Sag Harbor resident and editor
of the Long Island Herald, David Frothingham, condemned public slave sales
and labeled one 1796 auction in Whitestone, Queens, a "disgrace to humanity."[59] In 1799 abolitionist pressures compelled the New York Legislature to
pass "An Act for the Gradual Abolition of Slavery," which provided that all
female slave children born after 4 July 1799, were free at age twenty-five and
male slaves at age twenty-eight. In 1817 New York finally outlawed slavery
within its borders by enacting legislation that completely abolished it by 1827.[60]

In the end, the tragic violence of the War for American Independence was
both destructive and liberating. It disrupted lives but created a more equitable
society. It demolished churches but eventually produced greater religious freedom. It devastated property but eventually liberated chattel slaves. Ultimately,
the pain and suffering Suffolk County's inhabitants endured during the
Revolution was not forgotten, as many residents worked to propel their communities out of the "state of wretchedness" envisioned by George Washington
in 1776 and into the age of modern republicanism.

Notes

1. George Washington, General Orders, July 2, 1776, in *The Writings of George
Washington from the Original Manuscript Sources, 1745–1799*, ed. John Fitzpatrick
(Washington, D.C., 1932), 5: 211.

2. Michael Kammen was one of the first scholars to call for a greater examination
of the tragedy of the war. Michael Kammen, "The American Revolution as a Crise de
Conscience: The Case of New York," in Richard M. Jellison, ed., *Society, Freedom and
Conscience: The Coming of the Revolution in Virginia, Massachusetts, and New York*
(New York, 1976).

3. Myron H. Luke and Robert W. Venables, *Long Island in the American Revolution*
(Albany, 1976), 2, have argued that "New England's powerful cultural, religious and
social pull" on Suffolk residents was an important determinant in their response to "the
great controversies of the 1760s and 1770s." For the early New Englanders in Suffolk,
see Dixon Ryan Fox, *Yankees and Yorkers* (New York, 1940).

4. Richard Moss, *Slavery on Long Island: A Study in Local Institutional and Early
African-American Communal Life* (New York, 1993), 71–73. For more on Suffolk's
slaveholding statistics, see *Census of Suffolk County, 1776, Excerpted from Calendar of*

Historical Manuscripts Relating to the War of the Revolution (Lambertville, N.J., 1984), and Helen Wortis, "Blacks on Long Island: Population Growth in the Colonial Period," *Journal of Long Island History* 11 (1974): 40–41, 44.

5. According to Geoffrey Rossano, Suffolk's local governing class, such as the one that dominated the town of Huntington, was "based on [the] concentration of wealth in relatively few hands, electoral deference to descendants of founding families, high levels of plural office holding, and extended tenure in government service." Geoffrey Rossano, "Oligarchs and Democrats: The Revolution in Huntington Town Government, 1765–1800," *The Quarterly of the Huntington Historical Society* 21 (1981): 4–23, and "Class and Clan: The Origins of a Colonial Oligarchy in Huntington, Long Island 1650–1775," *Long Island Forum* 46 (1983): 105–35. Rossano also described Suffolk's colonial sociopolitical order in modern terms as "deference democracy," or as he explains, "an elitist structure based on a hierarchic view of society," in which "deference to the wealthy elite was an implicit duty for the bulk of the electorate." Rossano, "Tale of Two Towns," *Long Island Forum* 58 (1985): 136–65.

6. For a brief genealogy of the Smith families of Suffolk, see Frederick Mather, *The Refugees of 1776 from Long Island to Connecticut*, (Albany, 1913), 564–77.

7. For the origins and development of Presbyterianism in Suffolk County, see Robert Nichols, *Presbyterianism in New York State: A History of the Synod and Its Predecessors* (Philadelphia, 1963).

8. Charles Street, ed., *Huntington Town Records, 1658–1873* (Huntington, N.Y., 1887–1889) 2: 521–23; hereafter cited as *HTR*.

9. Ebenezer Prime was Huntington's pastor for fifty-eight years (1721–1779); Samuel Buell was East Hampton's pastor for fifty years (1749–1799).

10. For the Anglican Church in Suffolk, see Robert Cray, "Anglicans in the Puritan Domain: Clergy and Laity in Eastern Long Island, 1693–1776," *Long Island Historical Journal* 2 (1990): 189–200.

11. The most forceful was Huntington's "Declaration of Rights," which stated that "every freeman's property is absolutely his own, and no man has the right to take it from him without his consent"; Henry Onderdonk, *Revolutionary Incidents of Suffolk and Kings Counties, with an Account of the Battle of Long Island, and the British Prisonships at New York* (New York, 1849; reprint, Port Washington, N.Y., 1967), 13–18.

12. At this time, 236 men in Suffolk refused to sign the Continental Association; that number constituted approximately 8% of the eligible male population between the ages of sixteen and fifty years. The Association was a pledge to boycott British imports, to form extralegal committee structures, and to execute the measures recommended by the Continental Congress and the Provincial Convention; Onderdonk, *Revolutionary Incidents*, 18. A copy of the "Continental Association" that circulated in Suffolk appears in Mather, *Refugees of 1776*, 140–41; for the names of signers and recusants, see *idem.*, 1054–65.

13. Nichols, *Presbyterianism in New York*, 46; Jane Des Grange, comp., *Long Island's Religious History* (Stony Brook, N.Y., 1963), 35.

14. Edward Countryman, *A People in Revolution: The American Revolution and Political Society in New York, 1760–1790* (Baltimore, 1981), 104–108; 149.

15. Thomas Helme, Brookhaven, N.Y., to New York Provincial Congress, 3 Aug. 1775, in Onderdonk, *Revolutionary Incidents*, 20; *Journal of the New York Provincial Congress*, June 8, 1776, 27; Gen. David Wooster to Governor Trumbull, Oyster Pond, Aug. 14, 1775, in David Wooster, *Genealogy of the Woosters in America, Descended from Edward Wooster of Connecticut* (San Francisco, 1885.). For the occurrences in Brookhaven at the start of the Revolution and the proceedings of the committee of safety, see "Proceedings of the Committee of Safety of the Town of Brookhaven 1775," Manuscript Division, New York Public Library; and photostat of "Brookhaven, L.I., Committee of Safety, etc., Minutes," Pennypacker Collection, East Hampton Free Library, East Hampton, N.Y.

16. Nicoll Havens served as town clerk for eighteen years (1759–1776) and town supervisor for seven years (1770–1776). From 1770 to 1776 four members of the Havens family held the town's top public offices.

17. For the activities and muster rolls of the Suffolk County militia, see Silas Wood, *A Sketch of the Towns on Long Island* (Brooklyn, 1828), 141–42; Peter Ross, *A History of Long Island* (New York, 1903) 2:560–73; Reginald Metcalf and Rufus Langhans, *Mustering and Parading: 200 Years of Militia on Long Island, 1653–1868* (Huntington, N.Y., 1982), 16–20; and Onderdonk, *Revolutionary Incidents*, 20–29. There are several reasons for the east-west dichotomy over the Revolution that evolved on Long Island before the British occupation. First, unlike Kings and Queens Counties, whose societies gravitated west towards Manhattan, Suffolk's orientation extended north across the Sound. As a result, Suffolk's economic, social, and political ties were with Yankee New England not British-inclined New York. Second, Suffolk's geographical isolation produced a relatively homogenous society that distrusted outsiders and fostered a strong sense of autonomy. Finally, eastern Long Island was overwhelmingly Presbyterian and remained suspicious of matters that endorsed "Anglicans and royalty." For more on the differences between eastern and western Long Island, see Luke and Venables, *Long Island in the Revolution*; James Bunce and Richard Harmond, eds., *Long Island as America: A Documentary History to 1896* (Port Washington, N.Y., 1977), 69–75; and Rossano, "Tale of Two Towns."

18. For the Battle of Brooklyn, see John Gallagher, *The Battle of Brooklyn, 1776* (New York, 1995).

19. The British occupation of Suffolk provided the army access to badly needed provisions, protected the flank of the main British army in New York City, and secured a base of operations along the Atlantic seaboard.

20. Orders of Gen. Oliver De Lancey to Col. Phineas Fanning, Sept. 2, 1776; and Orders of Gov. William Tryon, undated, in Onderdonk, *Revolutionary Incidents*, 45–46, 60.

21. Mather, *Refugees*, 176; *HTR* 3: 72.

22. In New York the British seem to have been more successful recruiting soldiers from outside of than inside Suffolk County. In 1777 they were allegedly able to enlist 1,500 militia men in Queens County alone. In Cortlandt Manor in Westchester County, members from one out of every three families joined the British army. Although we may never know the motives of these soldiers, historian Sung Bok Kim asserts that "pecuniary considerations" were a possible factor. Nevertheless, the use of force to get men to enlist throughout New York coincides with British impressment polices in the region in general. For threats of "detaching" Suffolk men from the local militia, see Men Ordered by General De Lancey to be Enlisted in the King's Service, Sept. 5, 1776, *HTR*, 3:14–16; A Copy of what was sent through Suffolk County by Order of Governor Tryon, in Onderdonk, *Revolutionary Incidents*, 59–60; Mather, *Refugees*, 174. For the recruitment of militia in other New York counties, see Sung Bok Kim, "The Limits of Politicization in The American Revolution: The Experience of Westchester County, New York," in *Journal of American History* 80 (1993), 881–882; and James B. Whisker, *The American Colonial Militia: The Colonial Militias of New York, New Jersey, Delaware, and Maryland* (Lewiston, N.Y., 1997), 32–45. For the forcible enlistment of men by the British outside of New York, see Walter Edgar, *Partisans and Redcoats: The Southern Conflict that Turned the Tide of the American Revolution* (New York, 2001), 59–60.

23. For a discussion of martial law on British occupied Long Island, see Joseph Tiedemann, "Patriots by Default: Queens County, New York and the British Army, 1776–1783" *William and Mary Quarterly* 43 (1986), 49–62, hereafter cited as *WMQ*.

24. Stephen Conway argued that British abuse of civilians stemmed from several causes ranging from the need to supplement rations to a lack of respect for Americans in general; see Conway, "The Great Mischief Complain'd of": Reflections on the Misconduct of British Soldiers in the Revolutionary War," *WMQ* 47 (1990): 370–390; and his "To Subdue America: British Army Officers and the Conduct of the Revolutionary War," *WMQ* 43 (1986): 381–407.

25. General De Lancey's Orders for All Fat Cattle and Sheep in Suffolk County, Sept. 5, 1776; Orders from John Morrison, Commissary of Forage, Sept. 27, 1776, *HTR*, 3: 16–17; General Erskine's Proclamation Commanding Surrender of the Rebels, Aug. 29, 1776, in Onderdonk, *Revolutionary Incidents*, 13.

26. "Account of Rails Burnt by Col[one]l. Thompson's Command Whilst in Huntington, Winter, 1782–1783," *HTR*, 3:100.

27. Although only a child in 1776, Silas Wood includes his own observations and recollections of the British occupation in his book, *Sketch of Long Island*, 120.

28. "Smithtown Ledger," Smithtown Historical Society, Smithtown, N.Y.; "Revolutionary War Records," Town Clerk's Archives, Town of Huntington, N.Y.; see also, Wood, *Sketch of Long Island*, 120; "An Account of Damages sustained by the Inhabitants of Huntington, 1782," *HTR*, 3:97–99. Neither the "Smithtown Ledger" nor Huntington's "Revolutionary War Records" specify if the amounts are listed in British sterling or New York currency.

29. For calculations regarding the number of refugees, see Mather, *Refugees*, 187.

30. Henry Hazelton, *The Boroughs of Brooklyn and Queens and Counties of Nassau and Suffolk, N.Y., 1609–1924* (New York, 1925), 1: 217. In attempts to prevent spying and smuggling, authorities on both sides of the Sound tried to regulate communications and travel between Connecticut and Long Island. For copies of regulations and petitions concerning travel to and from Long Island, see Mather, *Refugees*, Appendix D-F, 873–988.

31. For accounts of the whaleboat warfare in and around the Long Island Sound, see Benjamin Tallmadge, *Memoirs of Colonel Benjamin Tallmadge* (New York, 1858); William Mulvihill, "The Battle of Sagg Harbor." *Long Island Forum* 51 (1998): 14–19; and Mather, *Refugees*, 220–24.

32. While imprisoned in New York, he became infected with smallpox and died within a month.

33. *Rivington's New-York Gazetteer*, Mar. 10, 1779, in Onderdonk, *Revolutionary Incidents*, 81; Orders of General De Lancey, Aug. 27, 1779, in Ross, *History of Long Island*, 2: 476.

34. Orders of Gen. De Lancey, Sept. 1, 1776, in Onderdonk, *Revolutionary Incidents*, 45; P.R.O., Colonial Office 5/1109, photostat in the Long Island Collection at the East Hampton Library, East Hampton, New York; Colonel Livingston to Governor Trumbull, Sept. 10, 1776, typescript in the Long Island Collection at the East Hampton Library. The British army issued the oath to Suffolk's inhabitants again in 1778. List of Persons Who Took the Oath of Loyalty in Huntington, 1778, *HTR*, 35–45; Letter of Governor Tryon, Sept. 5, 1778, in Onderdonk, *Revolutionary Incidents*, 76. Two thousand six hundred seventy-seven male inhabitants took the oath in 1778; Dwight Holbrook, *The Wickham Claim* (Riverhead, N.Y., 1986), 84.

35. For more on the organization and operations of the Culper Spy Ring, see Morton Pennypacker, *General Washington's Spies on Long Island and in New York* (Brooklyn, N.Y., 1939).

36. Orders of General De Lancey, Aug. 27, 1779, in Ross, *History of Long Island*, 2: 476; General De Reidesel, Brooklyn, N.Y., to Brig. Gen. De Lancey, Long Island, N.Y., July 16, 1781, *HTR*, 3: 68–69. At the time of the Revolution, Lloyd's Neck fell within the borders of Queens County, but it was situated less than a mile directly north of Huntington Village and was routinely involved in that town's local affairs. In 1886 the Lloyd's Neck peninsula was transferred from the jurisdiction of the Town of Oyster Bay, Queens County, to the Town of Huntington, Suffolk County.

37. Geoffrey Rossano, "Tale of Two Towns, The War Years," *Long Island Forum*, 48 (1985) 8: 164.

38. Myron Luke, "The Blydenburgh Manuscript: Smithtown Ledger of Revolutionary War Reparations," *Long Island Courant* 1 (1965): 35.

39. For the negative attitudes the British held toward American civilians in occupied regions, see Conway, "The Great Mischief Complain'd of" and his "To Subdue America," passim.

40. July 19, 1780, *Journal of the Continental Congress*, in Onderdonk, *Revolutionary Incidents*, 93; Ross, *History of Long Island*, 2:477.

41. William B. Willcox, ed., *The American Rebellion: Sir Henry Clinton's Narrative of his Campaign, 1775–1782* (New Haven, Conn., 1954), 47–48, 479.

42. Nichols, *Presbyterianism in New York*, 66.

43. Receipts of Col. Benjamin Thompson to John Sammis, Mar. 1, 1783, *HTR*, 3: 116. Fort Golgatha was one of seven British forts in Suffolk. Because Huntington served as the hub of British activities in Suffolk, two other forts were also erected in and around the village: Ft. Franklin, just to the north of the village at Lloyds Manor and another large redoubt to the east of town. All of the forts were targets for the American guerillas sailing whaleboats across the Sound from Connecticut.

44. *New London Gazette*, Jan. 2, 1778; *New York Gazette and Weekly Mercury*, February 16, 1778; *Rivington's New-York Gazetteer*, Feb. 26, 1778, in Onderdonk, *Revolutionary Incidents*, 71.

45. For details on the "illicit trade," see Mather, *Refugees*, 200–14.

46. *New London Gazette*, Sept. 20, 1782, in Onderdonk, *Revolutionary Incidents*, 107; "A meeting of the Inhabitants [of Huntington], Aug. 28, 1783," *HTR*, 3:117.

47. "Burning of the Soldier's Huts, Mar. 11, 1783," *HTR*, 101–102; Onderdonk, *Revolutionary Incidents*, 108.

48. Mather, *Refugees*, 192–93.

49. Kenneth Stryker-Rodda, "Genealogical Gleanings from the Account Book of Elias Pelletreau of Southampton, Long Island," *Journal of Long Island History* 5 (1965): 28.

50. In 1779 the New York State Legislature passed the Act of Attainder and rescinded the civil rights of the state's most troublesome Loyalists, confiscated their property, and banished them from the state forever. The four Suffolk County men named in the act lived the rest of their lives in exile: Richard Floyd in New Brunswick, Canada, George Muirson and Parker Wickham in Connecticut, and Henry Lloyd II in England. Harry B. Yoshpe, *The Disposition of Loyalist Estates in the Southern District of the State of New York* (New York, 1939), 18, 46–48; Holbrook, *Wickham Claim*, 91, 108–10.

51. Henry Onderdonk, "Suffolk County in Olden Times," *Journal of Long Island History* 6 (1966) 16–36.

52. Mather, *Refugees*, 340, 347–348, 719; Ross, *History of Long Island*, 1:175.

53. Gordon Wood, *The American Revolution: A History* (New York, 2002), 113.

54. This trend was even more dramatic in the early nineteenth century, when there was a different supervisor elected in Huntington every year from 1810 into the 1820s.

55. E. Wilder Spaulding, *New York in the Critical Period: 1783–1789* (Repr., Port Washington, N.Y., 1963), 33; Edward Palmer, *Tercentenary Celebration of the First Presbyterian Church, Southold, New York, 1640–1940* (Southold, N.Y.: 1940), 13; Des Grange, *Long Island's Religious History*, 13–14, 31; Robert Cray, "Forging a Majority: The Methodist Experience On Eastern Long Island, 1789–1845," *New York History* (1986): 288, 295, 298.

56. Gordon Wood made similar arguments regarding common attitudes towards slavery in the colonial period; Gordon Wood, *American Revolution*, 126–27. Richard S. Moss, *Slavery*, xv.

57. For a list of manumissions in Huntington, see Stanley Klein, comp., *Manumission Book of the Towns of Huntington and Babylon, New York: With Some Earlier Manumissions, 1800–1824* (Huntington, N.Y., 1997); James Bunce and Richard Harmond, eds., *Long Island as America: A Documentary History to 1896* (Port Washington, N.Y., 1977), 83–84; *HTR*, 3:142; Mather, *Refugees*, 512–513, 607–608.

58. Tomas Tredwell, "A Long Islander's Opposition to the Constitution," in James Bunce and Richard Harmond, *Long Island as America,* 92–96.

59. Ralph Ireland, "Slavery on Long Island: A Study of Economic Motivation,*" Journal of Long Island History* 6 (1966): 12.

60. Grania Marcus, *Discovering the African-American Experience in Suffolk County, 1620–1860* (Setauket, N.Y., 1988), 130–31; Moss, *Slavery*, 172–73.

4

Richmond County, Staten Island

Phillip Papas

Richmond County, which comprises the present Borough of Staten Island, is thirteen miles long and eight miles wide; located near the entrance to New York harbor, it is approximately ten miles southwest of Manhattan. The Narrows separates the county from what is today the Borough of Brooklyn on Long Island. Dividing Richmond from New Jersey to the west and south are the Kill van Kull, Arthur Kill (or creek), and Raritan Bay.

After the Dutch surrendered New Netherland to the English in 1664, Staten Island came under the jurisdiction of the province of New York and in 1683 was organized into Richmond County. In 1729 centrally located Richmondtown became the county seat. The island contained two manorial estates: the fifty-one-hundred-acre Cassiltowne Manor and Capt. Christopher Billopp's sixteen-hundred-acre Bentley Manor.[1] At the time of the Revolution, Staten Island was divided into four towns: Northfield, Southfield, Westfield, and Castleton.[2]

The population of Staten Island grew from 727 in 1698 to nearly 3,000 on the eve of the Revolution. Settlement was widely scattered along its shoreline and inland waterways. It is difficult to calculate the ethnic composition of colonial Staten Island. The only study of this topic, which was made by historian Field Horne, has concluded that the island's population in 1706 was at least 38 percent Dutch, 21 percent British, 17 percent French, and 24 percent African American.[3] Slavery was a conspicuous institution on the island. Slaves comprised anywhere from 10 percent to 24 percent of Staten Island's population. There were typically an average of no more than three slaves per farm, however, affluent residents owned between five and ten slaves.[4]

The majority of Staten Islanders were prosperous middle-class farmers, who grew grains such as wheat, corn, rye, and barley; kept vegetable gardens; and maintained fruit orchards, salt meadows, and woodlots. Staten Islanders also engaged in domestic manufacturing to supplement their agricultural incomes; enterprising residents owned grist- and sawmills, operated ferries, managed taverns and inns, engaged in the fishing and oyster trades, sold timber, and maintained shipyards. Staten Island's products were sold in the urban markets of New York City as well as in Perth Amboy, Elizabethtown (now Elizabeth), and Woodbridge, New Jersey. The ports of New York and Perth Amboy connected Staten Islanders to the commercial networks of the transatlantic world.[5]

By the late colonial period, the Anglican Church (or Church of England) wielded great political influence. Of the six Staten Islanders who served in the New York Assembly from 1750 to 1775, five were Anglicans, and one was a member of the Dutch Reformed Church, who was elected in 1761 with the support of the island's Anglican congregation.[6] The island's leading families before the Revolution—the Billopps, Dongans, Micheaus, and Seamans—were Anglicans. These families "pretty much governed the island" through an intricate network of intermarriage and local political deference.[7]

Religion was an important factor in determining revolutionary loyalties. According to historian Philip Ranlet, "about 53 percent" of Staten Islanders who signed an oath of allegiance to the king in July 1776 "appear to have been Anglicans."[8] Presbyterians and members of the Dutch Reformed Church joined the Whigs (or Patriots) and supported independence as a way to break the Anglicans' political hold over the island and to disestablish the Church of England. Self-preservation led Staten Island's Moravians (or Brethren) to become Loyalists. They had not only flourished under British imperial rule but by the Revolution tensions existed between them and the local Reformed congregants. Thus, as did the Anglicans, the Moravians feared the consequences of a new political and social order that would follow a Whig victory in the Revolution.[9]

During the Revolution, vulnerable Staten Island was a Loyalist stronghold. Like Kings County, it was proximate to the center of British power in New York City, dependent upon the urban market, and defenseless against the British navy. Following the British occupation of the island in early July 1776, it also became a haven for Loyalists, especially those escaping from Whig-controlled areas in New Jersey. The overwhelming majority of Staten Islanders had hoped that calm heads would prevail during the pre-Revolutionary disputes over imperial taxation and that a political reconciliation with Britain could be reached. The Whigs' attempt to force the islanders to embrace the Patriot cause further alienated residents. This essay will focus on the islanders' defiance of the colonial resistance movement and examine how almost seven-and-a-half years under British occupation, rough treatment by British regulars, Hessians, and Loyalists, and war-weariness turned many Staten Islanders from defenders of the king to people who accepted the Revolution.

The Events of 1775

Staten Islanders refrained from taking an active part in the protests against British taxation during and after the Stamp Act crisis. Instead, they deferred judgment on political matters to a small group of prominent, well-respected members of the community led by Christopher Billopp and Benjamin Seaman. Billopp, who was elected to the New York Assembly in 1769, came from a family that had long-established ties to the provincial governments of New York and New Jersey. Benjamin Seaman, who was Billopp's father-in-law and a justice of the county surrogate court, had sat in the Assembly since 1756. Both men were Anglicans, who favored reconciliation and who wielded much influence on Staten Island.[10] When the New York Assembly convened in January 1775, Billopp and Seaman voted with the majority to repudiate the First Continental Congress's measures; the Congress was an illegal body that had usurped the status of the constitutional colonial assembly. They also voted against thanking New York's Continental congressmen for their service and opposed sending a delegation to the Second Continental Congress.[11]

Staten Islanders were especially opposed to the Continental Association and the network of local committees of inspection (or observation) that enforced the boycott. As did many other New York agrarians, Staten Islanders objected to the measure, because it closed down the lucrative transatlantic export market to their products, threatened to cut off their access to highly desirable British manufactured goods and specie, and because the loss of British goods from the colonial market meant an increase in the price of domestically produced items. Staten Islanders evaded its provisions by smuggling, which was a long established practice on the island.[12]

The first real test of the Association in New York came on February 2, 1775, when the merchant vessel *James* arrived from Glasgow, Scotland. New York City's Committee of Sixty, which had been created to enforce the Association, ordered the ship to depart the port without breaking cargo. Although the ship's captain complied with the Committee's demand, the *James* returned the next week escorted by a British naval vessel. After two days of protests, the *James* again left New York with its cargo onboard.[13] Immediately following the *James*'s departure, rumors circulated that the *James* had stopped at Staten Island, and with the assistance of several residents, the captain had unloaded a portion of the ship's cargo. Given that the island had had a long history as a smugglers' haven, these rumors were probably true.

The island's failure to abide by the Continental Association led several committees of observation in eastern New Jersey to coerce Staten Island. On February 13, 1775, the Committee of Observation in Elizabethtown, New Jersey, banned all trade with the island until its residents signed the Association. One week later, the Committee of Observation in Woodbridge, New Jersey, threatened to suspend all trade with Staten Island. This tactic succeeded. By July 1775 Staten Islanders reportedly had "in general signed the Association."[14]

In early March 1775, New York City Whigs requested that a Provincial Convention on April 20 select delegates to represent New York at the upcoming Second Continental Congress and that each county send deputies to that Convention. On April 11, a meeting for this purpose was held on Staten Island. There, Christopher Billopp convinced the majority of those in attendance to repudiate the Congress, which made reconciliation more difficult to achieve.[15] Thus, Staten Island did not send deputies to the Convention.

The Provincial Convention met on April 20 and chose a twelve-member delegation to the Second Continental Congress. When the Convention adjourned on April 22, news of the bloodshed at Lexington and Concord reached New York City, inflaming tempers and causing a wave of protests.[16] Staten Islanders were stunned at the hostilities in Massachusetts and at the mob violence it precipitated, and nervous residents still hoped for political reconciliation. One islander was distressed to see that "the affairs of America are far from being settled" and hoped "a Mode of reconciliation between Great Britain & her Colonies" could be achieved. Rev. Richard Charlton, an Anglican minister, called for "a Speedy suppression to insulting Mobs, and a restoration of Loyalty and obedience to our Parent State." Christopher Billopp and Benjamin Seaman joined twelve other Assemblymen in a message to the British army's commander-in-chief, Gen. Thomas Gage, that called for a ceasefire and a negotiated settlement to the crisis.[17]

On April 28, 1775, New York City's Committee of Sixty called on each county to elect delegates to a Provincial Congress. In addition, on April 29, the Committee issued the General Association, by which signers pledged to support the actions of the Provincial and Continental congresses. On May 1 Staten Islanders chose a five-man delegation of moderate-to-conservative community leaders to represent them in the Provincial Congress. Self-preservation was probably the motivation for this sudden turnaround. According to Rev. Hector Gambold of the Moravian Church, residents "had 'till the last week generally opposed . . . having any Thing to do with the Congress," but the threat of "armed Force" by the Whigs compelled them to elect a slate of delegates to that governing body.[18]

The men elected to represent Richmond in the Provincial Congress were Richard Conner, a native of Ireland, a Moravian, and a future captain in the Third Company of Christopher Billopp's Brigade of Loyalist Militia; Aaron

Cortelyou, Benjamin Seaman's son-in-law and a leader in the Moravian congregation, who later actively assisted the British army with logistics and information; John Journeay, an Anglican acquaintance of Benjamin Seaman; Richard Lawrence, a shipwright, whom Gen. William Howe appointed in July 1776 to the position of master carpenter of Staten Island's shipyards; and Paul Micheau Jr., the county clerk, who was also Benjamin Seaman's son-in-law. Throughout the summer of 1775, these congressmen favored reconciliation. Thus, on June 2 they voted for a resolution introduced by conservative Benjamin Kissam of New York City, which called for "a reconciliation between Great Britain and these Colonies on constitutional principles" and for the appointment of a committee "to prepare a plan of such accommodation."[19]

The presence of British warships in New York harbor was one of the most serious issues facing the Provincial Congress. To prevent violence it authorized the continued sale of fresh provisions to these vessels, so long as these supplies did not end up in the hands of the besieged British army in Boston. The Congress also strictly limited the types of goods and outlined procedures for this trade. Staten Islanders, however, evaded these regulations. On September 2, for instance, a New York City resident notified the New York Committee of Safety, which was sitting for the adjourned Provincial Congress, that "sundry persons in Richmond County" were supplying livestock and other produce to British ships.[20]

The New York Committee of Safety launched an investigation, which pointed to John Wetherhead, a native of Britain and a leading New York City merchant. On September 17, 1775, from aboard the British warship *Asia* in New York harbor, where he had gone several months earlier to escape the mob violence in the city, Wetherhead addressed the Committee of Safety's suspicions. Although he admitted having been on Staten Island with an unidentified British officer, who "purchased some stock from two or three persons," Wetherhead did not reveal the identities of the Staten Islanders who had sold the provisions, nor whether they had been forwarded to Boston. He even sarcastically hinted that these islanders were responsible for saving New York City from destruction. "For my part, I thought myself happy, and do still think so," he wrote to the Committee of Safety, "that the stock was procured, as it in some measure tended to quiet the minds of the (British) officers," who might have taken "some steps . . . that would have been very fatal to numbers in the City." With no further information and no means of apprehending Wetherhead, the committee dropped its investigation.[21]

In October the Provincial Congress ordered the counties to hold elections for delegates to the Second Provincial Congress, which was to convene on November 14. Five counties—Charlotte, Cumberland, Gloucester, Queens, and Richmond—failed to do so. The first three counties eventually overcame poor communication and pressing local issues to send delegates. In the Queens elections, the Loyalists defeated the Whigs.[22] But Richmond residents defiantly refused to hold an election.

On December 2, the Provincial Congress ordered the Richmond County Committee of Safety, which was controlled by Loyalist sympathizers, to "cause an election to be held, without delay." Two weeks later islanders voted over-whelmingly against sending a delegation to the Second Provincial Congress. The committee explained that Staten Islanders had agreed to send delegates to the First Provincial Congress in the expectation that that body would work for reconciliation, but they had been disappointed by Congress's actions, which might instead provoke "a war with Great Britain" that could be harmful to the island.[23]

The Provincial Congress then used economic sanctions against Staten Island. On December 21, 1775, it announced that the island was in "breach of the General Association and of an open contempt of the authority of this Congress" and ordered the county Committee of Safety to make "a list of the names of those who oppose" holding elections for the Provincial Congress. If the committee did not forward the list within fifteen days, the island would face commercial interdiction. This tactic worked. On January 19, 1776, Staten Island elected moderate Whig Adrian Bancker, who was the brother of the New York merchant Evert Bancker and a member of the island's Dutch Reformed con-gregation, and reelected the Loyalist Richard Lawrence, who had served in the First Provincial Congress.[24]

Staten Island and the Defense of New York

In early 1776 persistent rumors circulated throughout the New York port area that Gen. William Howe, who had replaced Gage as the British army commander-in-chief, planned to abandon Boston and make New York City the focus of British military operations. Any successful American defense of New York required securing Staten Island. Its proximity to Manhattan, Long Island, and New Jersey; the ability of the British navy to control its coast; and the Loyalism of many of its residents made Staten Island an ideal military base of operations for the British.

Washington promptly appointed Maj. Gen. Charles Lee to defend New York. Lee quickly fortified several key water approaches to the city.[25] However, he failed to secure Staten Island, leaving it exposed to the British. The New York Committee of Safety protested, but Lee, who lacked naval support and was short of men and heavy artillery, decided against fortifying the island. Instead he favored securing its livestock against British depredations. To carry out this task, the New York Provincial Congress, which had few troops to spare, asked the New Jersey Whig government to order Col. Nathaniel Heard of Woodbridge, New Jersey, "to secure the live-stock of . . . [Staten] Island from depredation . . . by guarding it on the island till we have opportunity to determine on the expediency of removing it." The Provincial Congress also asked the Elizabethtown Committee of Observation to deploy some militia to support Heard's troops.[26] In the meantime, Brig. Gen. William Livingston of the New Jersey militia, who would later serve as governor of New Jersey (September 1776–July 1790), dispatched three hundred men to protect the livestock on Staten Island and to gather intelligence.[27]

On February 12, 1776, Staten Islanders awoke to the sight of Livingston's troops patrolling the island. Colonel Heard with seven hundred men arrived four days later. Several Staten Islanders harassed and insulted the soldiers, while others threatened them with death if they tried to confiscate weapons or remove livestock. A disgusted Heard consequently arrested four respected members of the community—Richard Conner, Isaac Decker, Abraham Harris, and Minah Burger—on charges of "inimicality" and sent them to Elizabethtown, where the local Committee of Observation placed them in jail to await trial.[28] Colonel Heard sent the prisoners there because he probably thought convicting the four would be impossible in Loyalist-leaning Richmond.

Colonel Heard eventually returned to New Jersey, and he left behind a few men to guard the island's coast; but his four arrests further angered Staten Islanders and stiffened their Loyalism. One resident complained that Heard's arrests demonstrated the lengths to which Whigs would go to force persons to "abide by the Laws of Congress." The New York Provincial Congress sympathetically explained to Staten Islanders that Heard had been dispatched to the island only to protect their livestock. Congress also informed the Elizabethtown Committee of Observation that in New York "all persons charged with any conduct inimical to the United Colonies, or transgressing any resolves, rules, or regulations of the Continental or Provincial Congress" were to be remanded to "the County Committee of the County in which such delinquents reside." Congress then requested that the chairman of the Elizabethtown committee hand over the four Staten Islanders and any evidence obtained against them to the Richmond County Committee of Safety, under whose jurisdiction the men were to be legally tried.[29] This was promptly done.

The trial, which took place on March 7, was a farce. Most of the witnesses called to testify against the suspects either failed to come forward, proclaimed their ignorance, or faced a barrage of insults while on the stand. One witness complained to the Provincial Congress that the county committee had allowed him to endure "insufferable abuse" from the defendants and their supporters "while under examination."[30] In the end, the charges against the four men were dropped, and they were released. New York Whigs condemned the county Committee of Safety's handling of the trial as "improper and ineffectual."[31]

On March 7, 1776, General Lee left New York for Charleston, South Carolina, where he was to oversee that city's defenses. Brig. Gen. William

Alexander (or Lord Stirling) succeeded him in New York City.[32] On March 19 Washington informed Stirling that the British had "abandon'd" Boston two days earlier. He added: "Where they Intend to make a descent next, is altogether unknown, but supposing New York to be an Object of much importance . . . I must recommend your most strenuous and active exertions in preparing to prevent any designs or Attempts they may have against It."[33] Stirling worked quickly to complete the port's defenses; he also monitored Staten Island's residents. When he received reports that a Staten Islander named John James Boyd had made "expressions injurious to the country, and in favour of Ministerial tyranny," Stirling immediately ordered Boyd arrested and brought before the New York Provincial Congress. Although Congress released Boyd because it found him to be "unimportant and insignificant," Whig troops continued to monitor his activities and those of his fellow Staten Islanders.[34]

After they abandoned Boston, the British sailed for Halifax, Nova Scotia, instead of New York. On March 20 Stirling returned to New Jersey to oversee that province's defenses. There, Stirling remained a strong advocate for securing Staten Island, which was important to the defense of both New York and of eastern New Jersey. He proposed using Jersey troops to occupy the island's heights. In a letter to Gen. William Livingston, Stirling stressed that it was "highly Necessary" to occupy "some Commanding height on Staten Island" in order to "Guard" New Jersey.[35]

Unfortunately for the Patriot cause, Stirling's efforts to defend Staten Island did not go well. On April 1, 1776, Stirling warned Washington that the island remained open to a British invasion. New Jersey's mobilization of troops was slow and disorganized. Gen. William Heath in late March assumed command in the New York port area and asked General Livingston to hasten the occupation of Staten Island. Heath stressed that the defense of New York and New Jersey depended "in a very great Measure . . . upon our being well possessed of Staten Island." Meanwhile, in New Jersey, Stirling, frustrated by the lack of progress being made on the island, sought personally to take charge of defensive preparations there.[36]

On April 3 Maj. Gen. Israel Putnam of Connecticut assumed command of New York's defenses. Putnam quickly dispatched three companies of Maryland and Virginia riflemen to Staten Island, where they were to receive their orders from Stirling. To prevent British naval commanders from resupplying their vessels with fresh drinking water, Stirling posted riflemen near the Watering Place, an area containing several natural springs on the island's northeastern coast. Others were positioned on the heights overlooking the Narrows. Fresh reinforcements arrived throughout April. Some of these Whig soldiers worked on the island's fortifications; others had orders to arrest and disarm suspected Loyalists; and others patrolled the coast to prevent Staten Islanders from contacting British ships.[37] Whig troops arrested Darby Doyle, a ferry operator who lived near the Watering Place, and charged him with "selling provisions to, and holding correspondence with the enemy." On another occasion, Susannah McDonald, whose husband Alexander was a captain in the Loyalist Royal Highland Emigrants in Halifax, suffered "a vast many insults & abuses" from Whig troops who often searched her home for weapons, letters from her husband, and military intelligence.[38]

These actions of the Whig troops made Staten Islanders even angrier. Residents were frustrated, too, by the failure of Patriot authorities to compensate them fairly and promptly for the army's use of their homes, produce, livestock, woodlands, and labor. In addition, several residents complained that their fields and gardens had been "over-run and eaten up by the Rebels" without regard for their property rights. On April 6 Christian Jacobson, a prominent Moravian and chairman of the county Committee of Safety, warned New York Whigs that if they expected to obtain Staten Islanders' cooperation, they must start to respect residents' lives and property.[39]

On April 13 Washington arrived in New York and assumed command of its defenses. He ordered three of his subordinate officers to establish signal stations on the "Heights and Head Lands at the entrance of the Harbour." The stations were to use a system of flags and fires to warn of the approach of the British fleet. One of these signal stations was located on the heights of Staten Island overlooking the Narrows.[40] Washington also suggested that the New York Provincial Congress make arrangements for "the Removal of the Stock of Cattle and Horses" from Staten Island to prevent the island's livestock from falling into British hands. Congress ordered the county Committee of Safety to send to New Jersey all the livestock, except those animals that the residents deemed "indispensably necessary." Because of the committee's history of lukewarm support for the Patriot cause, Washington directed Capt. Ephraim Manning of the Third Connecticut Regiment, which was already posted on the island, to "drive the Stock off, without waiting for the assistance or direction of the Committee there [Staten Island]." Residents, however, refused to cooperate. Gov. Jonathan Trumbull of Connecticut later remarked: "Staten Island are mostly Tory's—they are ordered to send off their stock, but they found means to delay & delay, so that, we had but Just got off the fat Cattle, when the Enemy, as they wished, came on & prevented our taking off the Lean."[41] Thus, uncooperative Staten Island residents foiled Washington's plan to remove the island's livestock before the British arrived in the port.

The British Arrival

General Howe reached New York harbor on June 25, 1776, aboard the frigate *Greyhound*, four days before the main British fleet from Halifax arrived off Sandy Hook, New Jersey. During onboard meetings with Gov. William Tryon of New York and some local Loyalists, including several Staten Islanders, Howe was briefed on the military situation of the New York area. Although Howe had originally planned that his forces should land at Gravesend Bay, Long Island, Gen. James Robertson, one of his staff officers, persuaded him to go instead to Staten Island. Its location at the entrance to the harbor; abundance of produce, livestock, and natural springs; vulnerability to British naval power; and its largely Loyalist populace made the island a better encampment.[42]

At eight o'clock in the morning of July 2, Gen. Howe ordered three warships and the first division of transports to proceed to the Watering Place on Staten Island. As the ships sailed through the Narrows, they met with limited resistance from Whig troops stationed on the western edge of Long Island. The Patriots could also have inflicted heavy damage on the British ships with heavy artillery from the heights of Staten Island, but there were "no cannon upon these posts." The Whigs' main priority for defending New York had been to fortify Brooklyn Heights, which overlooked the East River and the city. They therefore concentrated most of their limited forces and heavy artillery at that location. When the British forces appeared, the undisciplined few Whig troops stationed on Staten Island quickly retreated.[43] British soldiers landed on the island without opposition.

The landing of nine thousand British troops on Staten Island was fully accomplished by July 4, 1776. Islanders welcomed them with supplies and assistance. One British officer reported that many of the island's residents "shew the Greatest Satisfaction on our Arrival, which has relived them from the most horred Opresion that can be conceaved."[44] Two days later, the members of the Staten Island colonial militia assembled at Richmondtown and offered their services to General Howe; also more than five hundred Staten Islanders, nearly all of the island's adult male population, took an oath of allegiance administered to them by Governor Tryon. On July 9 Tryon enlisted volunteers for a local provincial corps and a company of light horse for defense of the island. Christopher Billopp was commissioned a lieutenant colonel and given command of this corps, which was called Billopp's Corps of Staten Island Militia (or Billopp's Brigade). Isaac Decker was appointed captain and commander of the company of light horse.[45]

Some Staten Island Patriots meanwhile fled to New Jersey. Members of the Mersereau family went to Newark, where they eventually established a spy network that reported to Washington on British troop movements and concentrations in eastern New Jersey. However, those Whigs who failed to flee the British occupation hid their political sentiments or faced public harassment, the confiscation of their homes and property, and in some cases imprisonment. General Howe commandeered the home of Adrian Bancker for use as his headquarters. Dr. John T. Harrison later remembered one Staten Island Whig, who had chosen to remain on the island. "The British turned him out of his property," Harrison recalled, "and he may be said to have suffered everything but death." British troops also arrested and detained Barent Dupuy Sr., in a guardhouse. His son, Barent Jr., would often "go to visit him . . . and carry him snuff, . . . which the sentries and officers would not allow," remembered another Staten Islander.[46]

On July 12 Adm. Richard Lord Howe, General Howe's brother, arrived. On August 1 generals Henry Clinton and Charles Lord Cornwallis, with three thousand soldiers from the ill-fated attempt to capture Charleston, South Carolina, reached Staten Island. On August 12 a fleet from Europe brought supplies and ten thousand British and Hessian soldiers. In addition, several fugitive slaves from Whig-owned farms in eastern New Jersey sought to take advantage of a proclamation that Virginia's exiled royal governor, Lord Dunmore, had issued in November 1775, promising freedom to any slave who ran away from his Whig master and joined the British army. These fugitives served the British military in an auxiliary capacity as guides, wagon drivers, orderlies, harbor pilots, laborers, and spies or joined Black Loyalist regiments that were organized on the island. By the middle of August, the British had amassed about twenty-five thousand men and nearly four hundred and fifty ships off Staten Island, the largest expeditionary force ever assembled until the allied invasion of Normandy on D-Day in 1944.[47]

During this military buildup, Admiral Howe, who favored reconciliation instead of military force, issued a proclamation announcing that he and his brother would serve as peace commissioners with power to grant pardons and to declare at peace any region, where royal authority had been restored. But Admiral Howe's attempts to open peace negotiations with the Americans failed. The Howes consequently made New York City their target. However, fearing that capturing the city without first removing enemy troops and artillery from Brooklyn Heights could lead to a repeat of the debacle in Boston, General Howe chose to begin military operations against the city by securing western Long Island. Although the theater of military operations thus shifted from Staten Island, the British still considered it strategically valuable. It continued to serve as a long-term staging area for British military operations and on it was a hospital for its sick and wounded. General Howe ordered a detachment of regulars to remain on the island to assist Billopp's Brigade to defend against Whig attacks from eastern New Jersey.[48]

The British Occupation and Partisan Warfare

Throughout the war, the British stationed a small number of regulars and some Hessian units on Staten Island. The island was also the headquarters of several prominent Loyalist regiments, including Cortlandt Skinner's New Jersey

Volunteers and John Graves Simcoe's Queen's Rangers. Loyalists from Whig-occupied areas in eastern New Jersey fled to the safety of British protection on Staten Island, where many joined a provincial regiment or purchased land and became permanent residents.

Loyalist and Hessian units stationed on Staten Island repeatedly made forays into eastern New Jersey. They terrorized Whig partisans and carried off livestock, weapons, ammunition, produce, valuables, and prisoners. In turn, New Jersey Whigs formed vigilante groups that often slipped passed British guards and gunboats patrolling the island's coast at night and made retaliatory strikes against residents and their farms, causing widespread destruction. Thomas Macdonogh, a Loyalist, complained that the estate of his widowed mother-in-law Rachel Dawson, "lay contiguous to the posts of the Army," and was "subject to Incursions from Jersey, and though capable of yielding great Advantages yet little or no Benefit was derived from it during the Calamities of the War, as nothing could be preserved from plunder." Another Loyalist, Job Smith, noted that in 1780 his two boats were burned, and his house was "seized by the rebels." During one such raid, some New Jersey Whigs disguised their faces with black soot, entered the home of Peter Houseman, an island farmer, and demanded his valuables. When he refused, he was struck on the head with a heavy object and left to die.[49]

Regular Whig forces also made incursions onto Staten Island from eastern New Jersey on three separate occasions. The first came on October 15, 1776, when a detachment of troops under Brig. Gen. Hugh Mercer penetrated as far east as Richmondtown; the second occurred on August 22, 1777, and was led by Brig. Gen. John Sullivan; and the third took place on January 15, 1780, when Lord Stirling led three thousand men across the frozen Kill van Kull.[50] According to the English traveler Nicholas Cresswell, these Whigs incursions—whether by vigilantes or regular troops—made residents "very uneasy."[51]

Staten Islanders also had to endure depredations to their property by the British, Hessian, and Loyalist troops living among them. Residents complained frequently about the theft of property and the destruction of homes, fences, barns, woodlots, gardens, and fields. One resident recalled that British troops "destroyed all the fences, and when they [British] returned from Jersey they destroyed them again." The British military's enormous need for fuel led to the deforestation of "Hundreds and Hundreds of acres" on the island. Loyalist New Jersey Volunteers under the command of Abraham Van Buskirk and Joseph Barton frequently stole livestock and plundered fields and gardens.[52]

Islanders also suffered from acts of brutal violence at the hands of British regulars, Hessians, and Loyalists. By the late summer of 1776, British troops were frequently accused of sexually assaulting female Staten Islanders.[53] Lt. Col. Francis Lord Rawdon, a British officer, laughed at residents' complaints of sexual assault: "The fair nymphs of this isle [Staten Island] are in wonderful tribulation, as the fresh meat our men have got here has made them as riotous as satyrs. A girl cannot step into the bushes to pluck a rose without running the most imminent risk of being ravished, and they are so little accustomed to these vigorous methods that they don't bear them with the proper resignation, and of consequence we have most entertaining courts-martial every day."[54] In addition, members of the occupation forces also committed acts of murder. Soldiers from the provincial Queen's Rangers mortally wounded Christian Jacobson, a former chairman of the county Committee of Safety, when they broke into his home looking for valuables. The soldiers were eventually caught, found guilty by a court martial, and hanged.[55]

Staten Islanders had profited as early as 1775 from the sale of supplies to the British military. But wartime regulations designed to control the price of goods the Quartermaster Department purchased cut into these profits. Residents also disliked regulations on the type, price, and amount of produce they could sell to the British army. They resented, too, the fact that British authorities restricted the markets in which farmers could sell their goods. Moreover, requirements that islanders provide the troops with hay, grains, and cordwood added to their dissatisfaction.[56]

Throughout the war, residents lived under martial law. Except for occasional meetings of the town supervisors, the island's colonial civil government ceased to function. The British also shut down county courts, leaving residents with no legal recourse in civil or military disputes. In February 1778, with the impending threat of a French entry into the war, the British ministry sent a peace commission to America headed by the Earl of Carlisle. After the commission failed to end the war, it recommended to Lord George Germain, the British colonial secretary, that civil government should be restored in British-occupied areas of America. This proposal would have been an important first step in a new pacification policy.[57]

In March 1780 Germain appointed Gen. James Robertson as the new governor of New York. In February 1781 Robertson moved to revive civil government on Staten Island, when he created a Police Court and appointed Lt. Col. Christopher Billopp to the office of Superintendent of Police. Billopp was given authority to "hear and determine Controversies, maintain Peace and good Order, and regulate the Police . . . until Civil Government in all Forms can take Place." Billopp enforced military regulations issued by the British commandant at New York, dealt with civilian complaints against the military, and heard cases involving civilians. In essence, the duties of the Police Court and the Superintendent of Police were similar to those of military police.[58]

On October 19, 1781, British Gen. Charles Lord Cornwallis surrendered to Washington at Yorktown, Virginia. Although this battle virtually ended the Revolution, the war continued for Staten Islanders. With the British still in control of the island, partisan warfare and depredations continued. During that time, the future of island Loyalists remained uncertain, and questions about the structure of local society in an independent America had yet to be answered.

Staten Island at War's End

The British defeat at Yorktown forced Loyalists to make a difficult decision: accept the Whig victory and the new republican state governments or go into exile. By August 1782, after Britain agreed to American independence, some Staten Island Loyalists sought new homes elsewhere in the British Empire rather than live under a government led by their enemies.

Those Loyalists, whom New York's republican government deemed dangerous, were banished from the state. In October 1779 New York had enacted the Act of Attainder (or Confiscation Act), which attainted and banished fifty-nine influential Loyalists of the state, including two prominent Staten Islanders: Christopher Billopp and Benjamin Seaman. The law aimed to undermine Loyalist power in New York and to raise much-needed funds for the war effort by the sale of confiscated Loyalist property. Given Staten Island's reputation for Loyalism, it is remarkable that only two residents were singled out for punishment. Because of the British occupation, the state could not immediately enforce the law against the two men. Once the British army evacuated the island in December 1783, the state officially laid claim to the Billopp and Seaman properties. But speculators who purchased the property at state auction found themselves entangled in legal disputes with the local residents, who had earlier bought sections of the estates from the two. The disputed claims over the confiscated Loyalist estates took several years to settle.[59]

In early December 1783, the last of the British forces evacuated Staten Island, which had been occupied longer than any other community in America. Most of the residents, whether Whig or Loyalist, who had remained on the island after the Revolution put aside their wartime differences and rebuilt the community. The Revolution did not have a drastic impact on Staten Island's socioeconomic structure. Residents remained predominantly middle-class agrarians. Except for the confiscation and sale of the Billopp and Seaman lands, there was no major redistribution of property. The island's population experienced an increase from about 2,847 residents at the beginning of the war to 3,835 in 1790. Of that number, 127 were free African Americans, and 759 were slaves.[60]

By 1784 civil government was fully restored in those areas of New York formerly under British occupation. On Staten Island, the county courts reopened, elections were held for local and state offices, and the town supervisors met regularly. Men from Whig families such as the Banckers and Mersereaus replaced the pre-Revolutionary leadership of Christopher Billopp, Benjamin Seaman, and their allies. Moreover, the religious affiliation of the island's post-

Revolutionary leadership shifted from Anglican to Presbyterian and Dutch Reformed. The residents of Staten Island, once maligned for their Loyalism, had made the successful transition to their nation.

Notes

1. Robert C. Ritchie, *The Duke's Province: A Study of New York Politics and Society, 1664–1691* (Chapel Hill, N.C., 1977), 34–35, 172; Michael Kammen, *Colonial New York: A History* (New York, 1975), 82; Charles W. Leng and William T. Davis, *Staten Island and Its People: A History, 1609–1929*, 5 vols. (New York, 1930), 1: 112, 128, 205; Harlow McMillen, "Richmondtown: The First 160 Years, Part I: Richmondtown as the County Seat," *The Staten Island Historian* 1st ser., 22 (1961), 3–5 (herein cited as *SIH*); Richard M. Bayles, *History of Richmond County, Staten Island, New York: From its Discovery to the Present Time* (New York, 1887), 90; Ira K. Morris, *Morris's Memorial History of Staten Island, New York*, 2 vols. (New York, 1898–1900), 1: 113, 118. For the creation of Cassiltowne Manor, see William E. McGinn, "John Palmer, Thomas Dongan, and the Manor of Cassiltowne," *SIH* 1st ser., 29 (1968), 9–12. For the history of Bentley Manor, see William T. Davis, *The Conference or Billopp House* (Staten Island, N.Y., 1926); and Field Horne, *The Conference House Revisited: A History of the Billopp Manor House* (Staten Island, 1990), 1–11.

2. By the late 1680s, Staten Island was divided into three administrative divisions: the north, south, and west divisions. The towns of Northfield, Southfield, Westfield, and Castleton were organized along the geographical boundaries of the three divisions and the Manor of Cassiltowne as well. See Bayles, *History of Richmond County*, 95, 326–327; and Dorothy Valentine Smith, *Staten Island: Gateway to New York* (Philadelphia, 1970), 41–43.

3. For census data, see Evarts B. Greene and Virginia D. Harrington, eds., *American Population before the Federal Census of 1790* (Gloucester, Mass., 1966), 95–102. Edward Countryman, *A People in Revolution: The American Revolution and Political Society in New York, 1760–1790* (Baltimore, 1981), 24, observed that between 1698 and 1771 the yearly growth rate of Staten Island's population was 1.9 percent, while that of the entire colony of New York was 3.2 percent. Field Horne, *A Social-Historical Context of the Voorlezer's House at Richmond Town, Staten Island, New York: A Guide for Interpretation* (Saratoga Springs, N.Y., 1986), 18; this is the only study to attempt to define the ethnicity of Staten Island's population at any given time during the colonial period.

4. See Horne, *Social-Historical Context of the Voorlezer's House*, 18; Graham Russell Hodges, *Root and Branch: African Americans in New York and East New Jersey, 1613–1863* (Chapel Hill, 1999), 104; Greene and Harrington, eds., *American Population*, 93, 100, 102. Ronald D. Jackson, "The Freedom Seekers: Staten Island's Runaway Slaves," *SIH* 2nd ser., 14 (1996), 1–12, 16; Edgar J. McManus, *A History of Negro Slavery in New York* (Syracuse, 1966), 42, 45. For a comprehensive list of Staten Island slave owners and their slaves, see Ronald D. Jackson and Evelyn E. Jackson, eds., *African*

American History in Staten Island: Slave Holding Families and Their Slaves, Raw Notes (Staten Island, 1995).

5. Charles L. Sachs, *Made on Staten Island: Agriculture, Industry, and Suburban Living in the City* (Staten Island, 1988), 20; Bruce E. Burgoyne, ed., *A Hessian Diary of the American Revolution* (Norman, Okla., 1990), 35. A British officer observed that on Staten Island "each house has a good farm and every man a trade." See Lt. Loftus Cliffe to Unknown, July 8, 1776, Transcript, Military Collection, American Revolution, Box 1, Folder 2, Staten Island Historical Society (herein cited as SIHS). For a discussion of Staten Island's colonial mill sites, see Loring McMillen, "Old Mills of Staten Island," *SIH* 1st ser., 10 (1949), 1–4, 9, 15–16; and Sachs, *Made on Staten Island*, 18. The island's colonial ferries are discussed in Kenneth Scott, "The Colonial Ferries of Staten Island," *Proceedings of the Staten Island Institute of Arts and Sciences* 14 (1952), 45–68 (herein cited as *PSIIAS*) and "The Colonial Ferries of Staten Island: Part II," *PSIIAS* 15 (1953), 9–31. Brief descriptions of the island's colonial taverns and inns can be found in Ira K. Morris, "Old Hotels of Staten Island," *Proceedings of the Natural Science Association of Staten Island* 14 (1893), 52–58. See also Harlow McMillen, "Richmondtown Prior to 1837—Innkeepers and Merchants: Part I," *SIH* 1st ser., 24 (1963), 12–15. Staten Island's fishing and oyster trades are treated in Leng and Davis, *Staten Island*, 1: 119, 631, 733. For the island's colonial shipyards, see Sachs, *Made on Staten Island*, 33; and Loring McMillen, "An Island Saga: The Mersereau Family, Part II," *Chronicles of Staten Island* 1 (1989–1990), 156 (herein cited as *COSI*). Staten Island's trade networks are outlined in Robert W. Venables, "A Historical Overview of Staten Island's Trade Patterns," *PSIIAS* 34 (1989), 1–24; and Sherene Baugher, "Trade Networks: Colonial and Federal Period (1680–1815)," *PSIIAS* 34 (1989), 33–37.

6. A history of Staten Island's Anglican parish—Saint Andrew's in Richmondtown—is presented in Charles S. Burch, "History of Saint Andrew's Church, Richmond, Staten Island," *The Grafton Magazine of History and Genealogy* 1 (1908), 1–24; and William T. Davis, Charles W. Leng, and Royden W. Vosburgh, eds., *The Church of St. Andrew, Richmond, Staten Island: Its History, Vital Records, and Gravestone Inscriptions* (Staten Island, 1925). The five Anglicans were: Christopher Billopp, John Le Count, Paul Micheau, Benjamin Seaman, and William T. Walton. Henry Holland, a member of the Dutch Reformed Church, thanked Staten Island's Anglicans for their political support by donating a bell and two silver collection plates to Saint Andrew's Church. See John J. Clute, *Annals of Staten Island: From Its Discovery to the Present Time* (New York, 1877), 141, 264.

7. Quoted in Charles E. Anthon, ed., "Anthon's Notes," *PSIIAS* 5 (1929–1930), 133.

8. Philip Ranlet, *The New York Loyalists* (Knoxville, Tenn., 1986), 71. This number included Staten Island Huguenots, and conservative Presbyterians (or "Old Lights") and Reformed Dutch (or Conferentie), who sought in the Anglican Church a refuge from the revivalism affecting their congregations during the Great Awakening (1739–1745). By the late 1730s, a large majority of Staten Island Huguenots had conformed to Anglicanism; Elders and Members of the French Congregation to the SPG, 1735, Excerpt, Charles W. Leng Collection, Box 2, Folder 60B, Staten Island Institute of Arts and

Sciences. For a discussion of the relationship between the Huguenots and Staten Island's Anglicans, see Jon Butler, *The Huguenots in America: A Refugee People in New World Society* (Cambridge, Mass., 1983), 169, 191–192; and Walter A. Bultemann, "The S.P.G. and the French Huguenots in Colonial America," *Historical Magazine of the Protestant Episcopal Church* 20 (1951), 156, 167–168, 171–172. See also Jean P. Jordan, "The Anglican Establishment in Colonial New York, 1693–1783" (Ph.D. diss., Columbia University, 1971), 207–209, 270.

9. In an effort to strengthen their congregations and to challenge effectively the Anglicans, Staten Island's Presbyterians and Dutch Reformed united in 1769; Loring McMillen, "The First Presbyterian Church of Staten Island, 1717–1776-1808: Part I," *COSI* 1 (1985), 4. During the 1768 elections for the New York Assembly, Rev. Hector Gambold wrote in the Moravian Congregation Diary that Rev. William Jackson of the Dutch Reformed congregation opposed the candidacy of Aaron Cortelyou because he was a Moravian. See Moravian Congregation Diary, May 10, 1768. I thank Elisabeth Sommer, Director of Research and Historical Interpretation at the Staten Island Historical Society, for bringing this document to my attention. Apparently, Presbyterians thought the Moravians "soft" on Anglicanism; Jordan, "Anglican Establishment in Colonial New York," 470–471.

10. For Christopher Billopp's biography, see Lorenzo Sabine, *Biographical Sketches of Loyalists of the American Revolution*, 2 vols. (Boston, 1864), 1: 229–230; Horne, *Conference House Revisited*, 17–18; and Loyalist Claim of Christopher Billopp, Transcript, Staten Island Loyalist Collection, Box 1, Folder 1, Staten Island Historical Society. Also see Charles F. Billopp, *A History of Thomas and Anne Billopp Farmar and Some of Their Descendants in America* (New York, 1907); Marjorie Johnson, *Christopher Billopp Family Genealogy: Captain Billopp (1631–1725) and His Descendants and the Allied Farmar Family* (Staten Island, 1991); and William A. Whitehead, *Contributions to the Early History of Perth Amboy and Adjoining Country* (New York, 1856), 53, 92–120. For Benjamin Seaman, see Charles L. Sachs, "Treasure Chest of Family History," *Seaport* (1992), 48–49; Sabine, *Biographical Sketches*, 2: 271–272; Leng and Davis, *Staten Island*, 2: 949; Morris, *Memorial History*, 1: 351–352; Mary T. Seaman, *The Seaman Family in America as Descended From Captain John Seaman of Hempstead, Long Island* (New York, 1928), 14, 16–17, 56, 78–80, 103; and the Loyalist Claim of Benjamin Seaman, Transcript, Staten Island Loyalist Collection, Box 1, Folder 1, SIHS.

11. Proceedings of the General Assembly of the Colony of New York, Jan.–Apr., 1775, in Peter Force, ed., *American Archives*, 4th Ser., 6 vols. (Washington D.C., 1843–1853), 1: 1286–1287, 1289–1290; hereafter cited as *American Archives*. Harlow McMillen, "Green, and Red, and a Little Blue: The Story of Staten Island in the American Revolution," *SIH* 1st ser., 32 (1975), 4.

12. See Anthon, ed., "Anthon's Notes," 154–155. For a discussion of smuggling in the New York City area, see Cathy Matson, *Merchants and Empire: Trading in Colonial New York* (Baltimore, 1998), 203–214.

13. Arthur M. Schlesinger, *The Colonial Merchants and the American Revolution* (New York, 1918), 490.

14. Elizabethtown, New Jersey, Committee of Observation's Interdiction of Staten Island, Feb. 13, 1775; Woodbridge, New Jersey, Committee of Observation's Interdiction of Staten Island, Feb. 20, 1775, *American Archives*, 1: 1234–1235, 1249. *New-York Gazette and Weekly Mercury*, July 20, 1775.

15. Committee of 60 Nominations for the Provincial Convention, Mar. 6, 1775, *American Archives*, 2: 138–139; Loyalist Claim of Christopher Billopp, Transcript, Staten Island Loyalist Collection, Box 1, Folder 1, SIHS; McMillen, "Green, and Red, and a Little Blue," 18.

16. Bernard Mason, *The Road to Independence: The Revolutionary Movement in New York, 1773–1777* (Lexington, Ky., 1966), 44, 178–179; Alexander C. Flick, *The American Revolution in New York: Its Political, Social, and Economic Significance* (New York, 1926), 49; Thomas Jones, *History of New York during the Revolutionary War and of the Leading Events in the Other Colonies at that Period*, 2 vols., ed. Edward F. De Lancey (New York, 1879), 1: 29–40.

17. The first quote is from Capt. Alexander McDonald to Walter and Thomas Buchannon, Nov. 4, 1775, *Letter-Book of Captain Alexander McDonald of the Royal Highland Emigrants, 1775–1779*, New York Historical Society *Collections* (1882), 217 (herein cited as *Letter-Book*); the second is from Ranlet, *New York Loyalists*, 71. Members of the N.Y. Assembly to Gen. Thomas Gage, May 5, 1775, *American Archives*, 2: 513.

18. See the General Association of New York, Apr. 29, 1775, in *Calendar of Historical Manuscripts Relating to the War of the Revolution in the Office of the Secretary State*, 2 vols. (Albany, 1868), 1: 3–4; and *American Archives*, 2: 471. See also Carl L. Becker, *The History of Political Parties in the Province of New York, 1760–1776* (Madison, Wis., 1909), 212–213, 215; Flick, *American Revolution in New York*, 317–318; Mason, *Road to Independence*, 63. Rev. Hector Gambold to Nathaniel Seidel, May 10, 1775; I want to thank Elisabeth Sommer, Director of Research and Historical Interpretation at the Staten Island Historical Society, for bringing this letter to my attention. See also Alexander C. Flick, *Loyalism in New York during the American Revolution* (New York, 1901), 59.

19. McMillen, "Green, and Red, and a Little Blue," 18; Clute, *Annals of Staten Island*, 140–141, 148, 170, 303–304, 357–358, 363, 396; *Calendar of Historical Manuscripts*, 1: 42. Proceedings of New York Provincial Congress (hereafter NYPC), June 2, 1775, *American Archives*, 2: 1271.

20. David Burger to the NYPC, Sept. 1, 1775, *American Archives*, 3: 624–625.

21. John Wetherhead to the N.Y. Committee of Safety, Sept. 17, 1775, *American Archives*, 3: 724–725.

22. Joseph S. Tiedemann, *Reluctant Revolutionaries: New York City and the Road to Independence, 1763–1776* (Ithaca, N.Y., 1997), 235.

23. NYPC to the Richmond County Committee of Safety, Dec. 2, 1775, *American Archives*, 3: 1762–1764; Flick, *Loyalism in New York*, 92, writes that the Richmond County Committee of Safety was "wholly inactive." The members of the Richmond

County Committee of Safety were: Christian Jacobson, chairman; George Barnes; Joseph Christopher; David Corsen; Moses Dupuy; Cornelius Dissossway; John Kettletas; David La Tourette; Lambert Merrill; Peter Mersereau; John Poillon; and John Tysen. Richmond County Committee of Safety to Nathaniel Woodhull, President of the NYPC, Dec. 15, 1775, *American Archives*, 4: 428.

24. Proceedings of the N.Y. Committee of Safety, Dec. 21, 1775, *American Archives*, 4: 435–436. McMillen, "Green, and Red, and a Little Blue," 23; and Flick, *Loyalism in New York*, 92.

25. Maj. Gen. Charles Lee to Washington, Feb. 5, 1776, *The Lee Papers*, New York Historical Society *Collections*, 3 vols. (1871–1874), 1: 272. For the life and military career of Maj. Gen. Charles Lee, see John R. Alden, *General Charles Lee: Traitor or Patriot?* (Baton Rouge, La., 1951); and John Shy, "Charles Lee: The Soldier as Radical," in George A. Billias, ed., *George Washington's Generals* (Westport, Conn., 1967), 22–53.

26. N.Y. Committee of Safety Proceedings, Feb. 10, 1776; N.Y. Committee of Safety to the N.J. Provincial Congress, Feb. 10, 1776; N.Y. Committee of Safety to the Elizabethtown Committee of Observation, Feb. 11, 1776, *American Archives*, 4: 1120–1121, 1123.

27. *New-York Gazette*, Feb. 19, 1776; and Rev. Edwin F. Hatfield, History of Elizabeth, New Jersey: Including the Early History of Union County (New York, 1868), 427.

28. Col. Nathaniel Heard to NYPC, Feb. 16, 1776; Richmond County Committee of Safety to NYPC, Mar. 7, 1776, *American Archives*, 4: 1163, 5: 102–103. Isaac Decker was a ferry operator and innkeeper. He was accused of supplying the British ships in New York harbor, opposing the election of delegates to the Provincial Congress, assisting the New Jersey Loyalist Cortlandt Skinner to escape arrest, and publicly speaking against the proceedings of the Continental and Provincial Congresses. Abraham Harris was charged with publicly condemning the Patriot cause and actively recruiting men for the British army. The charges of Loyalism against the farmer-mason Minah Burger and the former Provincial congressman Richard Conner were vague at best.

29. McDonald to Susannah McDonald, Feb. 22, 1776, *Letter-Book*, 250. NYPC to Adrian Bancker and Richard Lawrence, Feb. 19, 1776; NYPC to the Elizabethtown Committee of Observation, Feb. 21, 1776, *American Archives*, 5: 283–284, 293.

30. Hendrick Garrison to NYPC, Mar. 8, 1776, *American Archives*, 5: 136–137.

31. Quoted in Flick, *Loyalism in New York*, 93.

32. For Brig. Gen. William Alexander, see Paul David Nelson, *William Alexander, Lord Stirling* (Tuscaloosa, Ala., 1987); and Alan Valentine, *Lord Stirling* (New York, 1969).

33. Washington to Brig. Gen. William Alexander (Lord Stirling), Mar. 9, 1776, in W. W. Abbot, Philander D. Chase, and Dorothy Twohig, eds., *The Papers of George Washington*, Revolutionary War Series, 12 vols. (Charlottesville, Va., 1985–2002), 3: 497–498 (herein cited as *GWPRWS*).

34. Alexander (Stirling) to Capt. John Warner, Mar. 14, 1776; Proceedings of the NYPC, Mar. 14, 1776, *American Archives*, 5: 222, 383.

35. Nelson, *William Alexander*, 77; Valentine, *Lord Stirling*, 173; Mark V. Kwasny, *Washington's Partisan War: 1775–1783* (Kent, Ohio, 1996), 43. Alexander (Stirling) to Brig. Gen. William Livingston, Mar. 24, 1776, in Carl E. Prince and Dennis P. Ryan, eds., *The Papers of William Livingston*, 4 vols. (Trenton, N.J., 1979–1987), 1: 44–45 (herein cited as *PWL*).

36. Alexander (Stirling) to Washington, Apr. 1, 1776, *GWPRWS*, 4: 13–14. Brig. Gen. William Heath to Livingston, Apr. 1, 1776, *PWL*, 1: 46.

37. Bruce Bliven Jr., *Under the Guns: New York, 1775–1776* (New York, 1972), 211–212. Journal of Sergeant Henry Bedinger, Apr. 4, 5, 8, 9, 1776, in Danske Dandridge, ed., *Historic Shepherdstown* (Charlottesville, Va., 1910), 134–135, 139.

38. Proceedings of the N.Y. Committee of Safety, Apr. 9, 1776, *American Archives*, 5: 1455. Journal of Sergeant Henry Bedinger, Apr. 8, 1776, in Dandridge, ed., *Historic Shepherdstown*, 139. McDonald to Pedro de Mendonzo, Jan. 11, 1777, *Letter-Book*, 313.

39. Christian Jacobson to the N.Y. Committee of Safety, Apr. 16, 1776; Proceedings of the N.Y. Committee of Safety, May 2, 1776, *American Archives*, 5: 955–956, 1485. Lt. Loftus Cliffe to Unknown, July 8, 1776, Transcript, Military Collection, American Revolution, Box 1, Folder 2, SIHS.

40. The quote is from Barnet Schecter, *The Battle for New York: The City at the Heart of the American Revolution* (New York, 2001), 95. See Brig. Gens. John Sullivan, Nathanael Greene, and Alexander (Stirling) to Washington, *GWPRWS*, 4: 144–145.

41. Council of War, June 28, 1776; Gen. George Washington to John Hancock, July 3, 1776, *GWPRWS*, 5: 130–131, 193. Proceedings of the NYPC, June 29, 1776, *American Archives*, 6: 1439. Gov. Jonathan Trumbull to Jeremiah Wadsworth, July 4, 1776, William B. Clark and William J. Morgan, eds., *Naval Documents of the American Revolution*, 10 vols. (Washington, D.C., 1964–1996), 5: 918 (herein cited as *NDAR*).

42. Gen. Sir William Howe to Lord George Germain, July 7, 1776, in K.G. Davies, ed., *Documents of the American Revolution, 1770–1783*, 21 vols. (Dublin, Ireland: 1972–1981), 12: 157. Milton M. Klein and Ronald W. Howard, eds., *The Twilight of British Rule in Revolutionary America: The New York Letter Book of General James Robertson, 1780–1783* (Cooperstown, N.Y., 1983), 18, 33; Ranlet, *New York Loyalists*, 72; Maj. Charles Stuart to John Stuart, the Earl of Bute, July 8, 1776, *NDAR*, 5: 989.

43. Maj. Francis Hutcheson to Gen. Sir Frederick Haldimand, July 10, 1776, *NDAR*, 5: 1011.

44. Harlow McMillen, "The Oath of Allegiance Signed by the Inhabitants of Staten Island, on July 9, 1776," *SIH* 1st ser., 32 (1976), 51. Hutcheson to Haldimand, July 10, 1776, *NDAR*, 5: 1011. See also Flick, *Loyalism in New York*, 95.

45. McMillen, "Oath of Allegiance," 52; Gov. William Tryon to Germain, July 8, 1776, in E. B. O'Callaghan and Berthold Fernow, eds., *Documents Relative to the*

Colonial History of the State of New York, 15 vols. (Albany, 1856–1887), 8: 681 (hereafter *NYCD*).

46. John Bakeless, *Turncoats, Traitors, and Heroes: Espionage in the American Revolution* (New York, 1959), 123, 166, 177–181, 194–195, 277, 345, 364. Hutcheson to Haldimand, July 10, 1776, *NDAR*, 5: 1011. The quotes are from Anthon, ed., "Anthon's Notes," 147, 133–135.

47. Edward H. Tatum Jr., ed., *The American Journal of Ambrose Serle: Secretary to Lord Howe, 1776–1778* (San Marino, Calif., 1940), 28–30; Ira D. Gruber, *The Howe Brothers and the American Revolution* (Chapel Hill, N.C., 1972), 101–102; Harlow McMillen, *A History of Staten Island, New York, during the American Revolution* (Staten Island, 1976), 12; Piers Mackesy, *The War for America, 1775–1783* (Cambridge, Mass., 1964), 86–87. Hodges, *Root and Branch*, 148. Also see Todd W. Braisted, "The Black Pioneers and Others: The Military Role of Black Loyalists in the American War for Independence" in John W. Pulis, ed., *Moving On: Black Loyalists in the Afro-Atlantic World* (New York, 1999), 3–37; and Judith L. Van Buskirk, *Generous Enemies: Patriots and Loyalists in Revolutionary New York* (Philadelphia, 2002), chap. 5.

48. Ira D. Gruber, "Lord Howe and Lord George Germain: British Politics and the Winning of American Independence," *William and Mary Quarterly*, 3rd ser., 22 (1965), 233; Weldon A. Brown, *Empire or Independence: A Study in the Failure of Reconciliation, 1774–1783* (Baton Rouge, La., 1941), 113; Gruber, *Howe Brothers*, 98–99; Memorandum of an Interview with Lt. Col. James Patterson, July 20, 1776, *GWPRWS*, 5: 398–403; John J. Gallagher, *The Battle of Brooklyn, 1776* (New York, 1995), 81–82; and McMillen, *History of Staten Island . . . during the . . . Revolution*, 16.

49. Memorial of Thomas Macdonogh on Behalf of Rachel Dawson, Transcript, Staten Island Loyalist Collection, Box 1, Folder 4, SIHS; Excerpt from the Loyalist Claim of Job Smith (1786) in Peter W. Coldham, ed., *American Migrations, 1765–1799: The Lives, Times, and Families of Colonial Americans who Remained Loyal to the British Crown before, during, and after the Revolutionary War, As Related in their Own Words and through their Correspondence* (Baltimore, 2000), 342; Anthon, ed., "Anthon's Notes," 82–83.

50. McMillen, *History of Staten Island . . . during the . . . Revolution*, 31, 33–35, 40–41; Walter T. Dornfest, "Sullivan's Raid on Staten Island: Aug. 22, 1777," *SIH* 1st ser., 31 (1972), 97–102; Kwasny, *Washington's Partisan War*, 81–82, 160–161, 257–258.

51. Lincoln MacVeagh, ed., *The Journal of Nicholas Cresswell, 1774–1777* (New York, 1924), 217.

52. Anthon, ed., "Anthon's Notes," 139–140, 158; the quote is from p. 160. For the destruction of Staten Island's forests during the Revolution, see Kenneth Scott, "Cutting of Staten Island Forests during the Revolution," *PSIIAS* 17 (1955), 8–13.

53. Carol Berkin, *First Generations: Women in Colonial America* (New York, 1996), 184; Mary Beth Norton, *Liberty's Daughters: The Revolutionary Experience of American Women, 1750–1800* (New York, 1980), 202.

54. Lt. Col. Francis Lord Rawdon to the Earl of Huntington, Aug. 5, 1776, in Henry Steele Commager and Richard B. Morris, eds., *The Spirit of Seventy-Six: The Story of the American Revolution as told by Participants* (New York, 1995), 424.

55. Anthon, ed., "Anthon's Notes," 87.

56. McMillen, *History of Staten Island . . . during the . . . Revolution*, 30; Leng and Davis, *Staten Island*, 1: 180–181. One Staten Islander recalled that his father provided more than two hundred cords of wood to the British forces but did not receive payment for it. See Anthon, ed., "Anthon's Notes," 158.

57. Klein and Howard, eds., *Twilight of British Rule*, 7–9.

58. Ibid., 188–189. See also McMillen, *History of Staten Island . . . during the . . . Revolution*, 29.

59. Two Staten Island Loyalists—Richard Conner and Richard Lawrence—were sued under the Trespass Act of 1783 for their alleged participation in the confiscation and destruction of Whig property during the British occupation. Ranlet, *New York Loyalists*, 161, 173; Alexander C. Flick, *Loyalism in New York*, 146–147; Edwin G. Burrows and Mike Wallace, *Gotham: A History of New York City to 1898* (New York, 1999), 258; Horne, *Conference House Revisited*, 26–27; Harry B. Yoshpe, *The Disposition of Loyalist Estates in the Southern District of the State of New York* (New York, 1939), 48–50; Scott, "Cutting of Staten Island Forests," 11–12; and Leng and Davis, *Staten Island*, 1: 206. The Loyalist Claims (Transcripts) of Christopher Billopp and Benjamin Seaman in Box 1, Folder 1, Staten Island Loyalist Collection, SIHS.

60. Greene and Harrington, eds., *American Population*, 105.

Part II

The Revolution
in the Hudson Valley

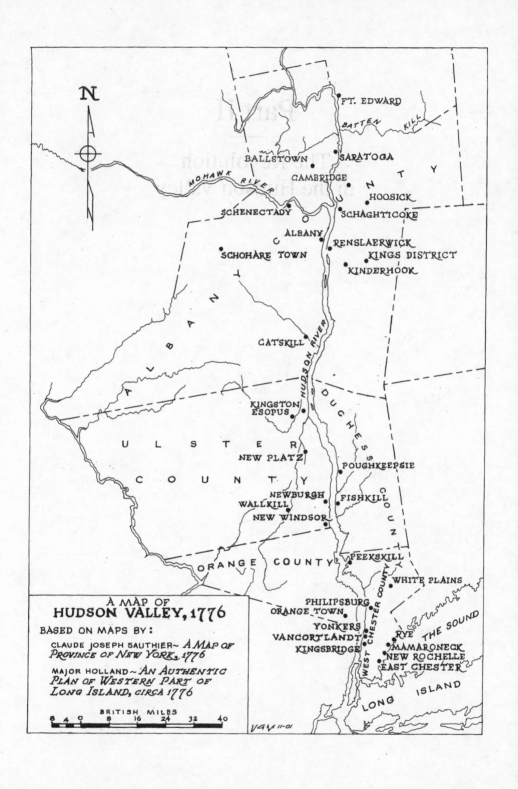

N

FT. EDWARD

BATTEN KILL

BALLSTOWN   SARATOGA

MOHAWK RIVER   CAMBRIDGE

HOOSICK

SCHENECTADY   SCHAGHTICOKE

ALBANY   RENSLAERWICK

C   KINGS DISTRICT

SCHOHARE TOWN   KINDERHOOK

A   HUDSON RIVER

L   CATSKILL

B   DUCHESS

A

N   KINGSTON
          ESOPUS

Y   ULSTER   COUNTY

NEW PLATZ   POUGHKEEPSIE

C O U N T Y

NEWBURGH   FISHKILL
WALLKILL
          NEW WINDSOR

PEEKSKILL

ORANGE COUNTY   WHITE PLAINS

PHILIPSBURG
ORANGE TOWN
          YONKERS   RYE   THE SOUND
          VANCORTLANDT
          KINGSBRIDGE   MAMARONECK
                    NEW ROCHELLE
                    EAST CHESTER

WEST CHESTER COUNTY

LONG ISLAND

A MAP OF
HUDSON VALLEY, 1776

BASED ON MAPS BY:

CLAUDE JOSEPH SAUTHIER~ A MAP OF
PROVINCE OF NEW YORK, 1776

MAJOR HOLLAND~ AN AUTHENTIC
PLAN OF WESTERN PART OF
LONG ISLAND, CIRCA 1776

BRITISH MILES
8 4 0   8   16   24   32   40

VGV 11-01

5

Westchester County

Jacob Judd

A publication prepared as part of New York's celebration of the one hundred and fiftieth anniversary of the American Revolution sought to summarize the results of that conflict. "When all the factors are taken into account the American Revolution was on the whole not an extremely radical movement. Except for the sundering of political ties with the British Empire, old usages were not torn up by the roots."[1] The veracity of this statement may be challenged by examining how the Revolution changed Westchester County. A civil war raged there from 1776 until 1783, a major transferal of property rights from the aristocracy to the average farmer took place following the conflict, and thousands of Loyalists were compelled to leave their homes.

During the war, much of Westchester was part of the so-called "Neutral Ground," an area located between the two armies, which neither side was able to control. Patriot and Loyalist clashes, along with major military engagements, occurred in the county from 1776 until the conclusion of hostilities in 1783. Here George Washington played a major role in the fighting during 1776 to 1777 and, in the later years of the conflict, Comte de Rochambeau and a French force were significant. The Revolutionary drama also included the capture of Maj. John André and the uncovering of Benedict Arnold's treacherous machinations.

The War for Independence brought profound political and economic changes to the county. The State of New York confiscated great manorial estates as well as smaller farms owned or controlled by Loyalists. Many properties were subsequently redistributed in smaller holdings to former Patriot tenants and to other approved purchasers. The Revolution also hastened the transferal of a substantial portion of the governmental powers formerly held by the landlords into the hands of local governmental units.

Colonial Westchester was larger than it is today, for it included what is now the Borough of the Bronx in New York City. It stretched from Dutchess County (whose southernmost portion is now Putnam County) in the north to the Bronx Kill in the south. To the east was Connecticut; to the west, the Hudson River; and to the southeast, the Long Island Sound.[2] Not only did Westchester border the Hudson River and Long Island Sound, it also contained a number of important rivers, such as the Croton, Pocantico, Saw Mill, Bronx, Hutchinson, Harlem, and East Rivers. These waterways provided easy access into the interior: waterpower to service saw, grist, and flour mills; and travel routes during those times when roads were impassable. The Hudson River opened the opportunity for trading with settlements on its west bank, with northern sections of New York as far as Albany, and with New Jersey. The Long Island Sound provided a pathway for trade with Connecticut and Long Island.

The wheat, rye, barley, Indian corn, and flax grown in the county soon found their way to New York City and beyond to the English sphere of trade. Westchester's agricultural and animal productions helped supply a major portion of the food needed by New York City's population. Forest products and trapped furs found ready markets. In addition to animal husbandry and agriculture, associated industries developed with grist, saw, and fulling mills; the development of water transport in the form of sails, skiffs, and local ferries; and the raising and driving of cattle. In sum, its geographical advantages, its proximity to New York City, its extensive frontage on the Hudson River and the Long Island Sound, and its rich agricultural base, all combined to make Westchester one of the most prized regions during the long period of warfare from 1776 until 1783.

Westchester was one of the few colonial counties where "manorial lords" held extensive land holdings. During the last half of the seventeenth century, prominent members of the Philipse, Pell, Van Cortlandt, DeLancey, and Morris families had acquired royal land grants, each for as much as 75,000 to 90,000 acres in Westchester and adjacent counties. By the Revolution a mixture of tenant farmers, freeholders (small-scale landowners), indentured servants, and slaves worked these lands. The population came from Dutch, English, Germanic, Huguenot, Jewish, Native American, Scandinavian, and African backgrounds. They worshiped in the Dutch Reformed, Huguenot, Anglican, Quaker, Presbyterian, and Congregational churches. While some groups, like the Huguenots and the Dutch, created distinctive communities, others melded into diverse entities.[3] Their eventual allegiances during the Revolution appear not to have been determined by religious or ethnic affiliations.

It is difficult to determine the exact population of the county in the 1760s, but sheriffs' returns for 1756 placed the European-American population at 11,919 with Native Americans and African-American slaves at 1,338. A later census of 1771 reported 18,315 European Americans and 3,430 slaves. The numbers of slaves owned by an individual master varied, but slave-owning families typically owned one or two slaves. Surprisingly, the little Huguenot community of New Rochelle, with a European-American population of some 290 in 1771, contained 156 slaves.[4] Westchester County slaves served in varied capacities: general field hands, house servants, mill-hands, and seafarers who operated or manned riverboats.

The region that became Westchester had been home to numerous Algonkian Indian groups. However, by the start of the eighteenth century most of these people had "vanished from Westchester as noiselessly as the morning mists disappear before the advancing day."[5] By the 1760s only scattered remnants remained in the area. Consequently, Westchester Indians played no role in the Revolution.

The county contained several settled localities: the Borough of West Chester (in the present Borough of the Bronx); and the towns and villages of East Chester, White Plains, Mamaroneck, Yonkers, New Rochelle, Rye, Bedford (near the border with Connecticut), and North Castle (about five miles southwest of Bedford). These communities lay outside the jurisdictions of the manors of Morrisania, Pelham, Fordham, Philipsburgh, and Van Cortlandt.[6] Other small settlements developed along the Long Island Sound and on the east bank of the Hudson River. They served as trading centers by providing farmers with everyday necessities and by acting as transportation transfer points for agricultural products.

Throughout the county were large and small farmsteads, located on manor lands, or held under individual ownership. The fortunate few who were able to buy property often had to borrow sums from the manor lords, who acted as the local bankers. Manorial landlords frequently rented out a farmstead of from fifty to three hundred acres for a period of one to three lives at a stipulated annual rent. Nonetheless, at the owner's discretion such tenants could be forced to vacate their farms.[7] The relationship between landlord and tenant occasionally led to disputes and outright conflict. Such controversies occurred on the Livingston estates in present Columbia County in the 1750s, and in the 1760s they spread to Philipse's Highland Patent and to the Roger Morris and Beverly Robinson estates in Dutchess County. Landlords had to contend with leaseholders who paid an annual rental; with squatters; and with those who paid a rental fee for land, even though they had not entered into a formal arrangement. Furthermore, at the northeastern corner of the county there were lands that were in dispute between New England real estate speculators and some large Westchester landowners.

When a Van Cortlandt attempted to eject a tenant from a farm in that corner of the county, a court suit followed in 1763 and a direct tenant-landlord clash in 1766.[8] Pierre Van Cortlandt, then living at the family manor house in Croton, complained that, "the Last Mob or Ryot here in the manor" began when a Van Cortlandt cousin sought to eject one tenant in order to replace him with another family. Pierre believed that these tenants "only want oppertunity Either to be screan'd from paying any Rents at all (or Such as they say shall be Reasonable) or from paying their Just Debts." In short, "rather than a contest between 'lords' and 'peasants,' the New York disturbances grew out of a competition between landholders and would-be landholders for material advantage."[9] During the Revolution, Van Cortlandt Manor lands straddled two areas, one controlled by Patriot forces and the other in the "Neutral Ground." As a result, even though the Van Cortlandt family became Whigs, the populace divided in their political allegiances during the years of conflict.

In general, Westchester farmers found the years from 1754 to 1763 to be profitable, for the Seven Years' War had increased demand for agricultural products. But the conflict was followed by an agricultural recession, whose repercussions were felt throughout the county. In 1764 the Rev. John Milner of West Chester noted that his parish was suffering economically from the "circumstances w[hic]h the late War & the present discouragements upon our trade" have produced.[10] His remarks referred to the decline in agricultural prices after 1763, for the Sugar Act (April 1764) had not yet taken effect. Indeed, the typical Westchester farmer did not protest against that act, for it had little economic impact on his life. However, there may have been dismay among those who had an active business in forest and lumber products that were traded with the West Indies.

The Stamp Act (1765) was a different matter. Almost all Americans would have to use stamps at some point in their normal activities. Explosive reactions spread throughout British North America. New York City was in the vanguard of the political and mercantile reactions. Many Westchester farmers, still suffering from the postwar recession, were soon convinced that their economic problems were attributable to the Sugar and Stamp Acts. As the months passed, more and more Westchester farmers were also pinched by the trade embargoes that many colonial cities had adopted in response to the Stamp Act. Such actions certainly did not relieve the economic plight of the local farmers. However, their reaction was not as demonstrative as in New York City or Albany.

The role tenant farmers played in politics was limited by suffrage requirements and local custom. Freemen and leaseholders could vote for such local officials as the constable, fence viewer, and assessor. In most instances, only freeholders could cast ballots in Assembly elections. This matter came to a head in the hotly contested election of 1768 in the Borough of West Chester.[11] The Stamp Act had been repealed in 1766, only to be replaced by the Townshend Acts in 1767. New Yorkers were sharply debating how to respond to Parliament's latest efforts at taxation and more stringent controls over the colonial economy, for the imperial crises of the 1760s had already begun to increase political factionalism within and without the legislature. As a consequence, in the 1768 Assembly elections, the DeLancey and Livingston factions contended vigorously for seats and power. In Westchester John DeLancey defeated Lewis Morris (a Livingstonite, a politician who belonged to the Livingston faction) for an

Assembly seat by only three votes. Following a bitter dispute as to whether freemen had the right to vote in Westchester, it was determined that they did not, and DeLancey was thus declared the victor. The election underscored just how deeply the Westchester electorate was divided in 1768.

Van Cortlandt Manor's head, Pierre Van Cortlandt, was a Livingstonite, who sought the manor's Assembly seat, which Pierre's cousin Philip Verplanck had held since 1733. The seventy-year-old Philip wanted his son, James, to succeed him, but Pierre was determined to acquire the seat for himself. In the ensuing 1768 election, Pierre won overwhelmingly. From that year until he stepped down as lieutenant governor in 1795, Pierre Van Cortlandt was a leading spokesperson for Westchester in New York politics.[12]

In addition to their role in Westchester, the leading landlords were often involved in New York City politics, and it was in that way that they became interested in provincial issues. Throughout the 1700s, the Philipse, Van Cortlandt, Morris, and DeLancey families had relatives serving in the New York Assembly and on the Governor's Council. They were most deeply involved in provincial politics and thus already aware in the early 1760s of the changing political climate. However, as political debate over Britain's imperial policies heated up, more people became involved, and the major county families began to split over resistance and independence. Thus, the two leading landholding families, the Van Cortlandts and the Philipses, ultimately became foes. In the mid-1760s, however, it would have been difficult to foresee such a development. Moreover, it is unclear exactly when the breach occurred among Westchester's aristocratic families. Legislators from the DeLancey, Philipse, Morris, and Van Cortlandt families sometimes divided on major issues early in the decade. However, because the leading families so often intermarried, it is difficult to link specific families with particular factions. For example, Pierre Van Cortlandt was related not only to the Livingston and Morris families, but also to the DeLancey and Philipse families. When Pierre entered the Assembly in 1768, he was considered to be a member of the Livingston faction, but he sometimes supported the DeLanceys on procedural matters. Nonetheless, from the mid-1760s as political opinion sharpened, Morris and Van Cortlandt Assemblymen usually opposed the positions advocated by the DeLancey-Philipse faction.

The people of the county and province divided over religious as well as political issues. Yonkers, Rye, and the Borough of West Chester were centers of Anglicanism. The Huguenots of New Rochelle, although they preferred Huguenot ministers ordained by the French Reformed Church, accepted Anglican ones when a Huguenot was not available. Tarrytown clung to the Dutch Reformed Church. Added to this religious mélange were itinerant ministers who carried their own brand of religion throughout the countryside. In such an environment a minister struggled to earn a living. The only ministers to obtain outside financial assistance were Anglican missionaries for the Society for the

Propagation of the Gospel in Foreign Parts (S.P.G.). But payments were slow in reaching the county, and Anglican ministers were frequently forced to appeal for payment of the funds they claimed were due them for their priestly activities.[13] Of all the denominational clergy, only the Anglican ministers consistently supported the King and Parliament and sought to keep their parishioners faithful to the Crown. They did so out of conviction, and also because a substantial portion of their income came from England. The Rev. Ephraim Avery of Rye reported that he "took a great deal of Satisfaction" in keeping his congregation from rising up against the Stamp Act.[14] Apparently, there had been some local agitation following the passage of that act.

The Townshend Acts caused little agitation in the county, but the situation changed dramatically following passage of the Tea Act (1773) and the Coercive Acts (1774). One prominent Anglican in Westchester who consistently supported royal control was the Rev. Samuel Seabury (1729–1796). A graduate of Yale College, he studied medicine at the University of Edinburgh, and was ordained by the Bishop of London in 1753. He was assigned as an S.P.G. missionary to the Westchester parish at New Rochelle in 1767. Previously, Seabury had become embroiled in a controversy over whether an Anglican bishopric should be established in the colonies. He wrote a series of essays in response to those who opposed the idea and sought not only to support Anglicanism's privileged position, but to bolster royal and parliamentary authority over the American colonies. He supported the Stamp Act and opposed any demonstrative action that aimed to thwart that measure. As early as 1770, amid the controversies over the Townshend Acts and New York City's Liberty Pole riot, Seabury informed the S.P.G. that, "the violent Party Heats which prevail in this Colony as well as in the Others, engross at present the attention of the People. But I think that even these Disturbances, will be attended with some Advantage to the Interest of the Church. The Usefulness & Truth of her Doctrines with Regard to civil Government, appear more evident from these Disorders, which other Principles have led the People into. This is particularly remarked & publickly mention'd with the late clamours for Liberty &c."[15]

When a call was issued in the summer of 1774 for a Continental Congress to develop a joint response to Parliament's latest actions, members of New York's Assembly had to decide whether to support creation of such a body and whether to choose representatives to it. It was in that context that Gov. William Tryon visited Pierre Van Cortlandt at Van Cortlandt Manor. Pierre's son, Philip, who would serve as a military officer during the Revolution and in the national government afterwards, recalled that "my Father was a member of the Legislature and one of the number opposed to the odious Incroachments of the Crown and when every art and address was made use of to seduce members to join their party." As Tryon and his father strolled in the garden, "the Governor commenced with observing what great favours could be obtained if my father would relinquish his opposition to the views of the King and Parliament of Great Brittain what grants of Land could and would be the consequence in addition to other favours of Emmense consequence." Pierre did not have to mull over this political bribery and, according to his son, bragged "that he was chosen a representative by unanimous approbation of a people who placed a confidence in his integrity to use all his ability for their benefit and the good of his country as a true patriot which line of conduct he was determined to pursue."[16]

Patriot fervor heightened in Westchester, when the New York City Committee of Correspondence urged the county to choose delegates to the First Continental Congress to be held in Philadelphia. Taking the lead, a group calling itself the "Freeholders and Inhabitants of Rye" urged the other towns to send representatives to White Plains on August 22, 1774, to select such delegates. The Borough of West Chester, where the Morris family held sway, not only sent representatives to White Plains, but adopted a series of resolutions, which included the assertion, "that all Acts of the British Parliament, imposing taxes on the Colonies, without their Consent, or by their Representative, are arbitrary and oppressive, and should meet the detestation of all good men."[17]

The August 22 meeting over which Frederick Philipse presided, chose to be represented by the delegates New York City had already elected: John Alsop, James Duane, John Jay, Philip Livingston, and Isaac Low. On September 24, "83 Inhabitants and Freeholders" of Rye declared that they were "much concerned with the unhappy Situation of public Affairs, think it our duty to our King and Country, to Declare that we have not been concerned in any Resolutions into or Measures taken with regard to the Disputes at present subsisting with the Mother Country." They went on to assert their continued loyalty and their desire "to live and die peaceable Subjects to our Gracious Sovereign, King George the Third, and his Laws."[18] Shortly thereafter, fourteen Rye residents objected to the above statement. It was clear that people there differed sharply over the need for a Continental Congress.

The actions of the Continental Congress, especially the Continental Association, inspired Reverend Seabury to begin writing his "Westchester Farmer" articles, which questioned the idea of independence. Seabury concentrated on the dire effects nonimportation would have on Great Britain and on agricultural pursuits in Westchester. He predicted that "clamours, discord, confusion, mobs, riots, insurrections, rebellions" would occur in Britain, Ireland, and the West Indies. Such upheavals would result from their not obtaining the flaxseed from New York. He reminded the farmers that "the sale of your seed not only pays your taxes, but furnishes you with many of the little conveniences, and comforts of life; the loss of it for one year would be of more damage to you, than paying the three-penny duty on tea for twenty."[19] In stressing how actions taken in Philadelphia would directly hurt them, Seabury sought to explain the emerging issues in ways they could readily understand.

The election of delegates to the Second Continental Congress also caused discord in Westchester. By March 1775 it was apparent from the arguments over Seabury's essays and from developments taking place in some townships that a sharp dichotomy of opinion had developed in the county. When Westchester was asked to choose representatives to the Second Continental Congress, twelve men from East Chester, West Chester, New Rochelle, and Mamaroneck determined that April 11 would be the day for "Taking the sense of the Freeholders. . . ." Those responding to this call came chiefly from the southern and eastern portions of the county. On the appointed day, about five hundred men appeared at White Plains, both supporting and opposing the Second Continental Congress. The two factions met first at different taverns in town. In the subsequent general meeting, the Loyalists took no part in the discussions or in the voting. After Lewis Morris had been chosen as Westchester's representative, Isaac Wilkins, speaking for the opposition, declared his "abhorrence of all unlawful congresses and committees" and his desire for a continued allegiance to King and Parliament. The Wilkins group then returned to their initial meeting place, where a statement was drawn up and signed by over three hundred participants, including Frederick Philipse. Lewis Morris rejected the protest by stating that "in this formidable catalogue of 312 sober and loyal" signers, there were 170 who were not voters and others who were too young to vote.[20]

A number of messages soon appeared in *Rivington's Gazette* urging "the Inhabitants of Cortlandt's Manor" not to participate in any activities leading to another Continental Congress. One such "Address" stated that, "We never consented to congresses nor committees, we detest the destruction of private property, we abhor the proceedings of riotous and disorderly people, and finally, we wish to live and die the same loyal subjects we have ever been, to his most sacred Majesty GEORGE the THIRD." A subsequent message sought to "Form An Association in Cortlandt's Manor" of loyal subjects. It declared, "If we have a right to complain of the British acts of parliament, we have a Governor, Council and Assembly, to represent our grievances to the King, Lords and Commons; we are assured that we shall be heard: We have no business with *Congresses* and *Committees*. Such methods only serve to irritate our best friends."[21]

Such statements were met by the following Patriot response: "Let me conjure you, to rise from your lethargy, assume the dignity of freemen; smite the serpents that have spread their poisons round you; burn your associations; and with dauntless intrepity, join the sons of freedom, who are the only temporal guardians of the human race."[22] Henceforth, the allegiance of the inhabitants of Van Cortlandt Manor was divided in the conflict. One may conjecture why some individuals became Loyalists and others, Patriots. The safest, most logical choice called for allegiance to King George. Apparently only the foolhardy supported the Whig cause. What psychological, emotional, and perhaps economic motivations drove individuals to make fateful, individual decisions may never be satisfactorily resolved.

Meanwhile, developments taking place in Philadelphia and New York City had a direct bearing upon local activities. In May Lewis Morris of Westchester joined the other New York delegates—George Clinton, Francis Lewis, Robert R. Livingston, and Philip Schuyler—in the Second Continental Congress. This newly appointed New York delegation signified a dramatic shift in political sentiment toward independence. The Continental Congress consequently lost no time in arranging for enlistments in local militia units, in forming a continental army, in choosing George Washington as commander of those forces, in organizing a postal service, in boldly planning for an invasion of Canada, and in issuing paper currency. The earmarks of independence were thus present.

In New York the colonial government began to fall apart, and a new revolutionary regime started to emerge. The regular Assembly, which had been growing increasingly more pro-British, ceased meeting in January 1775. Meanwhile, ad hoc committees of revolutionaries soon transformed themselves into a series of four Provincial Congresses that began meeting in April 1775. Pierre Van Cortlandt sat for Westchester in all four and was chosen to preside over the last three. In recognition of his firm support for the Patriot cause, a number of Manor residents placed a notice in *The New York Gazette and Weekly Mercury* in April 1775, specifically thanking Pierre and John Thomas for "their firm attachment to, and zeal on a late occasion for the preservation of the Union of the colonies, and rights and liberties of America."[23] Pierre was also a colonel in Westchester's Patriot militia. The Fourth Congress, then sitting at White Plains, ratified the Declaration of Independence on July 9, 1776. Because these provincial congresses had difficulty maintaining a functioning quorum, they delegated authority to smaller working groups, designated as committees of safety. Pierre Van Cortlandt assumed the chairmanship of the main Committee of Safety on January 3, 1776.

In its drive to render the fight a moral crusade against the evil Loyalists, the Westchester Committee of Safety sought to change the behavior of county inhabitants. It issued the following notice in August 1775: "*Resolved*, That all persons who shall sell or buy any Tea in this County, and all boatmen and others who shall purchase Tea at *New-York* or elsewhere . . . shall be considered and treated as contemners of the Resolution of the Continental Congress and this Committee, and as inimical to the liberties of this Country. *Resolved*, That it be recommended, and it is hereby recommended to the inhabitants of this County immediately to desist from Horse-racing and of all kinds of gaming."[24] The effort to inject moral reform into the Whig platform was similar to what Samuel Adams and other militants were doing elsewhere.

Because of the martial actions occurring around Boston in 1775 and early 1776, Westchester rebels feared that the British military might descend on the

Hudson Valley. Westchester was directly in the path between New England and the New York harbor area. The county also lay along the route British warships would have to use to sail up the Hudson River to Albany. Westchester, therefore, was critical to the defense of the Hudson Valley and the emerging state of New York. Before regular army units could be deployed, the burden of defense fell on the local militia. Indeed, of the four counties—Westchester, Orange, Ulster, and Dutchess—that provided the bulk of the militia, it was Westchester that bore "the major responsibility for the defense of New York above the North River."[25]

Early in 1776 New York's Provincial Congress created regiments of volunteers designated as Minute Men. At the same time, Congress also created on paper, at least, regiments of militia. Usually, the officers chosen as leaders of local Minute Men also served as officers in the militia. Although the Minute Men were apparently paid the same rate as the Continental forces, it is unknown what their particular duties were or in what actions they may have been engaged. Volunteers enlisted for very brief periods and seemed to come and go at will. The Westchester militia, however, formally became part of the American fighting force when the Provincial Congress activated them on July 21, 1776.[26] Primarily organized as a home guard, the militia would play only a limited role in the ensuing conflict.

The War for American Independence came to New York City in June 1776 with the arrival of a flotilla of warships carrying British regulars and Hessian soldiers. The Continental Congress had instructed Gen. George Washington to defend the city with a maximum of effort. He consequently placed a major portion of his troops across the East River on Brooklyn Heights and sought to throw deterrents into the paths of warships seeking to traverse the Hudson River. He also ordered construction of two fortifications, Fort Washington on the northern reaches of Manhattan Island and Fort Lee on the opposite bank of the Hudson. Westchester militia units were assigned to guard the eastern bank of the river.

Despite Washington's best efforts, between late June and mid-September 1776, British forces occupied Long Island and the major portion of Manhattan Island (but not Fort Washington, which was situated on the northwest corner of the island). Washington and his staff worried about where Gen. William Howe, the British commander-in-chief, would strike next. That attack came on October 12, when British forces sought to land on Throg's (Frog's, or Throgg's) Neck on the southeastern shore of the Long Island Sound in present-day Bronx. Incorrectly assuming that the site was a peninsula leading to the mainland and that it was behind American lines, the British plan called for a dash across southern Westchester to the northern part of Manhattan to quickly contain the rebel forces, which had not yet evacuated New York City. However, Throg's Neck was really an island, whose approaches to the mainland were guarded by Continental units with some militia support. While the British army maneuvered to bypass the entrenched American forces, Washington held a council of war on

October 16, at which time it was determined to move American forces north to a stronger position at White Plains, because " the enemy's whole force is in our rear at Frog's Point."[27] As the American forces evacuated Manhattan and the lower portion of Westchester around Kings Bridge, General Howe discovered a better landing site at Pell's Point (now Pelham Park in the Bronx). If Howe, upon landing there, had swiftly marched his men westward across Westchester, he could still have surrounded and trapped the major portion of the American army, which now lay between the city and his own army. He was stopped by John Glover and a small force of Massachusetts men in an action that "saved the American army from encirclement and complete destruction." When British troops, under the command of Lord Cornwallis, reinforced Howe, Glover's position became untenable, and he retreated. This battle of Pelham Bay was a "crucial engagement fraught with strategic significance," and served "as a stimulus to the fighting spirit of the entire army. . . ."[28] It so delayed the British that Washington's army escaped to northern Westchester.

There, the Americans created a line of defense in the hills overlooking White Plains. Israel Putnam was placed in command of a division on Purdy's Hill, William Heath on Hatfield Hill, and Washington at the center in White Plains. Another fortified line was also established on Chatterton's Hill, about a half mile away to the right of the main force. Separating that hill from the main force was the valley of the Bronx River. Defending the American position were some 1,600 men, including 300 militiamen. The Americans did not have long to wait for the anticipated attack. They watched as the British fighting force of over 14,000 men was positioned in the valley below Chatterton's Hill. An American officer described the scene: "Its appearance was truly magnificent. A bright autumnal sun shed its lustre on the polished arms; and the rich array of dress and military equipage gave an imposing grandeur to the scene as they advance in the pomp and circumstance of war."[29] Despite the overwhelming odds, the Americans held off wave after wave of attacks by British and Hessian forces. Under strong leadership from John Haslet and the Delaware contingent, the bulk of the American forces withdrew successfully. Washington's army had again escaped the British. According to Charles Stedman, a British officer, the American army upon leaving White Plains, "retired across the Crotton River to North Castle, setting fire, in their retreat, to all the houses on White Plains. Their position was now so advantageous, that any attack on them must have proved unsuccessful, for the river Crotton stretched along their front, and their rear was defended by woods and heights."[30] In abandoning White Plains, an overzealous officer, Major John W. Austin of Massachusetts, had issued an order for a number of homes to be burned. He was subsequently court martialed and discharged from the army.

With a British army entrenched on Chatterton's Hill, Washington quickly moved his wounded and as much equipment as possible to a stronger position in the hills of North Castle.[31] Instead of pursuing Washington into northern Westchester, Howe invested Fort Washington, which remained relatively unprotected at the northern tip of Manhattan Island. Although British forces surrounded the garrison on November 16, the American high command unwisely decided to defend it. The limited military usefulness of Fort Washington and Fort Lee (its companion across the Hudson River) had already been demonstrated on November 6, when British warships passed directly between the two fortifications. Even the American-created obstruction on the Hudson, a *chevaux de frise,* had failed to stop the British. Fort Washington fell quickly on November 16, and Fort Lee on November 20. Now the Hudson was open to the depredations of the British fleet, and the ground war shifted to New Jersey.

As royal government fell apart in the province, several local committees of correspondence were created to ascertain the allegiance of local inhabitants. The committees pressured Westchester residents to sign an oath of allegiance to the Patriot cause and to the Continental Association. Refusers were regarded as Tories and subject to house arrest, imprisonment, or banishment to Connecticut. Their arms were confiscated for use by the militia and continental forces. Among those arrested were Samuel Seabury and Frederick Philipse. In November 1776 Philipse sent a "Memorial" to the "Committee of Safety of the State of New York," objecting to his arrest and confinement in New Haven: "That your Memorialist has thus been deprived of his liberty without any particular matter being alledged against him, or ever having an opportunity of ever offering anything in his own defence." He asserted that he had not "taken any part in the present unhappy Contest, which could in any ways be construed unfriendly to the General Interest of America. . . ."[32] Soon after, the state committee permitted Philipse to return to his home at Yonkers on condition that he not provide any intelligence to the enemy, take up arms against the United States, or "say or do anything inimical to the American cause." The Westchester Committee of Safety took a dim view of his release and argued that his return home "would put it in the power of a professed enemy of the American cause not only further to disaffect the inhabitants of West-Chester County, but to put many of them in arms against the United States of America."[33] Shortly after returning to Yonkers, but before he could harm the American cause, Frederick Philipse and his family sought refuge within British lines in New York City. Although the Westchester committee had apparently feared that Philipse could persuade his tenant farmers to support the Crown, his tenants were divided: some being rebels; others, Loyalists; and still others, neutral.

At the end of 1776, the British army, aided by Loyalist groups, controlled Manhattan, Long Island, and lower Westchester, while American forces were stationed in the region north of the Croton River around Peekskill in Dutchess County. The area between the two armies became a no-man's-land, called the "Neutral Ground." The military reality belied this designation; the region was not neutral. The area was really a battleground for both armed forces and for marauding bands operating independently. Local farmers were subjected to periodic forays by both sides. Valuables were buried or sent away, and cattle and sheep had to be protected day and night. Farmers developed a clandestine cattle trade with New York City, where such animals brought a high price in specie or in British notes rather than in questionable rebel paper.

The "Neutral Ground" was also an inviting target for militarily led refugee Loyalists and for other loosely organized bodies, dubbed "Cowboys," if they were Loyalist in sentiment, or "Skinners" if they supported the rebel cause. Washington Irving succinctly characterized the two groups as "pretending to redress wrongs and punish political offenses; but all prone in the exercise of their high functions—to sack hen-roosts, drive off cattle, and lay farm houses under contribution; such was the origin of two great orders of border chivalry." In the process, "neither of them in the heat and hurry of a foray had time to ascertain the politics of a horse or cow; nor, when they wrung the neck of a rooster, did they trouble their heads whether he crowed for Congress or for King George."[34] The historian Catherine S. Crary has questioned why Westchester farmers and earlier historians had characterized James DeLancey's Raiders, one of the most prominent Loyalist military groups, as "Cowboys." She averred that DeLancey's Raiders acted according to the rules of warfare, and its officers were regarded as regular officers in the King's army. Crary also argued that most of their captured bounty was taken from known rebel families. Captain Samuel Kipp of North Castle (Chappaqua), an officer in DeLancey's corps, also asserted that they acted in accordance with military rules. "They occupied the Post in the Front of the Lines of the British Army during the whole war, without Pay or any other Reward than a consciousness of doing their Duty as faithful subjects." Crary nonetheless concluded that an "examination of the objectives and conduct of DeLancey's Cowboys does not justify a whitewash of their reputation or praise for their methods of warfare."[35]

Pierre Van Cortlandt's daughter, Cornelia, who was married to Gerard G. Beekman Jr., saw the Cowboys as a cruel menace. She wrote her father in April 1777, while residing near Peekskill, that one of the slaves had admitted to her that a scheme had been hatched by which a number of slaves would flee upon the appearance of the next raiding party. In October she and her husband reported on a visit that various units of the King's Rangers had made to their home. "Yesterday 10 Clock Coll. [Edmund] Fanning and Coll [John] Byard with two hundred of the New Levees March'd by this to destroy barracks N° 2 and the Village [Peekskill.] the Soldiers immediately rush'd in the house and ask'd who liv'd hear, we told them Beekman thay then past by then Came others and began to use abusive Langguage and said that the house was theirs, and that I was the daughter of the damdest rebel in the Province[.] all the Shouldiers knew that much of me and Call'd me a dammaition rebel bitch[.] Every moment, at that time Coll Fanning and Coll Byard came to the house to bid them keep their abuse, but they would not mind, Fanning told me not to be frighted that he would Pertict me that I should not be hurt."[36] This incident provides an interesting commentary. The daughter of New York's lieutenant governor continued to reside in her home, despite the violence that swirled about her. Rank and file redcoats treated the couple disrespectfully, but British officers, in the regular army and the Rangers, acted in a considerate manner. This may have been a civil war, but some officers still acted civilly.

By October 1777 the British could travel up the Hudson into state-held regions with impunity. They raided some river towns and bombarded others, including Tarrytown, Sing Sing, Croton, and Peekskill. This situation led the Continental Congress to authorize construction of a fortress to block these raids. This was the impetus behind the creation of West Point on the west shore of the Hudson.

British forces from New York City also periodically attacked Westchester's interior. Plundering continued. Although the Whig militia sought to protect farmers, residents on occasion realized they needed to band together informally to guard their own property. One such loosely organized unit eventually played a key role in uncovering the treason of Benedict Arnold. A recognized hero of many battles, who had commanded American forces in some of the war's fiercest fighting, General Arnold had been personally chosen by Washington to command the fortress at West Point in August 1780. Unbeknownst to the American high command, Arnold had been engaged for months in a secret correspondence with the British over the bounty he would receive for handing over important plans. As commander at West Point, he now sought to sell the plans for the fort for twenty thousand pounds. The British agent in the negotiations was Major John André, aide to Sir Henry Clinton, now British commander-in-chief.

On the night of September 21, 1780, under the cover of darkness, André left the British warship, the *Vulture*, for a rendezvous with Arnold on the west shore of the Hudson. Because the meeting lasted until 4 a.m., it was too close to dawn for rowers to risk taking André back to the ship undetected. At daylight André crossed the Hudson at King's Ferry using a safe conduct pass Arnold had provided. Riding a horse provided by Arnold, André rode toward the British lines around White Plains. Upon learning that an American unit was actively patrolling the road he was about to take, André thereupon turned southwest toward Tarrytown.

Militiamen frequently scouted the area for adventure and booty. Three such young men—John Paulding, Isaac Van Wart, and David Williams—hid beside the road north of Tarrytown. Along came a stranger on horseback. When challenged by Paulding, who was wearing a Hessian's coat, the stranger replied, "Gentlemen, I hope you belong to our party." Asked to identify the party, André replied, "The Lower Party." Convinced that these men were Loyalists, André added, "I am a British officer out of the country on particular business, and I hope you will not detain me a minute." Identifying themselves as Americans, the three ordered him to dismount, led him into some woods, and made him undress. In his riding boots they found the incriminating documents Arnold had given him.[37] Washington and a grateful Continental Congress treated the three captors as heroes. And thus in Westchester ended the war's most audacious plot of treachery.

If Arnold's betrayal pained Washington, he was cheered by the arrival at Newport, Rhode Island, in July 1780, of a French army under the command of Comte de Rochambeau. Because of the stalemate in the north, General Clinton had redeployed some of his forces to reconquer the south. Washington consequently determined to use the French army, along with American regulars, to attack the outlying fortifications around Kings Bridge to compel Clinton to recall some of his troops from the South. Rochambeau's forces began to leave Newport in June 1781, and the first French contingents reached Westchester by July 2. The French troops were garrisoned across northern Westchester from Peekskill to North Castle and Bedford. Another force gathered at Teller's Point at Croton in order to attack the British fortifications around Yonkers and lower Westchester and to encircle DeLancey's Rangers. The plan failed, for British forces in lower Westchester were stronger than the Americans had been led to believe. Washington consequently ordered a withdrawal of some of his men to Dobbs Ferry and White Plains. These new positions gave the Americans control of the "Neutral Ground" and placed them less than ten miles from the main British line in Westchester, thus curtailing the raids carried out by DeLancey's Rangers.

The bulk of the French army, which had remained at North Castle, was then deployed along the Bronx River and eastward toward White Plains. The French controlled the eastern part of the county from White Plains to New Rochelle, while Connecticut troops guarded the area near the Long Island Sound. However, the Hudson River still remained a defensive quagmire. On July 15 five British warships spotted two rebel sloops carrying supplies to American garrisons. When these sloops hastened toward shore, they ran aground near Tarrytown. Although the British vessels were standing nearby, a small group of French soldiers, who were stationed in the area, waded out to the sloops to unload them. Joined by a number of American dragoons, the French managed to save a substantial portion of the supplies. This event marked the first time that a French force had been directly engaged in fighting against the British.[38]

In the summer of 1781, Washington had about ten thousand American and French soldiers in Westchester. He consequently decided to harass Clinton at New York City and thus tie up British forces in that region. However, as soon as Washington learned on August 14, 1781, that Count De Grasse and a French armada were bound for the Chesapeake, he determined to march his and Rochambeau's troops to Virginia. As part of the plan, Sir Henry was deceived into believing that an American attack on New York City was imminent. While elaborate subterfuges were instituted to bolster the American positions in lower Westchester, especially around Kings Bridge, units of the American army began late on August 19 secretly to cross the Hudson at King's Ferry. They were joined there by French forces, which had crossed at Verplanck's Point. These united troops reached the Chesapeake in mid-September and participated in the Battle of Yorktown (August 30 to October 19, 1781). Meanwhile, the American redoubts at Dobbs Ferry were dismantled, and a portion of the American troops moved north of the Croton River. With the withdrawal of these units, lower Westchester was again left open to the depredations of DeLancey's Rangers.

Although the American troops still in Westchester learned on October 28 that Lord Cornwallis had surrendered nine days earlier, they continued to keep up their guard. Westchester, south of the Croton, remained an area that both Rangers and American Continentals periodically raided to obtain foodstuffs. A Westchester militia captain wrote to New York's Gov. George Clinton in December 1781 that "I must particularly inform you that our Situation is truly dismal; our strength exhausted, and our Poverty great; the Burden as heavy on all sides that it is impossible we can bear any further assistance as a County: I earnestly beg your Excellency's Attention to our Situation, that you will afford us the most ready Relief, as the least Delay may be productive of bad Consequences to the good people on the Frontiers being exposed to a ravaging Enemy making frequent Incursions Amongst us."[39]

Despite the cessation of large-scale hostilities between the main armies, guerilla warfare continued in Westchester throughout most of 1782, and the Americans sought unsuccessfully to capture James DeLancey and his leading officers. In October 1782, once it became known that conclusive negotiations were underway for a treaty between Great Britain and an independent United States, the last British fortified post, Fort Number Eight on the Harlem River, was evacuated. Whig militia units nonetheless continued to pursue DeLancey's men into the next year. Even after the last regular British forces were removed from Westchester on May 13, 1783, the Whig militia and DeLancey's men continued fighting one another. In July Washington finally sent a military force from New Windsor in Ulster County to quiet the situation. Eight American companies remained on guard in Westchester, until the British evacuated New York City on November 25.

The American victory brought change to Westchester, including dramatic transferences of land ownership. After the peace treaty, Frederick Philipse's fifty-thousand-acre estate was divided among many of his former tenants and other individuals who had actively aided the Patriot cause. In 1779 the New York State legislature had adopted an Act of Forfeiture, which confiscated the property of fifty-nine prominent New York Loyalists, including "Frederick Philipse, Esquire, now or late of the county of Westchester."[40] Historians argue over the major purpose of breaking up one of the great landed estates: Was this an effort at social experimentation or an act of retribution?[41]

The Confiscation Act of May 1784 spelled out procedures to be followed in the confiscation and sale of Loyalist estates. Most of Philipsburgh Manor was sold off under this act in two separate sales in 1785 and 1786. Former tenants had preemption rights to their farms, so long as they could demonstrate that they had taken an "active and decided part to maintain the same" and could obtain vouchers from twelve Westchester inhabitants as to their "known and undoubted attachment to the American cause."[42] Untenanted lands, or farms vacated by Loyalists, were sold as a separate category. One of the Commissioners of Forfeiture supervising these sales for the state was Brig. Gen. Philip Van Cortlandt, son of Lt. Gov. Pierre Van Cortlandt. This Patriot family added to their holdings when the Commissioners of Forfeiture sold the 500 acres comprising the Upper Mills portion of Philipsburgh Manor, to Philip's sister, Cornelia, and her husband, Gerard G. Beekman Jr. As a result of these sales, the estate was parceled out to 287 separate owners, each with an average farm size of 174 acres. Significantly, more than two-thirds of Philipse's former tenants became landowners through the exercise of their preemptive rights. A grateful New York State also made a gift of a farm of 277 acres in Westchester, formerly owned by a Loyalist, to Thomas Paine, the author of *Common Sense*, "in consideration for the eminent services rendered to the United States in the progress of the late war . . . and as a testimony of the sense which the people of this State entertain of his distinguished merit."[43]

In the years after Yorktown, the new nation endured a postwar depression that left both state and national governments short of revenue. A major dispute consequently arose over the establishment and collection of an impost duty. New York's Gov. George Clinton wanted to keep tariff collection under state control and opposed those who would grant the Continental Congress power to collect import duties. Indeed, in the years from 1784 to 1787 a number of important issues arose in the state legislature, which signaled whether one supported the Clintonian policy of state power or sought to enhance federal control at state expense. A county historian summarized the issues: "legislation dealing with the issuance of paper money, the Federal Impost bills, disqualification of Loyalists from serving in the legislature, election of delegates to the Constitutional Convention, and the debate on holding the ratifying convention."[44] Westchester typically sided with Clinton.

When the time came in 1787 to choose representatives for a state convention to ratify the proposed Federal Constitution, Westchester surprised almost everyone by voting for a Federalist slate of candidates: Philip Van Cortlandt, son of the lieutenant governor, along with Lewis Morris and Philip Livingston, both large landowners. The Federalists had made an all-out and successful effort to put their supporters in the state convention. Although the ratification of the

Constitution was a singular event in United States history, out of a potential 4,408 voters in Westchester, only 1,093 (or 24.8 percent) bothered to vote.[45] The Federalist slate in Westchester won by more than a 2-to-1 margin. Westchester legislators, who had provided Governor Clinton with a loyal following during the Confederation period, now left him in order to support the new Constitution.

The Revolution had thus wrought many significant changes in Westchester. The county had survived eight years of devastation, ruined fields, burned and vandalized homes, and lost lives. After the warfare had finally ended, many people resumed their peacetime lives. However, those who had openly or even furtively aided the enemy saw their properties confiscated, or sought refuge in Canada, Nova Scotia, or England. Of importance was the transformation of hundreds of former tenant farmers on Philipsburgh Manor into landowners. Westchester had undergone a revolution.

Notes

1. Division of Archives and History, *The American Revolution In New York: Its Political and Social Significance* (Albany, 1926), 249–50.

2. J. Thomas Scharf, ed., *History of Westchester County, New York, including Morrisania, Kings Bridge, and West Farms, Which Have Been Annexed to New York City* (Philadelphia, 1886), 1: 2–11.

3. Scharf, ed., *Westchester* 1: 9–20.

4. Edmund B. O'Callaghan and Berthold Fernow, eds., *The Documentary History of the State of New York* (Albany,1819), 1: 696–97; Jacob Judd, "Frederick Philipse III of Westchester County: A Reluctant Loyalist," in Robert A. East and Jacob Judd, eds., *The Loyalist Americans: A Focus on Greater New York* (Tarrytown, N.Y., 1975), 112–20; and Paula Carlo, "The Huguenots of New Paltz and New Rochelle" (Ph.D. diss., The City University of New York, 2001), 410.

5. Scharf, ed., *Westchester* 1:20.

6. According to the charters creating manors in New York, the "Lord" retained all governing rights, along with total control of the lands under his jurisdiction, and the right to choose the ministers for churches he may have helped to establish.

7. Judd, "Frederick Philipse III," 112–120; Jacob Judd, ed., *Correspondence of the Van Cortlandt Family of Cortlandt Manor, 1748–1800*, in *The Van Cortlandt Family Papers*, (Tarrytown, N.Y., 1977), 2: xli–xlii, 4–10.

8. E. Marie Becker, "The 801 Westchester County Freeholders of 1763: And The Cortlandt Manor Land-Case Which Occasioned Their Listing," *New-York Historical Society Quarterly* 35 (1951): 283–321.

9. Pierre Van Cortlandt to [Unidentified], Apr. 1766, in Judd, ed., *Van Cortlandt Family Papers* 2: 339–41; and Patricia U. Bonomi, *A Factious People: Politics and Society in Colonial New York* (New York, 1971), 224–26.

10. Frank Dean Gifford, "The Church of England in Colonial Westchester: A Study of the Work of the S.P.G. in the Parishes of West Chester, Rye, and New Rochelle" (Ph.D. diss., New York University, 1942), 453.

11. Don R. Gerlach, *Philip Schuyler and the American Revolution in New York 1733–1777* (Lincoln, Nebr., 1964), 153–56, 323–331.

12. Judd, ed., *Correspondence of Van Cortlandt Family* 2: 4–10.

13. Gifford, "Church of England," 448–522; G. N. D. Evans, ed., *Allegiance in America: The Case Of The Loyalists* (Reading, Mass., 1969), 3–9; Bernard Bailyn, *The Ideological Origins of the American Revolution* (Cambridge, Mass., 1967), 223, 226–27.

14. Carl Bridenbaugh, *Mitre and Sceptre: Transatlantic Faiths, Ideas, Personalities, and Politics 1689–1775* (New York, 1962), 13–14.

15. Carl Bridenbaugh, *Mitre and Sceptre*, 252–57; Samuel Seabury, *Letters of a Westchester Farmer*, ed. Clarence H. Vance, (Publications of the Westchester County Historical Society [White Plains, 1930]), 8: 13–14. The quote is from Gifford, "Church of England," 486.

16. Jacob Judd, ed., *The Revolutionary War Memoir and Selected Correspondence of Philip Van Cortlandt*, in *Van Cortlandt Family Papers* (Tarrytown, N.Y., 1976), 1:33–34.

17. Scharf, ed., *Westchester* 1: 205.

18. Scharf, ed., *Westchester* 1: 205, 208.

19. Seabury, *Letters of a Westchester Farmer*, ed. Clarence Vance, 43–49.

20. Otto Hufeland, *Westchester County during the American Revolution, 1775–1783* (Harrison, N.Y., 1974), 61.

21. Ibid.

22. Scharf, ed., *Westchester* 1: 219–20.

23. Michael Kammen, *Colonial New York: A History* (New York, 1975), 366; Bernard Mason, *The Road to Independence: The Revolutionary Movement in New York, 1773–1777* (Lexington, Ky., 1967), 178–212. The quote is from Judd, ed., *Van Cortlandt Papers*, 2: xliv–xlv.

24. Peter Force, ed., *American Archives*, Fourth Series (Washington, D.C., 1840), 3:150.

25. Harold Drimmer, "The Westchester Militia in the American Revolution," *Westchester Historian* 17 (1997): 3.

26. Ibid.

27. Christopher Ward, *The War of the Revolution* (New York, 1952), 256.

28. George A. Billias, "Pelham Bay: A Forgotten Battle," in *Narratives of the Revolution in New York* (*Collections* of the New-York Historical Society, 85 (1975): 106, 118–119.

29. Ward, *War of the Revolution*, 262.

30. Westchester County Historical Society, "The Battle of White Plains from the British Viewpoint," *Westchester Historian* 61 (1985): 34–39.

31. Hufeland, *Westchester*, 56–60.

32. Jacob Judd, "Frederick Philipse III of Westchester County: A Reluctant Loyalist," in Robert A. East and Jacob Judd, eds., *Loyalist Americans*, 32–33.

33. Peter Force, ed., *American Archives*, Fifth Series (Washington, D.C., 1853), 3: 1205–1207.

34. Washington Irving, *Wolfert's Roost and Other Stories* (New York, 1910), 8–9.

35. Catherine S. Crary, "Guerrilla Activities of James DeLancey's Cowboys in Westchester County: Conventional Warfare or Self-Interested Freebooting?" in East and Judd, eds., *Loyalist Americans*, 14–19.

36. Judd, ed., *Van Cortlandt Papers* 2: 243–49.

37. Carl Van Doren, *Secret History of the American Revolution* (New York, 1968), 313.

38. Hufeland, *Westchester*, 393.

39. Hufeland, *Westchester*, 409–10.

40. *New York Journal and the General Advertiser*, Nov. 29, 1779.

41. Judd, "Frederick Philipse III," in East and Judd, eds., *Loyalist Americans*, 36.

42. Beatrice G. Reubens, "Pre-Emptive Rights in the Disposition of a Confiscated Estate: Philipsburgh Manor, New York," *William & Mary Quarterly*, 3rd Ser., 22 (1965): 441–42.

43. Henry B. Yoshpe, "The Disposition of Loyalist Estates in Westchester County," *Westchester Historian* 61 (1985): 78.

44. William B. Michaelsen, "Westchester Ratifies the Constitution," *Westchester Historian* 64 (1988): 109.

45. Michaelsen, "Westchester Ratifies The Constitution," *Westchester Historian* 64 (1988): 111.

6

The Central Hudson Valley:
Dutchess, Orange, and Ulster Counties

Thomas S. Wermuth

The central Hudson Valley was one of the most contested battlegrounds in the War for American Independence, for the Hudson River separated the ardently revolutionary New England from the rest of the states and also linked Canada to New York City. In 1777 the Burgoyne campaign, which began in Canada and was defeated in Saratoga, drew men and resources from the central Hudson Valley. The American victory at Saratoga has been recognized widely as the "turning point" of the Revolution. From 1780 to 1781 George Washington's headquarters at Newburgh and New Windsor were his last encampments, and at Newburgh Washington squashed the threatened military conspiracy against civilian government. Moreover, throughout the war the region was the "bread-basket" of George Washington's army, and the area's fields, flocks, and herds kept his troops, and, at times, the troops of his enemy, fed. In addition, several thousand valley men fought in the war, whether for the Continental Army, the New York militia, or, less frequently, for the King.

The military contest for control of the river valley continued for several years, affecting local society in the central Hudson Valley. Many of the region's residents initially saw the Revolution as a struggle against a tyrannical British government that was attempting to subvert traditional liberties and rights. As the Revolution dragged on, others concluded that the conflict meant something else as well. Indeed, various groups promoted their vision of what the revolution was, or, more precisely, what they thought the Revolution *should* be. For some people, the war years brought the possibility of political empowerment, as many who had hitherto been denied access to power found in the revolutionary upheaval the opportunity for political advancement. Young, enterprising middle-class men, such as

127

Dutchess County's Dirck Brinckerhoff and Jacobus Swarthout, who had enjoyed few political opportunities before the war, now emerged to challenge the power and prestige of the landed aristocracy that had dominated the Hudson's east bank. Modestly born Ulster lawyer, George Clinton, shocked New York's elite by being elected the first governor of New York State in 1777. For still others the revolution represented an opportunity to challenge the existing social order. The war revived the tenant conflicts that had troubled the eastern bank of the Hudson in the years before 1774. Laboring men and women spearheaded boycotts against profiteering Patriot shopkeepers and seized staple products during periods of economic distress, demanding economic justice from local dignitaries. This essay will examine the transformation that the military struggle caused in the central Hudson Valley counties of Orange, Ulster, and Dutchess.

The Mid-Hudson Valley: The Setting

On the eve of the Revolution, the mid-Hudson Valley was one of the most fertile and productive farm regions in British North America. Its grain, flour, and dairy products were sent to the West Indies, Europe, and South America. The port towns of Poughkeepsie (in Dutchess County on the Hudson's east bank) and Kingston (in Ulster) were thriving little commercial entrepots that served as regional hubs in the vibrant agricultural trade with New York City. Nevertheless, the backcountry away from the river had much in common with Washington Irving's "Sleepy Hollow," small towns, where little happened, and change, when it occurred, happened slowly and imperceptibly.[1]

The mid-Hudson's west bank included the counties of Orange and Ulster, which the Dutch had settled in the mid-seventeenth century. The English followed soon thereafter, and many French Huguenots and some Germans also came to the area. Slavery took hold early, and by the Revolution some 15 percent of the population of the Hudson's west bank consisted of African-American slaves.[2] Despite this diversity, on the eve of the Revolution, much of the west bank remained ethnically and culturally Dutch, perhaps three generations removed from Europe. Dutch customs prevailed. The Dutch Reformed Church dominated. When the Second Continental Congress was approving the Declaration of Independence, Dutch was spoken more regularly than was English in many west bank towns. Indeed, as late as 1774, Kingston (a mere two years away from becoming the state capital) still kept its official town records in Dutch.[3]

Ulster and Orange Counties were populated by freehold farms. Although the "Great Hardenbergh Patent" comprised the western part of Ulster, it lay primarily in the Shawangunk Mountains and beyond and had few tenants. A few families, such as the Hasbroucks and Hardenberghs, dominated local politics and society, but the Hudson's west bank was a society of "roughly equal men," who owned their own land and marketed the produce of their farms and shops.[4]

Dutchess County faced Orange and Ulster across the river on the Hudson's east bank. The Dutch and Germans populated the central and northern parts of the county, but the English predominated in the south. Many of these English settlers were recent eighteenth-century migrants from New England and northern Long Island. As did Ulster and Orange, Dutchess did have some small communities, thriving port towns, and also many freehold farm families. But what characterized the Hudson's east bank, from Westchester north to Rensselaerwyck, was the continued existence of a manorial system, in which landowners used their economic power to politically control the county.[5]

Such landlords as Robert R. Livingston, Beverly Robinson, and Roger Morris possessed leases for more than five hundred tenant families in Dutchess County, many of whom owed their manor lords traditional services and duties that were more characteristic of medieval England than eighteenth-century North America. For example, leases might run for several generations, demand that tenants grind their wheat at the landlord's mill, work several days a year for the lessor, and require symbolic payment of portions of rent in fowl and fruit.[6]

The usual tensions between landlords and tenants were exacerbated by this manorial system. Tenant uneasiness expressed itself in different ways: simple resentment; the nonpayment of rents; intimidation of the landlord's agents; and, at times, outright rebellion. In 1741 and again twenty-five years later, fighting broke out between tenants and landlords on several of the manorial estates.[7]

The Great Dutchess Tenant Uprising of 1766 was significant. Beverly Robinson's attempt to expel both New England squatters and tenants who were withholding rents caused the rebellion that included upward of one thousand participants (about 20 percent of the adult male population) and that resulted in pitched battles between forces of the landlords and rioters. Although this event was unrelated to the growing crisis with Britain, the mutual distrust that landlords and tenants had for each other only increased, and that helped shape the relationship of both groups to the Revolution as it unfolded.[8]

The Revolutionary Crisis Begins

Unlike in New England and New York City, there was little organized anti-British activity in the central valley before 1774. Indeed, there were few attempts to challenge British authority or policy. Much like the rest of the northern colonies, however, this changed rapidly with passage of the Coercive Acts in 1774. In communities throughout the midvalley—from bustling port towns like Poughkeepsie and Kingston, to smaller, sleepier villages like New Windsor and Amenia—committees of safety, observation, and inspection sprung into action. For example, the Kingston Committee of Safety expressed its dismay at Parliament's attempt in the Quebec Act (1774) to establish "the Romish Religion in America." This committee was equally shocked by the "avowed design of the

ministry to raise a revenue in America." The New Windsor Committee of
Observation objected to levying taxes "on us without our consent" and asserting absolute legislative authority over the colonies. The committee resolved that
such efforts were "subversive of our natural and legal rights as British subjects,
and that we would be deficient in point of duty to our King and the British
Constitution were we to yield in tame submission to them."[9]

When the war began in 1775, the people of the Hudson Valley began to choose
sides. From the start, both Ulster and Orange Counties enjoyed unusually high
responses to Patriot "oath of allegiance" petitions. Indeed, throughout the course
of the war, though Loyalism was present in both counties, devotion to the revolutionary cause was quite strong. Although several distinct ethnic groups—
English, Dutch, German, and French Huguenots—lived in the region, there is no
evidence that any group was more predisposed to Patriotism or Loyalism; indeed,
the one clear fact is that there were few Loyalists in either county.[10]

Although Loyalism was weak in Dutchess as well (particularly when com-
pared to nearby Westchester County), the situation was nonetheless more complicated than the one on the west bank. When war began, both landlord and
tenant were wary about taking sides in the crisis. While the Livingstons and
Beekmans, who owned much of the county's land, generally supported the new
Patriot Provincial Congress and demanded compromises from Parliament, they
also sought to control the protest movement, so that the social and political order,
which they dominated, was not disturbed.[11]

For a variety of reasons, tenants viewed the Revolution even more warily.
First, some Dutchess County tenants were chary about siding with landlords
who had oppressed them before 1775, even though other landlords did convince
their tenants to side with them. Second, there were rumors that British agents
were promising tenants ownership of the land they presently held in leasehold
if they fought with the British. Finally, many tenants in southern Dutchess were
simply indifferent to the struggle. Possessing no political and relatively little
economic power, they were absorbed in the daily toil of farming and expressed
little interest in the conflict. Although William Smith thought that tenants in certain Dutchess towns were "forty to one" against independence, this was most
certainly an exaggeration. Many were lukewarm Patriots, until New York State
offered them the possibility of becoming landowners, when it confiscated and
redistributed Loyalist property.[12]

Rise of the Revolutionary Coalition

Although the traditional leadership of the midvalley was at the forefront
of resistance to Parliament in 1774 and 1775, the beginning of the war opened
new opportunities for ambitious men who had been for many years on the periph-

ery of power. This process was most pronounced in Dutchess, where a power-
ful manorial landlord class still controlled most of the county-wide and town
offices. Landlord Beverly Robinson, who purportedly owned one-third of south-
ern Dutchess, was the first judge of the county and a member of the Whig
Provincial Congress; Phillip Livingston was the county sheriff; and Robert
Livingston Jr., was one of the county's representatives in the Provincial
Assembly. By 1776 new faces began to join the customary leadership of
Dutchess County: freehold farmers and tradesmen like Dirck Brinckerhoff and
Jacobus Swarthout, as well as tenants like Henry Luddington, who had developed local power bases, were elected to the committees in the counties.
Nonetheless, their renown had never approached the provincial-wide reputa-
tions of the Livingstons, Beekmans, or Robinsons. By 1777, with the traditional
leadership moving somewhat hesitantly on wartime issues of importance to
county residents, these new, middle-class leaders began to exert greater power
first in local Dutchess politics and then in the New York State Assembly.[13]

In Ulster and Orange Counties, a similar challenge to the "old guard" took
place. Although historian Edward Countryman is correct in his assertion that the
Hudson's west bank was a "society of roughly equal men," a handful of prominent and powerful families had exerted considerable social, political, and economic influence before the war. More often than not, members of the oldest,
most prominent families, including the Coldens, Hardenberghs, and Ellisons,
had held such prestigious political offices as sheriff, county supervisor, and had
been appointed commanders of the local militias. In this hierarchical, deferential society, family name, education, wealth, and prestige counted for much.[14]

As the Revolution unfolded, many of the west bank's old elite found themselves first sharing and then relinquishing their political and military power.
Merchants William and John Hasbrouck, leading members of two of the most
prominent families in the county, had been the commanders of Ulster's two militia regiments at the beginning of the war, but they were not reelected to commands they had held by appointment for twenty years. Neither received enough
votes from their volunteer units to compete for leadership.[15]

Ulster County politics offers a glimpse of the political struggles that characterized this region as it entered the Revolution. On the eve of the conflict, New
Paltz's Johannes Hardenbergh was a member of the Duzine (the governing board
of the town) as well as the wealthiest man in the town and perhaps in all of Ulster
County. A colonel in the Ulster militia for twenty years and a delegate to the
First Provincial Congress, Hardenbergh was the grandson of the original patentee of the "Great Hardenbergh" Patent, two million acres that sprawled across
western Ulster. In the elections for the county-wide Committee of Safety in 1775,
Hardenbergh's neighbors deferentially selected him a member and immediately
named him chair and treasurer. Although Abraham Hasbrouck, one of Ulster's
most prominent merchants was also on the committee, these two traditional

leaders were joined by new men like Robert Boyd and Johannes Snyder, whose social standing had previously not given them access to county-wide political power. Accustomed to being obeyed, Hardenbergh soon clashed with the more middling members of the committee. Eventually, after a series of squabbles, he realized he had to work with them if he wanted to remain in power.[16]

Although most disagreements between the Hardenberghs and the the Hasbroucks, on the one hand, and the rest of the committee, on the other, were generally procedural, they broke sharply on the issue of support for Ulster's George Clinton. The New York Assembly had recently appointed Clinton the general of the New York militia and put him in charge of Ulster's regiments. Members of the county's elite viewed him as an upstart; Col. John Hasbrouck (Abraham Hardenbergh's cousin and a substantial farmer) refused to serve in a regiment "commanded by Mr. Clinton." Johannes Hardenbergh went further and, abusing his authority as chair, refused to accept the Ulster Committee of Safety's resolution appointing Clinton one of Ulster's delegates to the Provincial Congress, where Clinton had much support among the delegates from Ulster, Orange, and Dutchess. The Provincial Congress reprimanded Hardenbergh, demanded an explanation for his refusal, and then appointed Clinton to the Ulster delegation in the Provincial Congress.[17]

Following continued disagreements with several other committee members, Hardenbergh was ousted from his position as treasurer of the committee. He complained about these political upstarts and refused to relinquish the £300 in the treasury. The committee threatened Hardenbergh with an "altercation" and ordered him to turn over the money. Hardenbergh not only relented, but he soon began cooperating in the new political environment, for which he and most other committee members had little training: democratic political discussion, debate, and compromise.[18]

Despite Hardenbergh's preference for deferential politics and his discomfort with popular decision-making, he was committed to the revolutionary cause. Other members of the colonial elite on the west bank were not so inclined, and they did not fare as well. Cadwallader Colden Jr., son of the lieutenant governor, made clear his disdain for democratic politics and his loyal support for the Crown. He suffered the consequences, when a delegation from the New Windsor Committee of Safety stormed his estate at midnight on June 21, 1776. The committee searched and ransacked his house and ordered him arrested. Colden hoped to remain under house arrest and even offered to pay for guards to stay at his home that night, but the committee refused. When Colden continued to insist upon house arrest, the committee threatened him with the humiliating alternative that he would "be rode upon a rail" to the local jail, if he did not accompany them willingly. This type of theatrical punishment had traditionally been reserved during the Colonial Period for prostitutes, wife-abusers, and other community miscreants, not for men of Colden's stature. To threaten one of the most substantial men in the midvalley with such a fate, and his apparent belief that the committee would make good on their threat, reveals the extent of the military conflict's challenge to the existing social and political order.[19]

In the place of this traditional elite there emerged in Ulster and Orange a group of talented, opportunistic men, such as Robert Boyd, Charles DeWitt, and Matthew Cantine, who had developed strong local support, but who lacked the wealth and pedigree of the prewar leadership. These newly elected officials in the midvalley were not simply new names; they were men who came from a lower socioeconomic status than the traditional elite. They held divergent views on political leadership and political participation and had a different understanding of the goals of the Revolution. For these men the Revolution offered the opportunity for political and social advancement, something that had been denied them before the war. These new political leaders now had the opportunity to assume political roles on the many committees of correspondence, safety, and inspection. Further, the dramatically increased size of the state legislature (the delegations from the mid-Hudson Valley doubled in size) opened up new opportunities at the state level.

The most dramatic example of the new political opportunities in the midvalley (or in any part of Revolutionary America, for that matter) was the meteoric rise of George Clinton. Clinton was not new to political power, nor was he a simple farmer making his first foray into politics. Born to a "well-to-do" (though not prominent) family on the Ulster-Orange border, Clinton had practiced law in Ulster and New York City, and served as the Ulster representative to New York's Provincial Assembly from 1769 to 1771. He often spoke in the years before the war against British policy and had forged careful and practical alliances with such prominent provincial-wide leaders as Phillip Schuyler and Robert Livingston.[20]

Clinton's rise was swift. In 1776 the New York Congress appointed him a brigadier general in the New York militia, an appointment that drew the scorn of Ulster's traditional aristocracy. Col. John Hasbrouck, commander of the Ulster militia, pointedly asked the New York Congress "how he [Clinton] comes to be promoted to so high a rank . . . and how it was brought about to supercede so many brave officers in the regiment." Clinton's unexpected triumph as New York's first governor in 1777 brought equally critical commentary from the New York elite. Clinton's former ally in the New York Assembly, Phillip Schuyler, a losing candidate, claimed that Clinton's "family and connections do not entitle him to so distinguished a predominance."[21]

The War in the Midvalley: 1775–1783

Although no fighting took place in the region during the first year of the war, from 1776 through 1783, control of the Hudson River Valley remained one of the primary strategic objectives of the British high command, and the valley's defense was equally important to Gen. George Washington. American control of this region bottled up the British in New York City and kept other British forces far to the north in Canada. In 1776 Washington, whose army would spend more than one-third of the Revolutionary War in or in close proximity to the Hudson River Valley, stated that "the importance of the river in the present contest and the necessity of defending it, are so well understood that it is unnecessary to enlarge upon them." Washington nonetheless proceeded to do so, citing its strategic transportation and communications significance as well as the importance of its agricultural production.[22] His concern for the defense of this strategic region led the Americans to construct an "Iron Chain" and boom across the river just north of West Point. This lightweight impediment was soon outflanked and destroyed by Sir Henry Clinton's forces and rendered useless. In 1776 Washington had also ordered the construction of three forts along the Highlands: Forts Montgomery, Clinton, and Constitution. By the summer of 1777 these three forts were still unfinished and only lightly garrisoned.

The British in New York City engaged in several small raids in the mid-valley in 1776 and 1777, including a half-hearted shelling of the as yet uncompleted Fort Montgomery in the summer of 1777. The key British campaign for control of the Hudson River Valley was an elaborate yet poorly coordinated plan consisting of a three-pronged invasion in 1777. The main force under Gen. John Burgoyne was to depart from Canada in summer and push southward through the Adirondacks to Albany, where it was to meet up with a combined British-Indian force that had been pushing eastward along the Mohawk Valley. The third force was to be an expeditionary unit from New York City under the command of Sir Henry Clinton. Clinton's troops were to move up the Hudson and meet Burgoyne or at least give him support. The military's lack of proper planning, coordination, and execution of this major invasion led directly to the British defeat at Saratoga, the "turning point of the war."[23]

Instead of using all his military resources to support Burgoyne, Sir William Howe, commander-in-chief of the British army in America, took a large force to capture Philadelphia and left Sir Henry Clinton only a small contingent to support the invasion from Canada. About two thousand Continental soldiers and elements of the Ulster and Orange County militia garrisoned Fts. Montgomery and Clinton. The state's new governor, Gen. George Clinton, commanded the posts. On the morning of October 6, after a night of fierce fighting, British troops captured both forts and spent the next several days destroying the forts and the iron chain across the Hudson. The main part of the American force managed to escape northward.[24]

Although the British victory was complete, Henry Clinton's troops suffered almost two hundred casualties and were delayed by the military action. They finally resumed their slow movement upriver and stopped at a number of points along the way, where they landed several small units for limited forays against local militia units. British forces reached Kingston, the state capital, ten days later.

Advance British units entered Kingston before dawn on October 16. Many Kingstonians had already escaped, and local militia forces had stood ready to conduct a delaying action against enemy forces. However, a British raiding party of several hundred troops under Maj. John Vaughn quickly drove these militia units west from the town in predawn fighting on the banks of Esopus Creek just a few hundred yards from the Hudson. Determined to punish the region, British troops burned large portions of the town before departing later that afternoon. Sir Henry Clinton pushed ten miles upriver over the next few days, dropping landing parties at various points (including the Livingston estate at Clermont) before heading south to New York City. By this time, Burgoyne had already surrendered his army at Saratoga, and Clinton's slow northward movement was now irrelevant.[25]

Although the next year witnessed only limited military action in the midvalley, the Hudson remained a primary target of both British and American strategies for the remainder of the war. Sir Henry attempted a second invasion of the river valley in May 1779, seizing Stony Point in Orange County. However, Washington kept his army between Henry Clinton and the northern river valley. In July "Mad" Anthony Wayne drove the British from Stony Point and sent them retreating southward down the river.[26]

It was the importance of the Hudson that had led Washington in 1778 to order construction of fortress West Point, which overlooked the Hudson in Orange County. He also ordered that a heavy and formidable great "iron chain," be erected to prevent any future British incursion up the river. The British did make one more attempt to gain control of the Hudson in 1780, when Henry Clinton opened secret negotiations with Gen. Benedict Arnold, the recently appointed commander of West Point, to gain control of the fort. Arnold's plans were discovered, when Clinton's aide-de-camp John André was captured. André was hanged in Westchester County as a spy, and Arnold was barely able to escape to safety in British-occupied New York City.[27]

In the last years of the war, the midvalley remained central to Washington's planning. Although the British were defeated at Yorktown in 1781, they continued to occupy New York City for two more years, and their continued threat to the river valley kept Washington and his army stationed nearby. The Continental army encamped in southern Ulster County, in and around the town of New Windsor, while Washington himself took up headquarters a few miles north on the Hudson at Newburgh.

Popular Politics and the Committee Movement

The years of military conflict had a significant impact on the mid-Hudson Valley. The gradual collapse of New York's colonial government throughout 1775 impelled extralegal committees of safety, observation, and inspection to fill the power vacuum. In most towns these committees developed alongside existing legally constituted town boards and governments. In many communities these committees exerted their influence not only in the political sphere, but also in the economic arena by regulating prices, controlling the importation and exportation of goods, and setting maximum and minimum wage rates for local labor.

The committees enjoyed formidable powers that grew increasingly broad over time in response to wartime needs. Initially, the committees' role was simply to organize and promote revolutionary support and to communicate with the populace about the latest developments in the imperial crisis. With the disintegration of the official provincial government in late 1775, however, the committees became quasi-legal institutions replacing the power of the crumbling old government. Although the committees' powers were curtailed with the creation of the New York State government in 1777, these bodies nonetheless enjoyed significant local authority throughout the late 1770s.

The various committees that emerged in the mid-Hudson Valley during the war were popularly elected and supported. Among the earliest committees of correspondence were those elected at the town meetings of the Kingston Corporation, Poughkeepsie town government, and the New Paltz Duzine. Participation in these meetings was not open to all residents; only freeholders could vote. The people initially elected to the committees tended to be chosen from the traditional community leaders, for the mid-Hudson Valley was still a hierarchical and deferential society. During the war, as old leaders moved up to state and continental positions or retired from active efforts, the social and economic status of committee members elected by freeholders changed substantially. A majority eventually came from the "middling-sorts." In this way, the freeholder-elected committees often served as avenues of advancement for aspiring political leaders, whose social background had heretofore denied them access to prominent elective office.[28]

The powers invested in the committees were often greater than those that town officials had possessed in the colonial period. In 1776 the Provincial Congress gave the committees the authority to tax and appoint tax collectors and assessors. During the war, the committees gradually gained additional political powers and became the governments of many midvalley towns. Besides control over local taxation and legislation, the committees also assumed judicial and police powers. Furthermore, committees employed local militia units as police to enforce their rulings.

Usually, the committees were able to employ community pressure against those suspected of unpatriotic actions or of any activity seen as threatening to the community. These punishments included public denunciations of those considered to be enemies of the cause, symbolic burnings of effigies, and boycotts of shopkeepers and tradesmen who were lukewarm to the Revolution. For example, the Kingston committee stated that if persons were guilty of actions endangering the community, "they should be punished in the public newspapers as enemies to the liberties and privileges of American subjects," and all residents should abstain from commerce with the offender.[29] The Ulster Association instructed county residents not to patronize establishments, businesses, or shops whose Patriotism was suspect, because "every shilling of property we put in their hands . . . enable them to purchase the chains to bind us in slavery."[30]

Committees encouraged political action in other ways. At times they sponsored the public destruction of Loyalist assets in such places as the Kingston public market.[31] The committee also acted against members of the county's oldest and most prominent families, who seemed to impede the war effort. Leading members of valley towns came under public attack; were dislodged from political office; suffered riots or demonstrations at their homes or places of business; or, more ignobly, were arrested and charged with being "enemies of the cause." Some victims undoubtedly were Tories; others simply lacked enthusiasm for the cause, while still others had put self first and engaged in economic activities that residents felt compromised the integrity of the local economies that were already endangered by the extreme war-time dislocations. As a result, the Revolution successfully challenged the political and social order that had heretofore shaped life in small valley towns.

The issues upon which committees expended the most energy tended to be economic. On the eve of the war, the local committees of observation had supervised economic activities in their counties and towns and enforced the economic measures required by the Continental Association. During the war, when shortages and inflation had become rampant, the local committees scrutinized the trade and economic activities of local shopkeepers, to ensure that they engaged in business practices that promoted the war effort and supported a vibrant local economy.[32]

These activities included regulating prices, preventing hoarding and price-gouging, and forcing shopkeepers to sell necessary foodstuffs at affordable prices. As early as 1776, local committees had begun enacting price controls on a variety of staple products, including wheat, flour, and salt. They also fined shopkeepers and merchants, who violated these price maximums, by confiscating their goods and foodstuffs. Finally, these committees forbade the exportation of certain staple products beyond town boundaries.[33]

As the military conflict dragged on, the committees heightened their efforts to control Loyalists, motivate neutrals, and prohibit economic activities that would weaken the American cause. In 1777 the Ulster Committee, which met regularly at Andrew Oliver's home, forbade the exportation of flour, meal, or grain outside the county. In 1778, at the height of the wartime shortages, the town leaders of Marbletown gave permission to export flour, but "not more than four barrels" per person and only on the condition that an equal value of salt be brought into the town. By 1779 the situation had grown so desperate in several west bank communities, that the export of wheat or its use in distillation was forbidden.[34] Even though it is impossible to know today how much illegal trade there was, committees worked viligently to suppress it.

The state government, too, began regulating the prices of various goods once it was created in 1777. Each year from 1777 through 1780, it established various price controls in an unsuccessful attempt to halt hyperinflation. The state set the prices of all grains, flour, vegetables, leather, shoes, and a variety of other products. In addition, the state regulated wages and labor, ordering that "the various kinds of labour of farmers, mechanics and others, be set and affixed, at rates not exceeding seventy-five per centum" over the normal wages for a given locality. Moreover, in 1779 and 1780 and again in 1782, midvalley political officials requested that the State Assembly provide greater assistance in regulating prices. Specifically, the Ulster and Dutchess County committees asked the Assembly to introduce new, even stricter price controls to regulate the soaring price of grain and other staples.[35]

Legislation was passed not only to cap prices and control inflation, but to regulate economic behavior within communities as well. Many believed, as did Dutchess County's Henry Luddington, that the scarcity of bread in that county in 1776 was not the result of natural forces but of the actions of the "wicked, mercenary intrigues of a number of ingrossing jockies." In order to set a proper example, committees of observation and safety made public examples throughout the war of those thwarting the committee's dictates.[36] For example, in 1777 New Windsor residents accused Mrs. Jonathan Lawrence of price-gouging and selling tea for two shillings a pound above the rate the committee had set. Mrs. Lawrence claimed that she only charged the committee set price of six shillings, "but will not let the purchaser have the tea unless he takes a paper bag to put it in at two shillings." When challenged by the local Committee of Inspection, she sent the tea to her husband, Jonathan, the commissary at nearby Fort Constitution. The committee consequently seized the tea, discharged Jonathan from his duties, rebuked the couple, and agreed to keep a careful eye on Mrs. Lawrence in the future.[37]

Crowds, Riots & Popular Revolution in the Mid-Hudson Valley

Even more significant than the actions taken by the committees in these years was the popular action that occurred throughout the midvalley in the 1770s and 1780s. As early as 1776, Kingston and New Windsor residents took matters into their own hands, for they thought that their elected officials were not going far enough in regulating the economy and prosecuting monopolizers and engrossers.[38] In response, the Ulster Committee reported in 1776 that "we are daily alarmed, and our streets filled with mobs." According to the Committee, the situation had grown so desperate in Ulster that if the legislature could not solve the economic woes affecting the central valley, local committees would have to assume authority in the name "of the People at Large."[39]

Between 1776 and 1779, popular action led to frequent boycotts, forced sales of necessary products, and riots in the mid-Hudson Valley. The first major riot occurred in Kingston in November 1776, when a crowd raided warehouses and stores seizing tea. Two weeks later, one of Ulster County's first families, the Ellisons of New Windsor, became victims when a large crowd came to William Ellison's store. After accusing him of price-gouging and engrossment, they seized all the salt "except one bushel," which they left for his family's use.

Even merchants who lived outside the three–county–area were not safe from this form of popular activity.[40] Two Albany merchants who had purchased tea in Philadelphia had the misfortune of sending it overland through New Windsor in 1777. A crowd of men and women besieged the transporters, seized the load, asserting that it was being marketed for more than the six-shilling limit the local committee had set, and sold it to themselves at that price. Crowds of local Dutchess women visited Poughkeepsie shopkeeper Peter Messier in the spring of 1777. Accusing him of selling tea above the Poughkeepsie Committee's imposed price-cap, the women used their own weights and measures to divide and distribute the tea among themselves. The women, accompanied by two Continental soldiers, offered Messier "their own price," one that was considerably lower than his selling price. The women returned twice more over the next several days to repeat these actions.[41]

The New Windsor and Poughkeepsie riots reveal that rioters often used the local committees' authority to justify their own actions. The rioters at Ellison's store reminded the shopkeeper of the committee's price regulations that he was allegedly breaking. The women who confiscated Messier's tea specifically stated that "they had orders from the Committee to search his house." However, it is essential to point out that in each of these activities, the rioters exceeded the committee's dictates. Neither riot was authorized by the local committee, and indeed, some committee members criticized the New Windsor riot.[42]

The activities of the committees in controlling prices and commerce, as well as in prosecuting hoarders, are clear indications of a public economic policy that aimed to regulate the workings of the free market and protect the community's interest. The importance of these activities was not the imposition of price controls, for many of the powers of market regulation and price-setting were already well accepted. However, while enforcing these regulations, the committees were functioning as local governments.[43]

The actions of the rioters in seizing foodstuffs were yet another matter. The rioters clearly held traditional economic beliefs that denied the role of an unregulated market in times of economic crisis. They questioned the unfettered use of private property, when they seized goods, making clear their belief that a shopkeeper was not the only person to decide what to do with his or her merchandise and that the community had a legitimate voice in its distribution as well. During the Revolutionary War, these beliefs and activities became associated, even synonymous, with patriotic behavior and loyalty to the community. Those who participated in the riots were claiming that by their actions they were expressing their loyalty to the cause, while their targets, such as William Ellison, were exhibiting signs of diminished patriotic allegiance and even of Toryism.[44]

Also remarkable was that many of the rioters were ordinary women who had no public, political role and who had limited control over property. During the Revolution, such women often took the lead in Hudson Valley riots. It was a crowd of women, for example, who first confronted Mrs. Lawrence in 1777 for price-gouging and who by so doing forced the committee to act. Furthermore, the crowd that three times raided Peter Messier's store in Poughkeepsie was composed mainly of women. At a riot in New Windsor, a local observer complained to a tea merchant that "the women! in this place have risen in a mob, and are now selling a box of tea of yours [the owner] at 6s per lb."[45]

The action of women regarding economic matters was not limited to seizures and crowd action. Women also used their power as wives and mothers to disrupt the war effort, if the committees failed to regulate the economy. In August 1776 the women of Kingston surrounded the meeting room of the Committee of Safety and declared that if the food shortages were not resolved, "their husbands and sons shall fight no more."[46] These riots were thus not only economic, but also had clear political implications. The site of the women's protest was neither the Kingston public market nor a shopkeeper's warehouse, but the meeting-house where the town's political authorities conducted business. Finally, these women were not just making economic threats of boycotts or disruptions, but promising political action if their demands were not satisfied.

Women, who had few political rights, were now exerting a public voice about those issues, in which the needs of the domestic sphere crossed those of the public sphere. Women's right to demand salt, tea, or flour at what they considered fair prices fell firmly within the socially and culturally constructed gender roles of eighteenth-century America. Like their counterparts in the French Revolution, women's political action usually formed around issues of family and domestic concerns (particularly food and supplies).[47]

Residents of the mid-Hudson Valley were divided over the best policy to follow in handling the economic dislocations created by the military conflict. Generally, price controls had been needed before the Revolution only in times of economic crisis and only on certain necessities. However, some farm families benefited from wartime inflation, since it increased the profits they earned on the sale of farm produce. Yet many other residents suffered from the depreciated currency and soaring prices changed at shopkeepers' stores. As a result, by the late 1770s, many midvalley residents led the state-wide battle to implement policies that would halt spiraling inflation. Indeed, from 1779 through 1782, calls from the populous midvalley, which did not face a direct military threat, became increasingly pronounced for government regulation of prices, quality, and distribution of various staple products.[48]

The movement for the community regulation of prices and wages and of the distribution of goods occurred because of wartime exigencies. Whether in the eighteenth or the twenty-first century, wars generally engender shortages of goods and demands for personal sacrifice and community-mindedness. As a result of revolutionary problems, both local and provincial authorities began regulating economic affairs. What is remarkable is not these practices per se, but the methods employed to implement them. Official town authorities who regulated prices also sponsored boycotts and denounced tepid Whigs who threatened the goals of the Revolution. The people out-of-doors also used extralegal popular action in the form of seizures, public denunciations, and riots that sometimes supported the local authorities, but that also at times exceeded what officials thought necessary.

Land Confiscation and Its Effects in Dutchess County

Although Dutchess County was beset by food and price rioting and by other popular demonstrations throughout the war, a revolution of even more far-reaching proportions was unfolding there. Indeed, Dutchess witnessed what was, arguably, one of the most dramatic episodes of the Revolution in New York: tenant unrest and the state's confiscation of landlord property.

The Revolution was not the first time that mid-Hudson valley tenants had · resorted to mass violence. Serious conflict had occurred as early as the 1740s, and the Uprising of 1766 was the only time before the Battle of Lexington that British regulars were used in the North American colonies against provincials. This agrarian conflict had little to do with the imperial crisis, but much to do with limited access to land and growing resentment among both longtime tenants and more recent settlers from New England.[49]

At the beginning of the war, both Dutchess County landlords and tenants were generally supportive of, but not enthusiastic about the Revolution. Although some contemporary observers believed that many tenants were Tories who hoped for a British victory that would lead to the confiscation of the large estates and the redistribution of this property among the tenants, there is no strong evidence to affirm that large numbers of tenants in Dutchess were Loyalists, although some undoubtedly were. Allegiances were unstable throughout the war, and Loyalism could also be found among the landlord class.[50]

In 1775 the traditional Dutchess elite continued to represent the county in colonial government. Indeed, landlords Beverly Robinson and Robert

Livingston were elected to the New York Provincial Congress in both 1775 and 1776. Nevertheless, the landed aristocracy was no longer the only voice speaking for the county. The Dutchess delegation in Congress was now almost double the size of the county's representation in the prewar Provincial Assembly and included such middle-class representatives as Dirck Brinckerhoff and Jacobus Swarthout. Although neither Brinckerhoff nor Swarthout were tenants, they were middle-class men drawn from a very different class than the landlord elite and had been elected in the tenant-dominated region of southern Dutchess. Despite these differences, at the outset, both landlord and middle-class representatives shared the common goal of resisting British imperialism and generally worked together in the New York Congress. Once the war began to affect adversely the economy of the Hudson's east bank, however, this alliance weakened. In time, the military conflict and the negative economic consequences that flowed from it sundered the fragile unity between the two groups.[51]

Some of the problems facing tenants on the Hudson's east bank were little different from those confronting freeholders who lived there or on the other side of the river. The economic problems created by the war and the British blockade of New York City had resulted in inflated prices for necessary goods, shortages of essential foodstuffs, and a state tax burden beyond the ability of many to pay. Because of the apparent failure of Dutchess County's traditional leadership to resolve these problems, the "old guard" was effectively pushed from power. In 1777 Robert Livingston lost his reelection bid to the State Assembly, and Beverly Robinson openly declared himself a Tory and fled his estate. Now that landlords had lost their monopolistic hold on political power, or were exposed as Tories, the clamor for the confiscation of Loyalist property began to grow among the county's landless class.[52]

The war had so eroded the tenuous economic conditions that many Dutchess tenants now perceived that freehold ownership of land was their only economic hope. If many Patriot leaders supported the confiscation and sale of Tory property in order to raise money for the war effort, many tenants of southern Dutchess did so because they believed it would lead to their independence and freedom as landowners. As political pressure for land redistribution grew, so too did the possibility that the old, simmering tensions between landlord and tenant might revive, unless some sort of official action on this front was taken. The new state government first approached this problem by confiscating Loyalist-owned manors. In late 1778 a petition from "freeholders and others, inhabitants of the county of Dutchess" stated that unless Loyalist lands were confiscated and redistributed, "tumults and insurrections" might result.[53]

Dutchess County Assemblymen took the lead in calling for land confiscation. Although it was John Morin Scott of New York City who had proposed in the Assembly in 1778 the first serious plan for confiscating Loyalist land, the Dutchess County delegation of Henry Luddington, Jacobus Swarthout, and Dirck

Brinckerhoff became the champions of land confiscation and redistribution. The statewide legislative battle over confiscation can be seen in microcosm in the Dutchess County delegation in the Assembly. Egbert Benson, a conservative revolutionary, who represented landlord interests in the new landscape of popular politics, fought against the confiscation and sale of land in the 1779–1780 Assembly debates. Dirck Brinckerhoff, representing Fishkill in southern Dutchess (where a majority of the householders were tenants) led the fight for confiscation and sale. The legislative battle resulted in a Brinckerhoff victory and the Confiscation Act, which allowed for the confiscation of Loyalist property throughout the state. Brinckerhoff emerged as a champion of tenant-claims for land; Benson, who had previously dominated the Dutchess delegation and been an important provincial-wide voice in the Assembly, lost his bid for reelection.[54]

Ultimately, the Confiscation Act provided for the sale of 496 forfeited lots in Dutchess. Over 80 percent of this land had belonged to the once dominant Loyalist landlords Beverly Robinson and Roger Morris. The law required that lots be no more than 500 acres in size, and 401 separate buyers purchased this land in Dutchess. Although many of these purchasers were already freeholders, some of Robinson's former tenants also purchased the lots they had once worked under lease. In this way, land redistribution of substantial proportion had occurred in the mid-Hudson Valley. Some 150,000 acres of land once possessed by just two landlords had been divided among several hundred residents, including tenants who had not previously owned land.[55]

If tenants demanded land, slaves demanded freedom. Slavery had been an integral part of the economic and social life of the mid-Hudson Valley since the early eighteenth century. Approximately 6 percent of Dutchess County's population in the decade before the Revolution consisted of slaves, and the proportion of slaves on the west bank was probably twice as high. The overwhelming majority of slaves were owned by small freeholders, and very few slaveholders owned more than a handful. In Ulster County, most freeholders did not possess slaves, but those who did averaged about three slaves per household, which was about the same number that the typical Dutchess slaveholder owned.[56]

Although most slaves in the midvalley worked on farms, many were skilled tradesmen and artisans. Hudson Valley slaves worked in grain and flourmills; labored in warehouses on the river docks; and served as teamsters moving goods around the valley and along the river. For the most part, female slaves worked around their owner's home. Michael Groth, the foremost student of slavery in the Hudson Valley, has found that few owners freed their slaves before the Revolution, even though some European Americans were already criticizing the institution.[57]

The rhetoric of the Revolution, with its emphasis on freedom from tyranny and the British attempt to "enslave" North Americans, was surely not lost on African Americans or on many whites. At the outset of the war, some New

Yorkers were already questioning slavery. New York Quakers petitioned the State Assembly very early in the conflict for an end to slavery, and Gov. George Clinton joined the New York Society for Promoting the Manumission of Slaves, which was established in 1785. Nevertheless, although the rhetoric of the Revolution emphasized personal liberty, the wartime need for labor and the heightened fear of slave insurrections overcame the arguments for manumission. Ultimately, the strongest opposition in the midvalley to abolition developed among slaveholding farmers who successfully resisted the ever-growing demand for emancipation for more than a decade after the Revolution.[58]

African-American slaves waged a most powerful battle against slavery in the midvalley, however. The number of slave runaways increased during the war, as slaves used the close proximity of the British army and the various wartime dislocations as their opportunity to flee. Newspaper advertisements seeking the return of runaway slaves reveal that at least sixty slaves escaped from owners in Dutchess County during the war, and the actual number was probably much higher. Some slaves even destroyed their owner's property before fleeing. "Rachel," a Dutchess County slave, fled her master in 1781 with stolen clothes and other belongings. She returned one week later, however, and set her owner's home on fire before escaping south behind British lines.[59]

Although slavery did not receive its death blow in the Revolution, the continued existence of the institution was debated often in the New York Assembly, which actually called for gradual emancipation as early as 1785. Although the Council of Revisions vetoed the bill, the emancipation of slaves in several other northern states, including the newly independent Vermont, kept the debate alive in the decade after the war. Slavery was gradually abolished in New York beginning in 1799 with the passage of an emancipation act. Farmers in Ulster, Orange, and Dutchess, however, remained opposed.[60]

War and Economic Opportunity in the Mid-Hudson Valley

Even though the wartime midvalley economy was characterized by shortages of staple products, hyperinflation, and an increasingly devalued currency, it also offered economic opportunities that were not lost on enterprising farmers and artisans.[61] The enemy blockade halted the importation of British textiles and thereby encouraged increased domestic production of clothing and other manufactured goods. Perhaps most important for Hudson Valley farmers, between 1781 and 1783, the encampment of Gen. George Washington and his Continental army around New Windsor created a large market for agricultural produce. The number of the troops changed from year to year (from only a few hundred to several thousand), but there was, almost without interruption, a body of men and women who needed to be fed, clothed, and supplied on a daily basis.[62]

Although this situation was atypical, most people of the area participated in economic activities to support the war. For example, even before the troops were encamped around New Windsor, the farmers of the region had been brought into a production network that supplied the army wherever it was stationed. As part of this system, the Continental Commissary Department built a series of supply routes and depots throughout the northeastern states of New York, Pennsylvania, and Connecticut.[63]

The extent of wartime production in the mid-Hudson region can be examined through the Coenradt Elmendorph Account Book. Elmendorph was an army commissary, instructed to make purchases for the military throughout Orange and Ulster counties. He was a resident of Kingston, a lieutenant-colonel in the Continental Line, and a person of some wartime prestige in the Hudson Valley. Elmendorph directed purchases, hired laborers to move the produce, employed the butchers and bakers to service the army, and was one of the Continental government's representatives in determining the price of goods for a given locality.[64]

Elmendorph's "Invoice of Supplies, 1778–1779" records in detail the types of goods he purchased, the quantity, the unit cost, and total price. He also listed the farmers from whom he purchased goods, their towns, the date of the purchase, and the payment his customers were to receive. This ledger reveals the market opportunities that the military conflict created for west bank farmers and the extent to which they took advantage of the prospects.

Elmendorph transacted business with 440 customers. Production of alcohol (primarily in the form of distilled grain whiskey and rum) earned the highest profits for local farmers in their dealings with the commissary. Liquor was part of a soldier's daily ration and was used in surgery as an anesthetic. It consequently accounted for nearly 40 percent of local earnings, even though far more farmers engaged in the production of beef or grains than of whiskey. Beef and pork accounted for about 35 percent of Elmendorph's purchases. One hundred and eighty-three farmers produced meat products, but only forty produced alcohol. Elmendorph also purchased grain from local farmers. Two hundred and sixty-six farmers sold, on average, sixty bushels of grain to Elmendorph.[65]

This evidence suggests that a large number of midvalley farmers were engaged in substantial production for the war. Although Patriotism and devotion to the cause cannot be discounted as a possible motivation, economic self-interest induced many farmers to sell. However, if farmers refused to sell, the army would have requisitioned whatever it needed anyway, leaving the farmer in no position to decide what he wanted to sell to the military and what he wanted to dispose of in other ways. The most significant aspect of this production, however, is the way it was marketed. Almost all of the produce was sold to an army agent who paid in cash or notes, an experience that was new to many mid-Hudson farmers, who were more accustomed to exchanging produce with neighbors or bartering with local shopkeepers.

The war years also witnessed an increase in domestic textile manufacturing. Before the Revolution, the North American colonies annually imported more than ten million yards of linen and cloth from England. The nonimportation movement and the Revolution changed that. Not only did the farmers of mid-Hudson communities agree not to import British manufactures, but they began wearing homespun and engaging in domestic manufacturing. To increase wool production the Ulster County Committee of Safety voted in 1775 to "improve the breed, and increase the number of sheep," and tried to secure a pledge from local residents not to kill any "sheep under four years old, or procure them to be killed by others; neither will we sell the best of our sheep to butchers, or others employed by them to purchase, whereby the breed of our sheep is so much injured." Anyone who sold or ate lambs or ewes was denounced as an enemy of the American cause.[66]

Furthermore, during the war, the Ulster Committee of Safety employed hundreds of women to sew stockings and blankets and to weave the fabric needed for military uniforms. The state government assessed local towns a quota of shirts, shoes, and other products, and it then sent to the towns the wool, cloth, or other raw products needed to produce these goods. The local committees distributed raw materials to local farm families, who spun and wove the finished products, which were then collected and sent to the army supplier. For example, in April 1777, the Provincial Congress paid £600 for stockings and blankets to the Ulster Committee, which then distributed the cloth and yarn to local farm families for production. Ulster also became a focal point for shoe manufacturing for the Continental army, as the various county committees collected and then sent hides to Marbletown, where the hides were tanned and then "put-out" to local cordwainers to manufacture shoes at eighteen to twenty shillings a pair.[67]

Even with these developments, the midvalley failed for several reasons to develop into an extensive postwar manufacturing region. First, the market for finished products was still small and dispersed, and after the war those urban areas, where the demand existed, could get their goods more cheaply from British producers. In addition, local merchants in the region (and elsewhere) favored investing in bonds, public certificates, real estate, and a variety of other areas, but not in developing a rural outwork system of manufacturing. These other mediums of investment were potentially much more profitable in the postwar period than a large-scale network of outwork production.[68]

Nevertheless, the midvalley connection to commercial markets received a boost from the war, as military contractors and merchants actively sought farmers' goods and thereby opened up a variety of opportunities and a competitive market hitherto unknown to many yeoman farm families. After the war, speculators from New York City, recognizing the possibilities that lay in developing the Hudson Valley into a sophisticated manufacturing region made their way north to implement their ideas. Daniel Parker and William Duer won military contracts and opened a series of stores in Orange and Ulster to purchase local grain. Dutchess County's Melancton Smith opened a store in 1783 near the old main army camp in New Windsor with the plan of promoting a continued high level of market production in the area. In this way, the war impelled farmers to view their production and trade in market terms.[69]

The .Revolutionary War had other profound effects on the mid-Hudson Valley economy. First, the valley, like much of the northeast, was flooded with a variety of paper currencies. Some small farmers had never used cash before, and most had never used it regularly. The war, therefore, helped produce a farm population increasingly astute in commercial matters. Before the war many farmers had dealt only with neighbors or their local shopkeeper. These exchanges were primarily for obtaining goods; the farm produce they exchanged was a tool to help obtain the goods they needed.

Although these economic developments were significant for the war period, the increased production of agricultural goods and textiles was not sustained in the years following the war. Essentially, this enlarged production, much like the increased use of cash was a response to immediate wartime needs. The relatively limited market for manufactured goods, as well as the existence of alternative, and more profitable, investments for those with capital, restrained, at least temporarily, the region's long-term economic development.

The Aftermath of War: The Mid-Hudson Valley after 1783

How had the Revolution changed the mid-Hudson Valley? The most famous fictional character to live through the struggle, Washington Irving's Rip Van Winkle, found that the Revolution brought about dramatic changes to his community. After he returned to town from the Catskills and some twenty years of sleep, he was befuddled by the unfamiliar surroundings and was briefly mistaken for a Tory. Indeed, he found that the "very character of the people seemed changed. There was a busy, bustling, disputatious tone about it, instead of the accustomed phlegm and drowsy tranquility."[70]

What did Rip detect to be the big difference? Politics! A new democratic spirit of debate and discussion (indeed, he is not uncoincidentally returning to town on election day!). Instead of a small group of Dutch elders sitting on the porch of the local tavern dictating the activities of this fictionalized town, villagers are debating and arguing politics, "haranguing vehemently about the rights of citizens-elections-members of congress."[71] In essence, what Washington Irving described in a fictionalized form was a far more democratic, egalitarian society, which he believed, had emerged in the central Hudson in the years following the Revolution.

Much happened during the Revolution to support this fictionalized view. In the first place, the war created new opportunities for political advancement. Before the war, the political leadership in each of the three counties under analysis came from a small, socially and economically prominent part of the population. New leaders emerged in all three counties. Some had been wealthy and prominent before the war, but many had been modest in their backgrounds and experience, even if they had been ambitious in their goals. These men used the new town and county committees, the dramatically expanded state assembly, and the broader franchise offered by the Revolution to advance themselves and their own self-interest.

A new "class" of leadership, represented best by middle-class leaders like George Clinton and Dirck Brinckerhoff, emerged and replaced established families that had led their towns and villages for generations. Many of these new leaders began their political careers serving on local committees of safety and inspection and quickly graduated to representing their neighbors in the New York Provincial Congress and the State Assembly. Yet, many of the old families remained powerful and influential. The Hasbroucks and Hardenberghs continued to wield great economic power and remained important political leaders on the Hudson's west bank, but they now did so in a vastly different political and social environment, one in which power was competitively struggled for and, often, shared.

Some of the most prominent prewar leaders of the mid-Hudson did not survive the war with their power intact. Some, like Dutchess landlord Beverly Robinson became Tories, forfeiting their elite status. Nevertheless, most of the truly powerful families in the midvalley retained their status and property. Even though the Livingstons of Dutchess suffered politically during the war (Phillip lost his reelection bid for county sheriff, and Judge Robert his seat in the Assembly), they reemerged in the years following the struggle as important political players in local, state, and national politics. The various branches of the Livingston family retained their large landholdings and tenants, and continued to enjoy enormous power through the nineteenth century.

Slavery in the mid-Hudson Valley survived the war virtually intact. Although the number of runaways increased, midvalley farmers were among the staunchest defenders of chattel slavery and resisted efforts to end the institution. Indeed, farmers in the three mid-Hudson counties were still fighting against the gradual emancipation bill in New York at the end of the eighteenth century.

Probably the most dramatic development of the Revolution in the mid-Hudson was the impact of the Loyalist land confiscation program. As described, hundreds of different buyers purchased lots carved from the estates of Roger Morris, Beverly Robinson, and others, many of the buyers being former tenants on these estates. Farmers, who once worked on land that had been leased for several generations and for which they were required to make improvements and perhaps work for several days for the lord, now owned their own five-hundred-acre lots with no obligations to former landlords. The fact that many of these new independent landholders lost title to their land over the next few years because of an inability to pay taxes or to meet loan payments does not detract from what had been one of the most important developments of the war and which surely was of great importance to these families. Although tenantry continued in Dutchess and the northern valley after the Revolution, the land redistribution of the 1780s opened opportunities for land ownership and free-hold status previously denied to hundreds of Dutchess farmers.

Notes

1. Peter Kalm, *Travels in North America: The English Version of 1770*, ed. Adolph B. Benson (New York, 1987), 335, 647, and Richard Smith, *Journal from New York to Albany*, reprinted in Nelson Greene, ed., *History of the Valley of the Hudson*, 2 vols. (Chicago, 1931), 1: 9, describe the midvalley in the eighteenth century. Economic life in the Hudson can best be viewed through town records and mercantile accounts. For the west bank, see *"Benjamin Snyder Account Book, 1765–1798,"* New–York Historical Society, N.Y.C. (NYHS), and the *"Kingston Trustees Minutes, 1736–1783,"* Ulster County Clerk's Office, Kingston, New York. For the valley's backcountry, see Martin Bruegel, *Farm, Shop, Landing: The Rise of a Market Society in the Hudson Valley, 1780–1860* (Durham, N.C., 2002), 13–31.

2. Nathaniel Bartlett Sylvester, *History of Ulster County* (New Philadelphia, 1880); Edward Ruttenber, *History of Orange County, New York* (New York, 1911). The best analysis of mid-Hudson Valley slavery is Michael Groth, "Slaveholders and Manumission in Dutchess County, New York," *New York History* 78 (1997): 33–50, and *idem*, "Forging Freedom in the Mid-Hudson Valley: The End of Slavery and the Formation of a Free African-American Community 1770–1850" (Ph.D. diss., Binghamton University, 1994).

3. Alice Kenney, *Stubborn for Liberty: The Dutch in New York* (Syracuse, 1975), 69–70, 88–89; Thomas S. Wermuth, *Rip Van Winkle's Neighbors: The Transformation of Rural Society in the Hudson River Valley* (Albany, 2001), 15–16.

4. Wermuth, *Rip Van Winkle's Neighbors*, 38–42. Edward Countryman, *A People in Revolution: The American Revolution and Political Society in New York, 1760–1790* (Baltimore, 1982), 26–27; the phrase is from Countryman and is particularly accurate when comparing the west bank to Dutchess County. Carl Nordstrom, *Frontier Elements in a Hudson River Village* (Port Washington, N.Y., 1973).

5. Patricia Bonomi, *A Factious People: Politics and Society in Colonial New York* (New York, 1971), 188–190; Staughton Lynd, "Who Should Rule at Home: Dutchess County in the American Revolution," in his *Class Conflict, Slavery and the United States Constitution* (Westport, Conn., 1980), 30–31; Henry Noble McCracken, *Old Dutchess Forever! The Story of an American County* (New York, 1956), 470–71.

150<space/>*Thomas S. Wermuth*

6. Bonomi, *Factious People*, 180–96; Sung Bok Kim, *Landlord and Tenant in Colonial New York* (Chapel Hill, N.C., 1978), 235–80.

7. In Ulster County in 1790, 3,945 of 4,590 farmers owned their own freehold, Census for the State of New York for 1855 (Albany, 1857). For the east bank, see Kim, *Landlord and Tenant*, 39–40; 235–37.

8. Bonomi, *Factious People,* 220–23; Kim, *Landlord and Tenant*, 381–96.

9. "Letter from an Anonymous Kingston Farmer" in Peter Force, ed., *American Archives*, 4ᵗʰ Ser. (Washington, D.C., 1837–1853), 1: 1230, herein cited as *American Archives*; Resolves of New Windsor Committee, *American Archives,* 2:131–33.

10. Countryman, *People in Revolution*, 104–105.

11. Lynd, "Who Should Rule at Home," 32–34; George Dangerfield, *Chancellor Robert Livingston of New York, 1746–1813* (New York, 1960), 60–62; and Philip L. White, *The Beekmans of New York in Politics and Commerce, 1647–1877* (New York, 1956).

12. *Historical Memoirs from July 12, 1776 to July 25, 1778 of William Smith*, ed. William Sabine (New York, 1958), 118; Lynd, "Who Should Rule at Home?" 34–35.

13. Countryman, *People in Revolution*, 313–316. For background on political divisions in Dutchess, including Brinckerhoff's rise to power, see Bonomi, *Factious People*, 245–46.

14. Wermuth, *Rip Van Winkle's Neighbors*, 38–40.

15. Robert Boyd to George Clinton, July 3, 1776, *Public and Private Papers of George Clinton*, 1:244–47; E. M. Ruttenber, *A History of New Windsor, Orange County* (Newburgh, N.Y., 1911).

16. "Minutes of the Provincial Congress, May 25, 1776," *American Archives*, 6:1333. Background on Hardenbergh can be found in Sylvester, *History of Ulster County*, 84–87, and Countryman, *People in Revolution*, 225.

17. This ongoing political intrigue can be followed in "Hasbrouck to New York Congress, Kingston, Mar. 8, 1776," *American Archives*, 4:137–38; "Minutes of the Provincial Congress, May 31, 1776," *American Archives*, 6:1349; and "Ulster Committee to New York Congress, June 14, 1776," *American Archives*, 6:898–900.

18. "Ulster Committee to New York Provincial Congress, July 4, 1776," *American Archives*, 6:1273–1274.

19. "Cadwallader Colden, Jr., to Ulster County Committee, June 27, 1776," *American Archives*, 6:1112. See also, Eugene Fingerhut, *Survivor: Cadwallader Colden II in Revolutionary America* (Washington, D.C., 1983), 53–54.

20. E. Wilder Spaulding, *His Excellency George Clinton: Critic of the Constitution* (New York, 1938), 39–41; John P. Kaminski, *George Clinton: Yeoman Politician of the New Republic* (Madison, Wis., 1993).

21. "Col. John Hasbrouck to New York Congress, Mar. 18, 1776," *American Archives*, 5:138; Countryman, *People in Revolution*, 198.

22. Washington's quote is cited in Louis V. Mills, "Attack in the Highlands, the Battle of Ft. Montgomery," *Hudson Valley Regional Review* (Sept. 2000), 39–40.

23. Mark Lender and James Kirby Martin, *A Respectable Army: The Military Origins of the Republic* (New York, 1981), 83–87.

24. Mills, "Attack in the Highlands," 39–40.

25. "General John Vaughan to Sir William Howe, Oct. 17, 1777," *Dutchess County Historical Society Yearbook* 21 (1936), 118–19.

26. Lincoln Diamont, *The Chaining of the Hudson: The Fight for the River in the American Revolution* (New York, 1989), 156.

27. Diamont, *Chaining of the Hudson*, 158–74; William Sterne Randall, *Benedict Arnold: Patriot and Traitor* (New York, 1990), 526–37.

28. "Minutes of Mar. 14, 1775, New Windsor Town Meeting," *American Archives*, 2:131–33. The resolves and proclamations of New Paltz are in *American Archives*, 2:832–33, 1183–84.

29. "Ulster County Committee Minutes," Apr. 7, 1775, *American Archives*, 2:298–99.

30. "Resolves of the Ulster Association, 1775," *American Archives*, 2:132–33.

31. The pamphlets were also burned in Marbletown; see *American Archives*, 1:1100, 1183–84; 1201.

32. For the "non-importation" agreements in Ulster, see Ulster County Association, Jan. 6, 1775, *American Archives*, 1:1100–1101. For the general background and purpose behind the "non-importation" movement, see Pauline Maier, *From Resistance to Revolution* (New York, 1972), 137–38.

33. These activities were not unique to the Revolution. Midvalley communities had a long history of regulating economic activities within their towns. See, for example, "Minutes of Corporation of the Town of Kingston," 12 Feb. 1748, Ulster County Clerk's Office.

34. Alphonse Clearwater, *History of Ulster County, N.Y.* (Kingston, N.Y., 1907), 281–82; Sylvester, *History of Ulster County*, 202.

35. Some of the prices were firmly set by the Congress, such as wheat at thirteen shillings per bushel, and "good merchantable wheat flour" at one pound sixteen shillings per hundred gross weight. Other prices, such as leather and various animal skins were set "in the proportion of the price they usually bore to raw hides." See *Journals of the Provincial Congress*, 1:455–57, Apr. 3, 1778, for a full listing of the regulation of prices. Ulster County's call for new price controls can be found in "Ulster County Association instructions to Assemblymen, 1779" Matthew Visscher Folder, Albany Institute; "Ulster

County to New York State Legislature, 1782," Box 4239, New York State Library, Albany; Dutchess County's requests can be found "Jacob Heermane to Council of Safety, Nov. 1777," *Journals of the Provincial Congress*, 2:457.

36. "Henry Luddington to New York Council of Safety, Dec. 3, 1776," *Journals of the Provincial Congress*, 2:355.

37. *American Archives*, 5:635, 638–39.

38. "Ulster County Committee to New York Convention," Nov. 18, 1776, *Journals of the Provincial Congress*, 2:229–230.

39. Ibid.

40. Barbara Clark Smith, "Food Riots and the American Revolution," *William & Mary Quarterly*, 3rd Ser., 51 (Jan. 1994): 15.

41. Correspondence of John Hathorn, Dec. 2, 1776, Ruttenber, *History of New Windsor*, 67–68; and Countryman, *People in Revolution*, 183.

42. Correspondence of John Hathorn, Dec. 2, 1776, Ruttenber, *History of New Windsor*, 67.

43. For examples of prewar economic regulations see the "Minutes of Corporation of the Town of Kingston" Mar. 2, 1772, [for regulation of wheat prices], and Mar. 2, 1728, Nov. 8, 1752 [for regulations on other economic activities], Ulster County Clerk's Office.

44. For a discussion of the political implications of revolutionary rioting, see Smith, "Food Riots," *William & Mary Quarterly*, 5–12. For suspicions that Ellison was unpatriotic because of his economic dealings, see "Boyd to Clinton, July 3, 1776," *Clinton Papers*, 1:244–47.

45. "James H. Kip to James Caldwell, New Windsor, July 14, 1777," *Journals of the Provincial Congress*, 506.

46. New York Convention Proceedings, Aug. 1776, *American Archives*, 5th Series, 1:1542–43.

47. Linda Kerber, *Women of the Republic: Intellect and Ideology in Revolutionary America* (New York, 1980), 44.

48. For New York farming interests that supported both inflationary policies and paper currency, see Matson, "Liberty, Jealousy, and Union: The New York Economy in the 1780s," in Paul Gilje and William Pencak, eds., *New York in the Age of the Constitution* (New York, 1992), 114–115.

49. Kim, *Landlord and Tenant*, 367–415; Bonomi, *Factious People*, 218–24; Philip Schwarz, *The Jarring Interests: New York's Boundary Makers, 1664–1776* (Albany, 1979).

50. Lynd, "Who Should Rule at Home?" 34. Lynd's research on the Revolution in Dutchess County remains the standard interpretation. The following section on the debate over land confiscation in Dutchess is informed by Lynd's research.

51. Countryman, *People in Revolution*, 215–17; Lynd, "Who Should Rule at Home?" 34–36.

52. Lynd, "Who Should Rule at Home?" 42–43.

53. Ibid., 46.

54. Ibid., 51–53; Countryman, *People in Revolution*, 173–74.

55. Lynd, "Who Should Rule at Home?" 52–53; 59–60.

56. Groth, "Forging Freedom in the Mid-Hudson Valley," 75; Federal Manuscript Census for New York, Ulster County, 1800.

57. Michael Groth, "Laboring for Freedom in Dutchess County," 60–62, in Myra B. Young Armstead, ed., *Mighty Change, Tall Within: Black Identity in the Hudson Valley* (Albany, 2003). For slave life in the mid-Hudson Valley in the eighteenth century, see Margaret Washington, ed., *Narrative of Sojourner Truth* (New York, 1993), 6–8. Truth spent the first thirty years of her life in Ulster County.

58. For an overview of the antislavery arguments during the Revolution, see Gary Nash, *Race and Revolution* (Madison, Wis., 1990); Groth, "Forging Freedom in the Mid-Hudson Valley."

59. Groth, "Forging Freedom in the Mid-Hudson Valley," 85–86; and idem, "Laboring for Freedom," 70–71.

60. Countryman, *People in Revolution*, 284–85; Groth, "Slaveholders and Manumission," 35–36.

61. For new policies of taxation, see Robert Becker, *Revolution, Reform, and the Politics of Taxation in America: 1763–1783* (Baton Rouge, La., 1980).

62. The extent of Ulster's production for the war can be seen in George Clinton's report for 1778, where he argued that the entire west bank, "Having long been the seat of the war," had been "ravaged plundered and greatly exhausted." "Clinton to F. M. Dana, Feb. 17, 1778," *Clinton Papers*, 2:824–25. Indeed, in 1778, the Continental army was fed almost exclusively on Ulster wheat; see *Olde Ulster*, 3:365–69.

63. Louis C. Hatch, *The Administration of the American Revolutionary Army* (New York, 1904), 86–115; Flick, *Revolution in New York*, 179–202.

64. This and the next several paragraphs are based on an analysis of the "Coenradt Elmendorph Account Book, 1778–79," New York State Library, Albany, and Ulster County Wills and Inventories, 1760–1791, Ulster County Surrogate Court, Boxes 9–49.

65. "Coenradt Elmendorph Account Book, 1778–79."

66. James Shepherd and Gary M. Walton, *Shipping, Maritime Trade, and the Economic Development of Colonial North America* (New York, 1972), 110–13, 182; "Ulster County Committee Resolves," Mar. 14, 1775, *American Archives*, 4th Ser., 2:132; and Alexander C. Flick, ed., *The American Revolution in New York* (New York, 1926), 184.

67. Flick, *American Revolution in New York*, 187. See also the reports of the commissaries of clothing in *Clinton Papers*. Commissar John Henry worked out of Shawangunk—see his report of Aug. 26, 1778, *Clinton Papers*, 3:693; 4:31–32. Commissar Peter Curtenius was in charge of the store in Wallkill. See his report in *Clinton Papers*, 3:692.

68. James Henretta, "War for Independence and American Economic Development," in Ronald Hoffman, John McCusker, and Russell Menand, eds., *The Economy of Early America: The Revolutionary Period, 1763–1790* (Charlotteville, Va., 1988), 81–86; Virginia Harrington discusses New York merchants' fondness for provincial bonds and real estate, not manufacturing in her *The New York Merchant on the Eve of the Revolution* (New York, 1935), Chapter 4.

69. For the Duer and Parker plans, see Duer to William Alexander, June 15, 1781, Alexander Papers, NYHS; Daniel Parker to Duer, June 26, 1781, Duer Papers, NYHS. For Smith's store, still in operation in 1785, see Duer Papers, Box 8, NYHS.

70. Washington Irving, *Sketch Book* (New York, 1915), 50–51.

71. Ibid., 51.

7

Albany County

Stefan Bielinski

Historians have referred to Albany County as "the crossroads of the American Revolution."[1] Although Albanians had always lived at a geographical juncture, after 1763 they were also at a crossroads in their own lives. They were torn between a heritage of living off the fruits of subsistence agriculture and of now being able to exploit farm and forest for profit. At the same time, new immigrants further increased the diversity of the county's population and challenged entrenched interests. Many of the newcomers had political and social alliances that brought them opportunities formerly reserved for New York-born elites. In 1775 the county's large settler population would be caught in a crossfire, as the Hudson-Mohawk corridor became an avenue of war and a major battleground. Rich in resources and in the line of military march, few Albany people could avoid the demands and dilemmas that powerful external forces now placed upon them. These were trying times for upriver people from all backgrounds and stations.[2]

By the eve of the American Revolution, Albany was the largest and most dynamic of the fourteen counties in the royal province of New York. Even though its physical size had been reduced dramatically by the recent formation of frontier Tryon, Charlotte, Cumberland, and Gloucester Counties, its population had more than doubled since 1756 to 42,706, a number that included 3,877 slaves but not the Native Americans who nonetheless still constituted a significant element of the population. In 1772 the county was organized into seventeen districts (roughly akin to towns), but the centrally located city of Albany, the county's most important trading center and entry point for new people, still politically dominated the county. This early American entrepôt was located at the crossroads of the Hudson-Mohawk corridors and was well on its way to becoming an important production center.

The county's other settlements radiated out from Albany city. Surrounding it was the large manor of Rensselaerswyck—a well-settled Dutch land grant— that in 1775 included three distinct plantations on both sides of the Hudson. At the time, more than a third of the county's people were residents of either Albany or Rensselaerswyck. Schenectady, which was located about eighteen miles from Albany city, had started as a farming community but was now a borough that was emerging as an independent market for Mohawk Valley products. East of Albany city, across the Hudson, were the old agricultural settlements of Kinderhook, Coxsackie, Schoharie, Half Moon, Hoosick, Schaghticoke, and the German Camp (or Germantown), which was part of Livingston Manor. North of Albany in the Hudson Valley were Ballstown, Saratoga, Cambridge, Kings District, and Great Imboght; these communities were more remote, more recently settled, and much less populated. Lansingburgh was located north of Albany and east of the Hudson but had not yet achieved district status. Smaller numbers of settlers were isolated at marginal locations in the mountain regions of the Heldebergs and the Catskills to the southwest of Albany and the Adirondacks foothills to the northwest, and in the hardscrabble uplands along the New England border.[3]

Albany's original European population was descended from the New Netherland Dutch. They had been joined in the early eighteenth century by German and Scottish newcomers and some English and Irish soldiers and opportunists. By the 1750s, all these newcomers had intermarried with the children of New Netherland to produce a substantial American-born population that was greatly augmented after 1763 by a significant wave of New Englanders, émigrés from other American colonies, and Europeans. African-American slaves, who constituted almost 10 percent of the total population, resided chiefly in the oldest and most settled parts of the county. In these areas, slavery was widespread but still concentrated around the wealthiest colonial families.[4]

Albany people were apprehensive and frustrated about the imperial relationship, even before the British ministry sought to impose new taxes to help pay for the Seven Years' War (1756–1763). They already had firsthand experience in that war with the depredations of large British armies and their disregard for American rights; they were also affronted by the closing off of the frontier in 1763 and 1768. The Stamp Act and other revenue-raising measures were reviled and resisted in the Hudson-Mohawk region. Then the royal government in New York parceled out most of the remaining unclaimed acreage in the area to British favorites, again frustrating Albany people in their desire for the uniquely American commodity—investment land! Albany men had fought against the French and were offended when preference was given to politically connected New Yorkers and the Indians. Standing firm against the royal government's plan to appoint a stamp tax collector for Albany, in early 1766 the city's "sons of liberty" lashed out at suspected applicants and produced a constitution signed by ninety-four men. They called on Schenectady and the other districts to join them. Although the charged atmosphere improved when the Stamp Act was withdrawn, across the county a division appeared between those aligning with the British government in New York and those who would follow a more independent vision of what was best for Albany. This new condition became more acute in the decade that followed.[5]

Although bitter memories of British mistreatment rankled many people in the region, it was Albany's own growth and development over the next ten years that brought affairs to a head. As crossroads and landings grew into actual communities, more products were needed to sustain the lives of a larger settler population. Ironically, it was the mostly European newcomers who initially sought to exploit the natural resources found in the American wilderness. At the same time, entrepreneurial Americans were eager to take advantage of new technologies and a talented labor pool of newcomers. However, these would-be investors were frustrated by British manufacturing prohibitions and by a perceived reluctance on the part of the royal government to make land grants to patent partnerships that consisted only of Americans.

Despite festering animosities, Albany County nonetheless boomed, as new settlers started to farm the land. Local landlords and entrepreneurs sought to turn farm and forest produce into commercial products instead of merely exporting cut and processed staples to resource-starved British factories and mills. Because New York's population was expanding rapidly, trade and commerce flowed from Albany south to New York City and north to British-controlled Canada. During the early 1770s, Hudson River skippers began to take their cargoes to the West Indies, while investors looked to forbidden markets beyond. Local entrepreneurs advertised in the *Albany Gazette*, which began publication in 1771. With population growth fueled by natural increase and by an influx of new business and professional people, new development features including roads and waterways, docks, mills, kilns, and yards appeared on the socioeconomic landscape as wide-open Albany reached for sustained economic growth.[6]

This new development was hindered by the imperial crises that followed implementation of the Tea Act in 1773. During the summer of 1774, a city-based Albany committee secretly voted to support sending New York delegates to the Continental Congress. In January 1775 a county "Committee of Correspondence, Safety, and Protection," which contained people from additional settlements, met publicly at an Albany tavern and agreed to send representatives to a Provincial Congress and to encourage the districts to form their own action committees. However, not all of the county's diverse communities dealt with the situation in the same way. The city of Albany and surrounding Rensselaerswyck took the lead in resistance activities. These long-established communities contained few Britons and were most prominent at county meetings. They also sought to have the county committee replace the civil government, whose officers were led by royal appointees. Schenectady formed its own committee that quickly sought to take charge on the Mohawk frontier. Most of the other less-populated districts set up their committees and chose delegates to the county committee. However, they strained to implement the county committee's decrees on the local level.

As the ice went out of the waterways and farmers prepared to plant crops, the action at Lexington and Concord, and, closer to home, the American capture of Crown Point and Ticonderoga, caught most Albany people unaware and unprepared. Some grasped the gravity of the new military situation, but most people remained focused on their usual economic activities. With royal government in New York in disarray, extralegal provincial congresses and local committees spurred the people into action.

Led by Chairman Abraham Yates Jr., and other Albany-based advocates of American liberties, the insurgent county committee led resistance activities. It urged the localities to organize, sign a nonimportation agreement, and to assure Patriot brethren beyond the Albany stockade that "we mean to Co-operate in this arduous struggle for Liberty to the utmost of our Power." The county committee took steps to collect relief materials, to identify potential enemies of liberty, and to support the formation of a new militia.[7]

In the spring of 1775, the Provincial Congress reconstituted the colonial militia to protect American liberties. By the end of summer, eighteen Albany County regiments were organized representing each of the districts. Merchant-landowner Abraham Ten Broeck was named commander of the county militia, and each unit was staffed with local officers commissioned by the Provincial Congress. As in colonial times, militia service was an ongoing obligation for white males. But now, the demands made on county residents increased dramatically, because the Albany committee frequently called on the militia to protect needed resources, intimidate and apprehend suspected Tories, and even to march into battle. Throughout the war years, units of the county militia were mobilized and sent in all directions from Albany. In the fall of 1777, virtually the entire county militia went to Saratoga, where Albany men helped thwart the British offensive. Although all adult males were eligible for militia service, militia companies functionally were composed of young or recently arrived men from the countryside, while their officers were prominent merchants and landholders and their sons. Adult artisans, transporters, and farmers frequently were exempted, because they were needed for the homefront war effort. At the onset of each emergency, an allotment of soldiers was drafted out of each militia unit and sent to Ticonderoga or the Mohawk Valley for active duty. The absence of these residents placed great strains on the family and community economies they left behind.

At the intercolonial level, a newly formed Continental army placed Gen. Philip Schuyler in command of the Northern Department. Four Continental regiments, called the New York Line, were filled with soldiers enlisted from the militia companies. The Continental Congress commissioned the officers. Commissary and quartermaster departments, created to provision and supply the troops, were headquartered in New York, in the mid-Hudson region, and in Albany. The Second Regiment of the Line represented Albany and the countryside to the north. It was commanded by Goose Van Schaick who was, like Schuyler and Ten Broeck, a veteran of the French and Indian War. Most of its officers were sons of prominent New Netherland ancestry families.

From the beginning of the conflict, a British attack from Canada was expected, and the Champlain-Hudson corridors figured to become scenes of battle. From their Albany homes, General Schuyler and Colonel Van Schaick took charge of filling out rosters, mobilizing defenses, helping establish supply networks, and dealing with the Iroquois, whose neutrality (if not support) was viewed as critical to the war effort and to the safety of the region. Merchants, artisans, transporters, and agriculturists were asked to contribute their specific talents and resources in defense of American liberties. Moreover, a widely representative Albany County committee pressed their neighbors from Cambridge in the north to Catskill in the south to participate in the war effort.[8]

In well-populated Albany, Rensselaerswyck, and Schenectady, the committee was successful in engendering support and in identifying and neutralizing those who opposed resistance activities. Merchants and shippers were watched to keep them from profiteering and dealing in restricted commodities. But in the expansive and more recently settled Albany countryside, some farmers (especially those newcomers without extensive kinship ties to older communities) sought to tend their fields and stock. Some rural districts answered county committee requests with petitions to be excused from participating in a military mobilization. Motives for nonparticipation were complex and only became clear as the conflict developed.

The county endured its first test later in 1775, when the Continental Congress ordered Schuyler to attack British strongholds to the north. Although the Continental army constituted the actual invasion force, the Albany militia was called on to garrison Fort Ticonderoga and other newly acquired northern outposts, to establish transportation links, and to maintain supply lines for the invading Americans. However, the initiative failed, placed a wintertime strain on Albany resources, revealed that many county people did not support such aggressive measures, and assured that the British would seek revenge in the months to come. The ill-fated campaign also brought to Albany County a large number of soldiers and their families who had left Quebec to find liberty. Many of these French-ancestry Canadians would find new homes in the upper Hudson and Mohawk Valleys. But until the return of peace, they were refugees.[9]

The beginning of 1776 was much different from the previous year, as most Albany people now began to grasp the gravity of the situation and to understand that they had reason to fear the future. New York's royal government had ceased to exist, leaving the Albany County Committee of Correspondence to take charge on the homefront. First, it launched a concerted effort to collect spare arms and ordnance in the county for the American army besieging Boston. It then began an active campaign, first against "non-associators" and then against a growing number of "disaffected" peoples who were now identified as "enemies of Liberty!" Overt Tories first left for Canada and later for British-occupied New York City. Others, like the Tunnicliffs, an extended family of recent English émigrés, withdrew to the Unadilla River, and to the more remote parts of the county. Others, including Abraham C. Cuyler, an Albany native and the last royal mayor, were apprehended and sent to New England, where they would pose less of a threat to the county's internal security. More recently arrived royal place-holders like Postmaster John Monier would be incarcerated in the newly established Tory jail or placed under house arrest. The removal of all these British adherents from active life left the committee in control of their property and of the persons they left behind.[10]

Watershed events during the summer of 1776 set up an irrevocable course of action. The Declaration of Independence, the British occupation of greater New York City, and the attack from Canada placed Albany County directly in the line of fire. Military preparedness took on a new urgency. Therefore, Schuyler began building roads and readying bateaux and other watercraft to carry soldiers and supplies to the anticipated front lines in the north. In the months that followed, the old fort and hospital at Albany were reinforced; an armory and powder house were erected; a barracks was built in Schenectady; Schoharie and Schaghticoke were fortified; and a blockhouse was established at Ballstown to protect the county's northern borders.

With the invasion of Canada in 1775, Albany had reverted to its historic role as a staging area for military operations. In the years that followed, large armies were massed at Albany and its environs. Most of these American soldiers came from other colonies and needed to be quartered, supplied, and provisioned. Continental commissary and quartermaster offices were set up in Albany and staffed with local merchants who were deputized to find and secure supplies and provisions from a large but increasingly depleted countryside. An outstanding prewar breadbasket, in the autumn of 1776 greater Albany experienced a stunted harvest caused by the pressure of an anticipated British attack; the reluctance of a large, unsympathetic (if not hostile) segment of its population who were hesitant to part with their crops; and the loss of many young farmers and husbandmen to military service.

The closing off of New York City and the lower Hudson Valley created serious shortages throughout the county. Once Albany farmers had diverted enough of their harvests to family subsistence, they had little left over for sale. Those who hoarded country products or sold imported items were likely to be branded as Tories and thus have their stocks and staples confiscated. Every household in the county felt the effects of scarcity, because all producers and vendors eventually lost control of their ability to do business.

The British occupation of lower New York sent hundreds of wealthy Patriots upriver to the safety of family holdings in the city of Albany and its countryside. Prewar commercial links were severed; dozens of individuals who had conducted business in Albany and New York City were now in exile upriver and unable to connect with the Manhattan port area. At the same time, vulnerable settlers on the large and undefended frontier were leaving their farms and retreating to the safety of the more settled areas. By the end of 1776, the county's most populated areas felt the burden of these increasingly demanding refugee groups.

The situation was grim. The American army had been pushed out of lower New York, and the peripatetic state Convention was struggling to form a new government. To compound these problems, Albany people understood that a more determined British offensive would take place in 1777. To check potential Tory incursions, in the fall of 1776 Ranger companies were organized and stationed at Ballstown, Coxsackie, Schoharie, and other vulnerable locations. Throughout the next spring, the county committee accelerated its efforts to maintain and improve supply and communications lines and to take an even firmer hand at rooting out the enemies of American liberty who still lived in the county.[11]

Influenced by disparately cautious newcomers from Albany and Massachusetts, the old farming village of Kinderhook stood out in its reluctance to support the American cause. Although Patriots were found in the local militia, the Kinderhook committee was unable to comply with Albany's directives and generally could not be counted on to fill militia or supply quotas or to suppress internal enemies. On several occasions, the county committee sent militia units and rangers to apprehend troublemakers. Among the most recalcitrant native sons were the Van Schaacks. Peter was a one-time New York attorney of some distinction, whose conscience prevented him from supporting any war. His older brother, Henry, was a complex character who evolved from Whig committee member to Tory prisoner and then exile in New England. Insulated by geography from the actual fighting, multiethnic Kinderhook never developed an effective revolutionary movement. Despite Albany's prodding, it was known as a Tory haven throughout the war. In the spring of 1777, the fear of Tory activities prompted General Gates to station Continental soldiers in the Kinderhook District. Because of its somewhat isolated inland location, multiethnic Kinderhook people were never directly stressed by military imperatives.[12]

Immediately east of Kinderhook was the King's District, which had been settled a decade earlier by Connecticut Whigs who had been frustrated in their attempts to secure a New York patent for land technically within the boundaries of Van Rensselaer Manor. These settlers represented a growing New England presence within eastern New York's emerging "Yankee Zone." In contrast to unresponsive Kinderhook, the revolutionary cause could count on "a thousand men" under arms in the King's District (today's Canaan, New York) and on its leaders to lend support and suppress Tories. Politically ambitious landholder Matthew Adgate emerged from this group as a revolutionary leader of statewide importance.[13]

Because large invasion forces threatened Albany from three directions in 1777, county people braced for an unprecedented but certain siege. During the summer, farmers in the outlying districts were instructed to take their remaining livestock and other animals beyond the range of British foragers. At old Saratoga, General Schuyler's extensive farmlands were not burned as tradition claims, but his estate was evacuated, and many of his terrified neighbors fell back to Albany, leaving fields and farms to the mercy of the invaders. At the same time, Schaghticoke farmers were offering to sell their abandoned crops to the Continental army.

At harvest time, the bounty of eastern Albany County Schaghticoke and Hoosick farms did not escape the notice of John Burgoyne's advancing and hungry army. On August 16, Hessian hunters headed for a supposed supply cache at Bennington. They were ambushed and routed by American forces along the Walloomsac River a few miles west of the new independent "nation" of Vermont. Among those killed in the engagement was Francis Pfister, a one-time British officer and engineer and one of a number of loyal British subjects who had settled in the greater Hoosick Valley just prior to the outbreak of war. He was a member of a Tory militia unit that threatened the New Englanders and native New Yorker Patriots. They were in the majority in the Hoosick, Schaghticoke, and Cambridge districts, but the advancing British armies had plundered their farms. After the so-called Battle of Bennington, most of these eastern New York Loyalists fled to Canada.

Burgoyne's massive army moved west across the Hudson River on September 13, 1777. Over the next month, one of the most significant military actions in American history unfolded across the farms of northern Albany County. Most farmers had already fled either south to Albany or north to British Canada. Militiamen, suppliers, and transporters from every part of the county played important parts in this great American victory. However, the battle left the landscape so devastated that it remained unproductive for many years. During the Saratoga campaign, Albany served as a staging area for the American defense. Soldiers and supplies were shipped north on newly made bateaux, while the sick and wounded turned the former British army hospital in Albany into a major medical center.[14]

With the simultaneous approach of British ships from the south, the Dutch and German farmers of exposed Coxsackie and Great Imboght (Catskill) districts were instructed to drive their stock into the forest to prevent capture, to pack their valuables for a speedy withdrawal, and to ship wheat and grains to the comparative safety of Albany City. Southern county farmers had been early supporters of the fight for American liberty. More than 220 freeholders signed the "Coxsackie Association" in May 1775, and the region contributed soldiers and supplies throughout the war. The Eleventh Regiment of the Albany County Militia protected the southern west bank and also fought at Saratoga. While local militia stood with Continental forces at Saratoga, the war came dangerously close to home in October, when British raiders from New York City burned the Livingston Manor House, less than fifty miles from Albany.[15]

Although the British had been repelled, Albany County was in a shambles. Its diverse peoples were dislocated, dismayed, and no longer able to live off of stored resources. The more settled areas were clogged with refugees, soldiers, and the sick and wounded. The outlying districts feared raids by Tories and Indians. In mid-December, a fire destroyed a number of homes in Schenectady, and inhabitants were left to beg for relief from Albany and the rest of the county. But it was clear that the people of the county would need to rebuild their society or they would starve and perish.

The spring of 1778 brought a new resolve to return to a more normal existence, to reclaim the land, to begin producing foodstuffs and staples, and to make in quantity the weapons, implements, and supplies needed for the American war effort. An immediate need, however, was for a functional civil government. The first meetings of the new state government in 1778 drew many of the county's leaders to Kingston. Meanwhile, municipal government resumed in the city of Albany. Governor Clinton appointed citywide officers. After a two-year hiatus, the Common Council met again on April 17 and began considering petitions from new and old Albany people for space to open stores, shops, and new production facilities.

Revolutionary leaders were anxious for greater Albany to resume agricultural operations as well. Across the county, saw and gristmills were refurbished, and their owners were pushed to turn out more boards and bags of flour. With fields and forests no longer directly menaced by the enemy, asheries, tanneries, and breweries also underwent similar revivals. In Albany workhouses (primitive factories) were established to make shoes and other leather products. Always at a premium, cattle and livestock were more closely monitored by Continental commissaries to prevent their disappearance. Weavers were tapped for cloth that local men and women made into sails, tents, and clothing. Metal craftsmen were called on to engage and organize apprentices to turn out shovels, nails, knives, and bayonets.

The destruction caused by the campaign of 1777 also stifled cultural and spiritual life. The only printers in the region had been Tories who fled to New York City, where they started a Loyalist newspaper. Budding Anglican congregations in Albany, in Schenectady, and in frontier chapels withered, because they carried the stigma of "Church of England." Their demise deprived English speakers of an important social institution. Impeded by wartime conditions, itinerant Lutheran pastors made even fewer visits to Albany County chapels, and the recently formed Presbyterian meetinghouse fell into limbo as well. But the functioning Dutch Reformed churches in Albany, Schenectady, Kinderhook, and Schaghticoke became a haven for those seeking spiritual as well as material relief. With the appearance of more soldiers, victuallers, medical people, army officers, and agents of the new state government, Albany became the center of operations in upstate New York. This new influx of talented outsiders included a cadre of lawyers who removed to Albany pending the end of the war. These newcomers joined with local leaders to lay the foundation for what would become the nerve center of the Empire State.[16]

The royalist cause in Albany County might have been much stronger had Sir William Johnson not died suddenly in the summer of 1774. The passing of that British stalwart left a leadership vacuum among the growing number of native English speakers in the Hudson-Mohawk region. Many of the county's newer residents who arrived after the Seven Years' War were Scots–Irish Highlanders or discharged British soldiers with strong ties to the Crown. They were not welcomed by an entrenched New York-born settler population of non-English background. Instead, they supported royal government and settled in the remote reaches of the county beyond the established settlements carved out by the children of New Netherland. By the end of 1776, many of these immigrants were overt Loyalists and either had been neutralized by the Albany committee or had fled the county. Even though a large number of loyal British subjects still remained in the Albany countryside, the Burgoyne invasion of 1777 seriously overestimated the level of support loyal farmers could provide. With the failure of the Burgoyne campaign, the new state sought to punish those who had supported it. A set of legislative enactments set up mechanisms (oaths) for identifying the disloyal, banishing them, and then sequestering and finally confiscating their property. The Act of Attainder of October 1779 condemned the state's fifty-nine most obvious Tories to death if found within the borders of New York. Included in this group were erstwhile Albany mayor Abraham C. Cuyler, Robert Leake, and Edward and Ebenezer Jessup, local landholders and Loyalist officers.[17]

In 1778 the State legislature had created the Commissioners for Detecting and Defeating Conspiracies to guard "against the wicked Machinations and Designs of . . . Foreign and Domestic Foes." Subsequent legislation defined the organization's responsibilities and established boards in different counties. Having brought internal enemies under control in the most settled areas during the two previous years, this body was the political tool Albany's revolutionary leaders needed to secure the more isolated parts of the countryside. As late as 1780 active Loyalists still posed a real threat in the outlying districts. Over the next two years, the Albany Commissioners rooted out Loyalists in the county. Informants were cultivated in each district, as the commissioners gathered information on potential internal enemies. Evidence on dozens of suspected Tories was evaluated. Militia detachments were sent into the countryside to bring in suspected Tories for examination. Many with ties to upstanding revolutionaries typically were required to post bail guaranteeing their good behavior. Strangers were ordered to leave the county. In February 1783 the commissioners dealt Albany's remaining Loyalists a final blow by banishing thirty-one prominent residents for refusing to sign the loyalty oath.[18]

Of particular concern were two enclaves of English religious extremists who had settled first in Watervliet and afterwards near the Massachusetts border in the King's District. These "shaking Quakers," or "Shakers," were pacifists who were denounced by their neighbors, especially after the Shakers refused to bear arms themselves, were implicated in plans to purchase munitions for the enemy, and began encouraging slaves to flee to the British who promised them freedom.[19]

The county's large African ancestry minority was concentrated around the wealthiest of the old Albany families most of whom lived around Albany and Schenectady. Patriot masters used slave men and boys to perform a range of war-related tasks, for which owners were sometimes compensated by the Albany committee. Female slaves continued to perform domestic chores for which they received little remuneration. During wartime, the already loose restrictions characteristic of slavery in the north became even more lax, for Patriot owners often were absent or preoccupied. Because of this breakdown in discipline, some slaves were able to earn wages that made them historically visible as individuals for the first time. During the late 1770s, references to small enclaves of free blacks began to appear in the historical records of Albany, Schenectady, and Watervliet. Men and women of African ancestry found themselves able to acquire enough wealth to purchase or lease house lots. Moreover, the presence of free blacks as soldiers in the armies stationed at and passing through Albany during the war, allowed Afro-Albanians to envision a future that might include freedom.

From the start of the conflict, patriot leaders were aware that the large slave population of unknown loyalty might pose a threat to the safety and security of the region. Unsolved mysterious events and violent disturbances were likely to be blamed on "Negroes." Much revolutionary rhetoric charged that all slaves were Tories who were likely to flee to the British at the first opportunity. Except for unfounded reports, the sole incidence of slave disloyalty came in March 1778, when a group of slaves was caught trying to leave Albany in a boat.[20]

The defeat of Burgoyne's army at Saratoga destroyed British ambition to mount another large-scale offensive. Instead, they adopted terror tactics across upstate New York to divert American forces away from more southern battlefields and to inhibit the Americans' ability to produce food and supplies for the larger war effort. From 1778 to the end of the war, British-inspired raiders attacked settlements on the New York frontier, especially exposed western settlements in Tryon County. But the fear of attack touched every community in Albany County as well. In Duanesburgh, a large proprietorship located between Schenectady and the Schoharie Creek, many of James Duane's tenants were unable to work their farms, mills, and asheries because of the constant fear of Tory raiders.

Albany County did not escape the torch entirely, for Tories and Indians attacked isolated farms in the years following Saratoga. In the autumn of 1780, Sir John Johnson led a large raiding party east from Niagara into the Schoharie Valley breadbasket, burning the fields in his path. On October 17 he engaged an American force at Middle Fort (Middleburgh), destroyed the settlement, and burned old Schoharie (Lower Fort). Then he torched his way to the Mohawk, leaving the Schoharie Valley smoldering in ruin, as German and Dutch farmers took to the hills, unable to protect their homes and fields. Also that month, another party of British and Indian raiders commanded by John Munro, a former Schenectady merchant, attacked Ballstown. Avoiding the stockade fort, the raiders destroyed several outlying homes and carried away more than twenty prisoners.[21]

These were dark days in the struggle for independence. Uncertainty bred suspicion, disputes, and denunciations. Justifiable fear of spies and plots haunted the people, especially after Tory raiders menaced a number of prominent revolutionary leaders. One of these was Gen. Philip Schuyler, who for years was rumored to be the victim of Tory kidnapping plots. By August 1781 he had gathered his family into a guarded compound at his Albany home, where a party of Tory marauders subsequently captured one of the guards, wounded another, and stole some silver.[22]

As the war was winding down, refugees returned to their homes in the county's outlying districts, and the militia reverted to its original peacekeeping role. In Schaghticoke, a well-populated agricultural satellite situated northeast of Albany, most of the landed farmers sided with their revolutionary kin in Albany, and the Fourteenth Regiment under Col. Johannes Knickerbacker stood guard against Tory incursions and would-be Vermont squatters. However, during the latter stages of the conflict, many of those suspected of Loyalism were actually recent émigrés from New England, who simply sought better farmland. However, the Commissioners on Conspiracies forced them to post bail guaranteeing good behavior or pressed them into service.[23]

In June 1782 General Washington and his advisors visited Albany to evaluate options for repelling a possible attack from Canada. Feted and granted the keys to the city, his party then went on to Schenectady. His presence bolstered morale and raised hope that the end of the long conflict was in sight. Washington returned the following summer and made an extensive tour of the entire region. Along his circuitous route, as people turned out to greet him, their mood shifted from depression to hope as Albanians now realized that the war was over.[24]

On a late August Market Day in 1783, the Albany air buzzed with energy and excitement. The city's main streets were busy and crowded with people in motion. The commotion began with the familiar sight of country people bringing grains, produce, and livestock to be valued at the city market. From all directions, farmers and husbandmen converged on Albany, their boats and wagons loaded with animals, farm, and forest products that for the past eight years mostly had been preempted by the military. With the Articles of Peace already in place, these farmers from the outlying districts understood that everything they produced would be much in demand. At every store and shop, country people were met by merchants and artisans eager to trade. Many of these businessmen were long familiar; some customers were hailing them as "cousin" and "uncle." But an even larger number of the anxious storekeepers had been in Albany for a decade or less. These new traders with strange sounding voices caught producers' ears, for they usually offered the most interesting items in exchange for country produce.

In the street, long-standing Albanians rubbed elbows with an extraordinary array of new people: immigrants from Europe, Yankees, and other Americans who were willing to pay inflated prices for the goods they needed, as they headed out to new homes in the north and west. For the first time in years, only a few uniformed soldiers were visible on the street, quite a contrast to the years since 1775, when hundreds of new men and boys in red and blue were jammed into the city. Some of these recently discharged Patriots were returning home, others were outsiders who had come to Albany to stay. Long-time Albany people, a flood of transients, government employees and officials, soldiers awaiting discharge, and many new people occupied vacant city buildings and petitioned the city council for permission to build on almost every parcel of available land.

Independence and the end of the war dramatically changed the county's political, social, and economic landscapes. Within two decades, old Albany had been carved into six additional counties, all of which were settled by people from New England and beyond. The land that now encompassed postfrontier Albany County was confined to the west side of the Hudson and was bounded by the Mohawk River in the north and the Heldeberg Mountains on the west. Nonetheless, the county's population continued to grow—reaching 25,155 by 1800 and 34,661 a decade later. By 1797 New York State government had settled permanently in Albany, and the city became the defacto state capital. Some of those who came to Albany as wartime refugees either returned home or moved on. But another wave of talented and ambitious newcomers was drawn to the center of New York State government and the upstate hub of budding medical, education, and publishing enterprises as well.

Immediately these newcomers joined in and competed with residents of old Albany in an effort to take advantage of new technologies, resources, and markets. Born of necessity during the struggle for independence, factories and mills now sprang up all over the county, particularly in the new manufacturing center of Watervliet (West Troy). These new industries were also prominent along the streams, which flowed through Bethlehem, Coeymans, and Guilderland and eventually emptied into the Hudson, and in the Heldeberg hill towns as well. With the coming of age of Stephen Van Rensselaer III in 1784, feudal Rensselaerswyck began to evolve into more modern forms, with cities, manufacturing complexes, military installations, schools, and canals—the outstanding features of Albany County's nineteenth-century landscape![25]

Notes

1. Alice P. Kenney, *Albany: Crossroads of Liberty* (Albany, 1976). See also Edward Countryman, *A People in Revolution: The American Revolution and Political Society in New York, 1760–1790* (Baltimore, 1981). Both are works of synthesis that comprehend the standard sources and traditional literature.

2. The general story of the Revolutionary War (and the War for Independence in particular) is well known and thus will receive only scant attention here. This essay instead will focus on the internal history of what had been Albany County during the years 1775–83, raising issues and following developments that shaped the formation of a distinctly American society in Albany County. My purpose here is to explain how and why colonists became revolutionaries, and then to relate their experiences to the overarching elements of a multifaceted war.

3. The most comprehensive county history relating to this period is George Rogers Howell and Jonathan Tenney et al., comp., *History of the County of Albany, N. Y., from 1609 to 1886* (New York, 1886). For Albany city, Rensselaerswyck, Watervliet, and Schaghticoke, see *The People of Colonial Albany Live Here* website at: http://www.nysm.nysed.gov/albany/, which is a massive, well-documented, and evolving exposition on the people of colonial Albany and their world. More specialized works consider parts of Albany County during the era of the Revolution. For Schenectady, see Willis T. Hanson Jr., *A History of Schenectady during the Revolution* (Schenectady, 1916): Edward H. Tebbenhoff's "The Momentum of Tradition: Dutch Society and Identity in Schenectady, 1660–1790" (Ph.D. diss., University of Minnesota, 1992), focuses on language and culture and is less concerned with the Revolution. Rita B. Klopott, "The History of the Town of Schaghticoke, New York, 1676–1855" (Ph.D. diss., State University of New York, Albany, 1981), includes a chapter on the war years, which claims the land ownership conflict with the New Englanders was more significant than any revolutionary issues. John H. Brandow, *The Story of Old Saratoga* (Albany, 1919), contains surprisingly little about the Saratoga homefront. For the Hoosick area, see Grace G. Niles, *The Hoosac Valley, Its Legends and Its History* (New York, 1912), and Philip Lord Jr., *War Over Wallomscoick: Land Use and Settlement Pattern on the Bennington Battlefield—1777* (Albany, 1989). For King's District, see David J. Goodall, "New Light

on the Border: New England Squatter Settlements in New York during the American Revolution" (Ph.D. diss., State University of New York, Albany, 1984). For Rensselaerswyck and Livingston Manor, see Sung Bok Kim, *Landlord and Tenant in Colonial New York: Manorial Society, 1664–1775* (Chapel Hill, N.C., 1978), an economic study, and Irving Mark, *Agrarian Conflicts in Colonial New York, 1711–1775* (New York, 1940), a class-based analysis. For the Schoharie Valley, see Jeptha R. Simms, *History of Schoharie County, and Border Wars of New York* (Albany, 1845), a very early, lore-laden compendium of information. For Ballstown, see Katherine Q. Braiddy, *Shadows: The Life and Times of Eliphalet Ball: The Founder of the Town of Ballston* (Ballston, 1991). For Lansingburgh, see Arthur J. Weise, *History of Lansingburgh, New York: From the Year 1670 to 1877* (Troy, N.Y., 1877). Weise also wrote readable but anecdotal histories of Albany and Troy.

4. Population analysis relies on statistics presented in Evarts B. Greene and Virginia D. Harrington, *American Population before the Federal Census of 1790* (New York, 1932), 88–105, a colony-by-colony compendium of very useful population statistics; and Robert V. Wells, *The Population of the British Colonies in America before 1776: A Survey of Census Data* (Princeton, 1975), an interesting analysis of those statistics. The key printed source for colonial New York census data is Edmund B. O'Callaghan, comp., *Documentary History of the State of New York*, vol. 1 (Albany, 1949), 687–97. Immigration at the end of the British colonial period is the subject of Bernard Bailyn, *Voyagers to the West: A Passage in the Peopling of America on the Eve of the Revolution* (New York, 1986), especially the first part of the chapter entitled "New York: Swarming to the North," 573–604. The most comprehensive source on Native Americans living in the area is Shirley W. Dunn, *The Mohican World, 1680–1750* (New York, 2000).

5. For a window on Albany-British army relations, see Stefan Bielinski, *Abraham Yates, Jr, and the New Political Order in Revolutionary New York* (Albany, 1975), esp. 3–13. Although quite dated, the most comprehensive printed source on the Stamp Act in Albany is Beverly McAnear, "The Albany Stamp Act Riots," *William & Mary Quarterly* (1947), 3rd ser., 4: 486–98. For more recent studies, see: http://www.nysm.nysed.gov/albany/solconst.html.

6. Maryland native Stewart Dean was one Albany skipper who sailed out of the Hudson; see William J. Wilgus, *The Life of Stewart Dean: A Character of the American Revolution* (Ascutney, Vt., 1942). For the short-lived but pioneering *Albany Gazette*, see Denis P. Brennan, "Open to All Parties: Alexander and James Robertson, Albany Printers, 1771–1777," *The Hudson Valley Regional Review* 10 (1993), 25–39.

7. For Yates and the Albany committee, see Bielinski, *Abraham Yates, Jr.*, and the sources cited therein. The principal narrative on the committee is still Barbara H. Voorhees, "The Albany Committee of Correspondence: 1775–1778" (M.A. thesis, Syracuse University, 1961). The committee minutes were published as *Minutes of the Albany Committee of Correspondence, 1775–1778*, 2 vols., (Albany, 1923). The second volume contains the "Minutes of the Schenectady Committee, 1775–1779" and a comprehensive index.

8. For Philip Schuyler, see Don R. Gerlach, *Proud Patriot: Philip Schuyler and the War for Independence, 1775–1783* (Syracuse, 1987). For the Continental army, see T. W. Egly Jr., *Goose Van Schaick of Albany, 1736–1789: The Continental Army's Senior Colonel* (Gloversville, N.Y., 1992), which comprehends his earlier work on the American military. The career of Abraham Ten Broeck is described in Emma Ten Broeck Runk, *The Ten Broeck Genealogy* (New York, 1897), 91–98. For Indian relations, see Ralph T. Pastore, "The Board of Commissioners for Indian Affairs in the Northern Department and the Iroquois Indians, 1775–1778" (Ph.D. diss., University of Notre Dame, 1972).

9. For the Canadian invasion, see Hal T. Shelton, *General Richard Montgomery and the American Revolution: From Redcoat to Rebel* (New York, 1994) and Michael P. Gabriel, *Major General Richard Montgomery: The Making of an American Hero* (Madison, N.J., 2002). A sense of the difficulty of supplying an army emerges in the letters of Albany storekeeper-turned-commissary Philip Van Rensselaer. See Catharina Van Rensselaer Bonney, comp., *A Legacy of Historical Gleanings* (Albany, 1873). Hanson, *Schenectady during the Revolution,* chapter 9, is particularly informative on the role Schenectady played in the Canadian invasion. For the Canadian refugees, see Allan S. Everest, *Moses Hazen and the Canadian Refugees in the American Revolution* (Syracuse, 1976). I take this opportunity to thank Professor Everest, a wonderful teacher, who piqued my interest in the impact of the Revolution on New York's people three decades ago.

10. The events of June 4 led to a roundup of prominent Tories. That incident is considered at http://www.nysm.nysed.gov/albany/or-be.html. The subsequent deportation of the mayor, other officials, and prominent businessmen removed an important leadership group and signaled the end of Whig toleration of pro-British sympathies. After that, Albany Loyalists were relegated to the remote reaches of the county. "Broken Homes: Widows, Abandoned Wives, and Single Women in Wartime Albany, 1775–83" is the subject of a chapter in my manuscript monograph entitled "The Other Revolutionaries: The People of Albany and American Independence, 1763–1783" (http://www.nysm.nysed .gov/albany/or.html).

11. For Ranger activities in Coxsackie, see Field Horne, *The Greene County Catskills: A History* (Hensonville, N.Y., 1994), 15. For committee efforts during these months, see Voorhees, "Albany Committee of Correspondence," 107–18. After adoption of the State Constitution, county courts were reestablished, and some civil offices were filled. However, Albany's most prominent civilian leaders had moved on to state-level activities. For Schoharie, see Simms, *Schoharie County and Border Wars,* chapters 7–8, 12–14.

12. Edward C. Collier, *A History of Old Kinderhook* (New York, 1914), chapter 6, loosely chronicles wartime events. More useful are the minutes of the Albany committee for its efforts to secure cooperation in Kinderhook. For the Van Schaacks and a window on events in Kinderhook, see Henry C. Van Schaack, ed., *Life of Peter Van Schaack* (New York, 1842) and his *Memoirs of Henry Van Schaack* (Chicago, 1892). Becoming progressively blind, pacifist Peter Van Schaack had returned home. Henry was a former Albany trader and provincial placeman whose marriage to the daughter of a British officer further connected him to the colony's pro-British leaders. Their sister married for-

mer Albany attorney Peter Silvester, a one-time Johnson retainer and the most conservative of revolutionaries. See Peyton F. Miller, *A Group of Great Lawyers of Columbia County, New York* (Hudson, 1904), 55–60, 75–83; Carl L. Becker, "John Jay and Peter Van Schaack," *New York History*, 1 (1919), 1-12; and Richard B. Morris, ed., *John Jay: The Making of a Revolutionary, Unpublished Papers, 1745–1780*, vol. 1 (New York, 1975), 331–333.

13. David Goodall used the term "Yankee Zone" to refer to the new New England settlements north to south from Lake Champlain to Livingston Manor. His "New Light," chapter IV, provides a basic narrative for developments in King's District. Adgate was an important county committee member and delegate to the New York congresses. See a recent conference paper by Jason K. Duncan entitled "Matthew Adgate," on file at the Colonial Albany Project office.

14. For a debunking of the "burning myth," see Gerlach, *Proud Patriot*, 281–83, a generally solid source for the Battle of Saratoga from a New York perspective. Schuyler's debilitating affliction with rheumatoid arthritis prevented him from taking a more active part in the campaign of 1777 or in the defense of his own property. For eastern Albany Tory activities, see Rick J. Ashton, *The Life of Henry Ruiter, 1742–1819* (privately printed, 1974). For conditions at the military hospital in Albany, see Dr. James Thatcher's *Military Journal during the American Revolutionary War from 1776 to 1783* (Boston, 1823), entry for Oct. 24, 1777. See also Mary C. Gillett, *The Army Medical Department, 1775–1818* (Washington, D.C., 1981), chapter 4.

15. An exceptional window on the southern Albany homefront is found in *Letters From a Revolution, 1775–1783: A Selection From the Bronck Family Papers At the Greene County Historical Society*, ed. Raymond Beecher (Coxsackie and Albany, 1973). Horne, *Greene County Catskills,* chaps. 4–5.

16. This section is based on an interpretive reading of the sources and narratives cited elsewhere in this essay. Especially interesting (yet puzzling for their contradictory information) are the numerous accounts and reminiscences of visitors to the Albany area. See, for example, the notorious Thomas Anburey, *Travels through the Interior Parts of America* (London, 1789); [author unknown], *The Sexagenary: or, Reminiscences of the American Revolution* (Albany, 1866); and Simeon E. Baldwin, ed., *Life and Letters of Simeon Baldwin* (New Haven, 1918), 86–180, an extensive commentary by a Yale-educated Albany schoolmaster. Conditions in Albany County are reported and discussed throughout *Public Papers of George Clinton, First Governor of New York*, vol. 2, edited by Hugh Hastings (Albany, 1900). See also Gerlach, *Proud Patriot*, chapters 10–11. Copies of all known narratives on early Albany are archived at the Colonial Albany Project office.

17. The latest word on the subject is Philip Ranlet, *The New York Loyalists* (Knoxville, Tenn., 1986), but it is little concerned with Loyalists in the Albany countryside or in its communities. For the pro-British mindset of the newcomers, see Bailyn, *Voyagers to the West*, especially as described in the final chapter, entitled "New York: Swarming to the North," 573–637. Also see, Alice P. Kenney, "The Albany Dutch: Loyalists and Patriots," *New York History* 42 (October 1961), 331–50. The most

comprehensive chronicle of anti-Loyalist measures still is found in Alexander C. Flick, *Loyalism in New York during the American Revolution* (New York, 1901).

18. *Minutes of the Commissioners for Detecting and Defeating Conspiracies in the State of New York: Albany County Sessions, 1778–1781*, 3 vols., ed. Victor H. Paltsits (Albany, 1909–1910; reprinted 1972), hereafter cited as *CDDC*. The Albany commissioners have been more closely studied by Sean O'Mara in "Defining and Regulating a Revolutionary Community: The Albany Board of the Commissioners for Detecting and Defeating Conspiracies," an unpublished conference paper on file at the Colonial Albany Project. Almost all of those listed on the "Return of the Persons banished at Albany" were born in Albany County, a testimony to the thoroughness of the inquisition. Printed in *Calendar of Historical Manuscripts Relating to the War of the Revolution* (Albany, 1868), 2:364. This was the last of a number of lists of the "disaffected."

19. The Commissioners' dealings with the Shakers are chronicled in their printed minutes, *CDDC*, 2:452–71, 504, 555, 592, 678–80, 724. As early as 1781, informants in King's District were passing along information about Shaking Quakers. For the Shakers, see Stephen J. Stein, *The Shaker Experience in America: A History of the United Society of Believers* (New Haven, Conn., 1992).

20. The evolution of a free black community in Albany is considered in Stefan Bielinski, "The Jacksons, Lattimores, and Schuylers: First African-American Families of Early Albany," *New York History* 77:4 (October 1996), 373–94, and on the Internet in an expanded form at: http://www.nysm.nysed.gov/albany/art/art-jls.html. Sources identifying and describing the activities of slaves and free blacks during this period include the records of government (particularly the Revolutionary committee and commissioners), assessment rolls and real estate records, church records, and account books. The March 1778 incident is described in Stefan Bielinski, "Slavery and Community: Afro-Albanians and the War," a manuscript chapter from an in-progress monograph available online at: http://www.nysm.nysed.gov/albany/or.html. An exciting new window on African-American women in the local economy comes from "African-American Consumers in the Segregated Economy of Albany," a chapter in Aileen B. Agnew, "Silent Partners: The Economic Life of Women on the Frontier of Colonial New York" (Ph.D. diss., University of New Hampshire, 1998), 80–122.

21. Revolutionary leader James Duane was an absentee landlord whose managers were ineffective in turning the more than fifty prewar tenancies into profit-making enterprises. See Edward P. Alexander, *A Revolutionary Conservative: James Duane of New York, 1733–1797* (New York, 1938), 54–59, 216–19. For Schoharie, see Simms, *Schoharie County,* and an even more romanticized derivative in William E. Roscoe, *History of Schoharie County, New York* (Syracuse, 1882), especially chapter 3.

22. For the attack on Schuyler's home, see Gerlach, *Proud Patriot,* 458–60. The folklore surrounding that event is chronicled in Division for Historic Preservation, *Schuyler Mansion: A Historic Structures Report* (Albany, 1977), 29–30.

23. For events in Schaghticoke, see Klopott, "Town of Schaghticoke," 90–101.

24. Philip Schuyler hosted Washington on both of his visits; see Gerlach, *Proud Patriot,* 479–80, 511–12.

25. Population statistics and information on the formation of new political entities have been culled from J. H. French, comp., *Historical and Statistical Gazetteer of New York State*, (Syracuse, 1860; reprinted 1980). For the city of Albany in the postwar period, see Stefan Bielinski, "Episodes in the Coming of Age of an Early American Community: Albany, N.Y., 1780–1793," in *World of the Founders: New York Communities in the Federal Period,* ed. Stephen L. Schechter and Wendell Tripp (Albany, 1990), 108–37.

Part III

The Revolution
on the Frontier

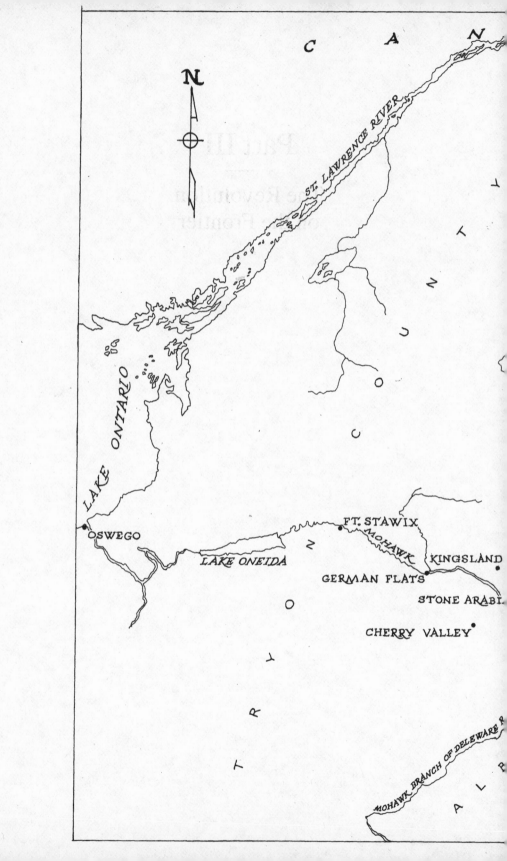

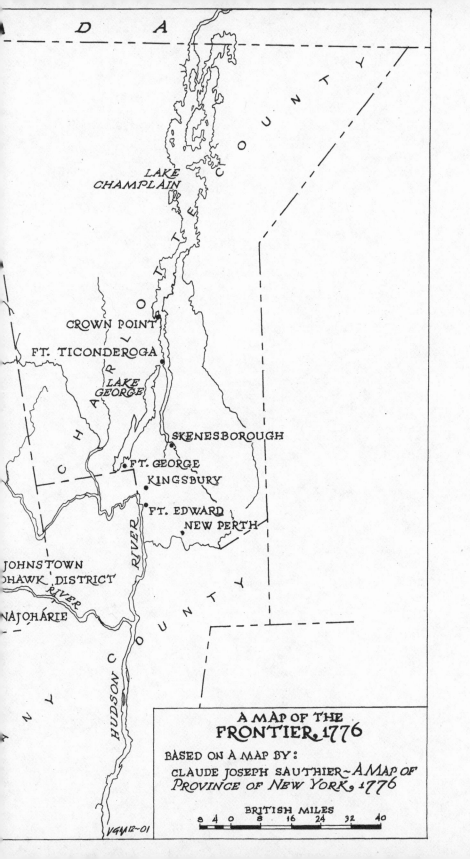

A MAP OF THE
FRONTIER, 1776

BASED ON A MAP BY:

CLAUDE JOSEPH SAUTHIER~ A MAP OF
PROVINCE OF NEW YORK, 1776

BRITISH MILES

8 4 0 8 16 24 32 40

VGM 12~01

8

Tryon County

Robert W. Venables

Tryon County was established in 1772 as a separate political entity within the British colony of New York, although the first white settlement in the area had begun in 1689 as part of Albany County. Tryon included all the lands claimed by the colony of New York west of the counties of Ulster, Albany, and Charlotte. The county's western border was the boundary line established by the Iroquois Confederacy and the British government at the 1768 Treaty of Fort Stanwix (now Rome, N.Y.).[1] On the eve of the American Revolution, the Iroquois Confederacy was the oldest "empire" in the region. The Iroquois Confederacy (the "Haudenosaunee," or people of the longhouse) was made up of a core of five nations: the Mohawks, Oneidas, Onondagas, Cayugas, and Senecas, reinforced through adoptions of other Indian individuals and nations such as the Tuscaroras. The colonists referred to the Tuscaroras, who had been adopted by 1722, as the sixth nation of the Confederacy, and hence the Iroquois were widely known as the Six Nations. The Iroquois had established trade and political influences beyond their homeland's borders both before and after European contact, and during the colonial period their extensive commercial and political influence was recognized by the relatively new empire, that of the British. The Revolution did not end imperialism among either the whites or the Iroquois, but rather led to new definitions of empire.

When the Revolution began, Tryon County was within the political domain of both the Iroquois Confederacy and the British empire—two separate but interdependent sovereign states. Specifically, Tryon County was within the age-old political domain of two of the Iroquois Confederacy's member nations: the Mohawks and the Oneidas.[2] This factor would complicate the political and military course of the Revolution in Tryon County. Although the Oneidas still

179

claimed the western reaches of the Mohawk River, by the outbreak of the
Revolution their primary settlements were west of the boundary line marked by
the 1768 Treaty of Fort Stanwix.

In Tryon the European-American families who adhered to the Patriot cause
had generally lived in this frontier county longer than those colonists who
became Loyalists. Many of the Patriot families had endured more than a gen-
eration of warfare with French Canada, during which their families' safety and
interests had often been ignored in far-away London. In contrast, the Loyalists
tended to be directly tied to Crown employment. Royalists rallied around the
most important Loyalist clan, the family of the late Sir William Johnson, the
Crown's Superintendent of Indian Affairs who had died in 1774. Patriots tended
to be those colonists who were outside the Johnson clan's immediate circle. In
general, ethnic identities were not as important as social, political, economic,
and family connections. For example, there were Germans on both sides, and
their individual choices were based on their connections. And even though a
majority of a particular family joined either the Loyalist or Patriot cause, one
or more members of that same family sometimes chose the opposite side or
neutrality.

The Patriots of Tryon County were divided into two basic factions: moderates and radicals. Moderates often had friendships within the Johnson clan.
These friendships were sometimes enhanced by ties through the Masonic lodges,
as in the case of moderate Jelles Fonda.[3] Before independence was declared in
1776, the moderates wanted to believe that all colonists desired reform within
the British empire, even though Loyalists might "differ with us, in the mode in
Obtaining a Redress of Grievances."[4] The radicals, on the other hand, resented
the Johnson clan and were determined to overthrow them. The radicals also
wanted to end Iroquois influence in the region; some radicals even sought to
drive Iroquois neighbors out of the county, even though these Iroquois had fought
alongside them against the French. The radicals avidly supported independence
and saw their pro-British opponents, both white and Indian, in simplistic terms
that evolved during the Revolution into outright hatred.[5]

The oldest families were, of course, Mohawk, and, like their neighbors,
they were divided into factions—Mohawk Loyalists, Mohawk Patriots, and
Mohawk neutrals. But gradually, between 1775 and the summer of 1777, the
actions of one Mohawk family in particular—the extended family of Molly and
Joseph Brant, who were in turn connected to the Johnsons—encouraged most
of the Mohawks to support the British cause.

As with so many other revolutions, friends sometimes became enemies, and
moderates on all sides—Iroquois and colonists alike—gradually lost control of
the Revolution after warfare broke out in Massachusetts in April 1775. By the end
of August 1777, political policies and military actions were being determined by
individuals on both sides who were increasingly willing to use brutality.

Colonial Background

In 1689 a Swiss, Heinrich Frey, entered the Iroquois Confederacy's terri-tory of the "Eastern Door" of the Mohawk nation. With the Mohawks' permis-sion, Frey became the first permanent white settler in the area by building a log cabin near Canajoharie Creek. Frey was both a farmer and fur trader, whose descendants played major roles in both the Patriot and Loyalist causes.[6] Two significant steps in the development of Tryon County's colonial frontier society occurred around 1722. That year, about thirty German families moved to the rich river flats fifty-five miles west of Schenectady and established a settlement called German Flats.[7] At about the same time, the Oneidas just west of these set-tlers adopted Tuscarora refugees from North Carolina. The resettlement of these Germans and Tuscaroras by two different, overlapping governments—one British and the other Haudenosaunee—demonstrates how the region could evolve under coexisting political systems, and that the future of this frontier set-tlement was not inevitably "either" EuroAmerican "or" Indian.

The distances between colonial settlements in the Mohawk Valley in the 1720s were great. Twenty miles from Schenectady were the settlements of Caughnawaga and Tribe's Hill, where the Fonda and Hanson families were dom-inant. Thirty-five miles from Schenectady were the settlements of Canajoharie, Palatine, and Stone Arabia, where the Frey and Loucks families were promi-nent. Finally, farthest west of all was German Flats, twenty miles from the near-est settlement and fifty-five miles from Schenectady and dominated by the Herkimer family. Colonists spent the next decades filling in the lands between these major white settlements, and settlers in the valley profited by supplying and transporting newcomers. The Mohawk provided an excellent route into the interior, and soon the valleys that branched off to the south were inhabited by scattered colonial families. In 1738 Cherry Valley, ten miles south of the Mohawk River below the German town of Palatine, was settled by a group of Scotch-Irish from Connecticut and other New England colonies.[8]

The Mohawks did not fear being engulfed by the colonists. They often gave away or sold some of their land. In fact, the Mohawks were boldly experiment-ing and altering their society, continually adapting European technology and ideas. This adaptation sometimes included layering Anglican Protestant Christianity upon their own religion.[9] In 1738 William Johnson arrived in the Mohawk Valley. He was an Irish colonist with significant family connections within the British empire. With generous gifts of land from the Mohawks, he built a vast manor estate and established Tryon County's most important family.[10]

During the French and Indian War, William Johnson gained military suc-cesses, a fortune, and the title of baronet, enabling him to be identified as "Sir." Sir William soon served the Crown as superintendent of Indian Affairs for the northern colonies. His closest advisors and friends were beneficiaries of his success. His friend Daniel Claus, a German who had been an indigent in Philadelphia just thirteen years before, married Sir William's oldest daughter, Nancy, in 1762. As deputy superintendent of Indian Affairs under Sir William, Claus served diligently in Montreal after the French and Indian War as the sole agent for the Canadian Iroquois.[11]

Guy Johnson, Sir William's nephew, acted as Sir William's principal assistant and secretary. In 1763 Guy married Sir William's second daughter, Polly. As a belated wedding gift, Sir William built them a handsome two-story stone mansion in 1766 on the edge of the north bank of the Mohawk River eighteen miles west of Schenectady. Sir William included over five thousand acres of land with the mansion and named the estate "Guy Park."[12]

Perhaps the most significant factor in the influence of Sir William Johnson was his intimate relation with a prominent Mohawk woman at Canajoharie, Molly (Mary) Brant. Born about 1736, Molly's Mohawk name was Gonwatsijayeeni ("Kon?watsi?tsiai e n?ni"), meaning "someone lends her a flower."[13] In the spring of 1759, Johnson's German wife, Catherine Weissenberg, died. She had borne him a son John and two daughters, Ann and Nancy. Molly Brant soon rose to prominence as Sir William's consort. Whether Molly Brant married Sir William in a Mohawk ceremony is unknown. Whatever the circumstances, in September 1759 she gave birth to their first of eight children. Molly Brant's influence among the Mohawks and within the entire Confederacy was considerable, because Iroquois women wielded considerable power through their clans.[14] Sir William, as supportive of his Iroquois relatives as he was of his white kin, encouraged Molly's younger brother Joseph, born in 1743.[15] As Molly's own influence increased over time, she became an elder leader or "clan mother" among these women.[16] Sir William had thus gathered around him an energetic biracial, multiethnic clan, as his able assistants were now his Mohawk wife and her considerable Mohawk connections; his children by both Catherine and Molly; his sons-in-law; and his close friends.

In the midst of the political crises of the 1760s, the Mohawk Valley continued to prosper. New churches were built to accommodate the growing population, while established congregations replaced their old frame and stone churches with new, larger edifices. Speculation in Iroquois lands continued to be the major investment for men such as John and Hendrick Frey, Jelles Fonda, and Nicholas Herkimer, as well as for Sir William Johnson. The fur trade prospered under the security of peace with the Iroquois. Farmers' wheat, butter, and pearl ash brought good prices at Albany and New York, and bateauxmen kept busy transporting goods up and down the river. An important indicator of the valley's postwar prosperity and growth was Sir William Johnson's successful petition of January 2, 1772, to the New York Assembly requesting that the area west of Schenectady be formed into a new county apart from Albany County. The Assembly granted the petition and created Tryon County, named after Gov.

William Tryon. Five districts were created: the Mohawk District north of the river around Fort Johnson; Stone Arabia (Palatine) directly west of the Mohawk District; Kingsland to the north; Canajoharie on the south side of the river; and German Flats farthest west on both sides of the river. On July 30, 1772, the new county was officially inaugurated, when Governor Tryon presided over a provincial council meeting at Johnson Hall. The governor and Johnson spent a few days reviewing the militia at Johnstown, German Flats, and Fort Herkimer, and then attended a four-day Indian conference at Johnson Hall.[17]

In July 1774, during another conference with the Iroquois Confederacy at Johnson Hall, Sir William suddenly died. His death came just as colonial protests over British taxation and imperial policy were about to propel Tryon County's multiracial, multiethnic population toward revolution.[18]

The Revolution

In 1775 there were about five thousand colonists in Tryon County. About 20 percent of these were tenant farmers of the Johnson family. There were also about five hundred Mohawks in the county.[19]

On March 16 Sir John Johnson, Guy Johnson, and the majority of the magistrates and grand jury of Tryon County signed a declaration opposing the Continental Association. Then, on April 19, the opening battles of the Revolution were fought at Lexington and Concord in Massachusetts. Now that political debate had been trumped by violent confrontation, Patriots in the Mohawk Valley reacted. Sometime between May 2 and May 15, a large crowd came together near the road that ran past Jelles Fonda's home and store on the north bank of the Mohawk, about eight miles west of Fort Johnson. The crowd had gathered to raise a Liberty Pole on behalf of the Continental Congress. No one in the crowd knew how the Johnsons and other Loyalists would respond. The answer came suddenly, as Sheriff Alexander White led mounted men directly into the midst of the crowd and dispersed the Patriots. Not a single shot was fired. No one was hurt. But Tryon County's Revolution moved from debate to confrontation, and moderation would thereafter give way to ever-escalating violence, ironically beginning on the land of the moderate Jelles Fonda.[20]

Committees of correspondence in the five districts in the county had been organized to exchange ideas sometime before June 1775. In the aftermath of Sheriff White's action, the local committees began calling themselves "Committees of Safety" as well as "Committees of Correspondence."[21] On May 24 four committees (Palatine, Canajoharie, Kingsland, and German Flats) met as the Tryon County Committee of Correspondence, also known as the United Committee. Only the committee members for the Mohawk District, the location of the Johnson clan, did not attend—perhaps because they had not yet entirely organized. The other committees assembled at William Seeber's tavern in Canajoharie to discuss Guy Johnson's opposition to the protestors. In addition to Christopher P. Yates, John Frey, Isaac Paris, and Andrew Finck (the charter members of the committee) the Palatine district was represented by six other men, including Peter Waggoner, an important farmer, whose many sons owned farms neighboring his; Harmanus Van Slyck, a member of a prominent county family that ran a gristmill and owned extensive lands; and Jacob Klock, the son of George Klock, a man accused by both the Mohawk Nation and the late Sir William Johnson of fraudulently obtaining Mohawk lands.[22]

Canajoharie, which included the entire south bank of the Mohawk River in Tryon County, sent six representatives, including Nicholas Herkimer, Ebenezer Cox, David Cox, and William Seeber, in whose tavern the meeting was held. The Coxes owned extensive lands directly on the Fort Stanwix Treaty Line. The intolerant and heady Ebenezer Cox was a skilled builder, who had erected a large gristmill for Nicholas Herkimer. A potential antagonism existed between these two Patriots, however, because a Cox relative, Julian Cox (perhaps his father) had been sued and arrested for a debt of £80 by Nicholas in 1767.[23]

Thirteen men from Kingsland and German Flats attended this United Committee meeting. They included George Herkimer, Nicholas's brother; Duncan McDougal, a relative and probably the brother of Daniel McDougal, who was a member from Palatine; William Petry, a close friend of the Herkimers; and Edward Wall, teacher at the Johnstown school established by the late Sir William Johnson. The United Committee discussed the increasing danger of an open split with the Johnson clan. The committee assigned David Cox, Edward Wall, and Duncan McDougal to go to Albany to secure some much-needed powder and to bring it back without being detected by Guy Johnson. The committee then adjourned.[24]

In May, Guy Johnson, who had succeeded Sir William as superintendent of Indian Affairs for the north, met with some Iroquois near Guy Park. The council was convened to hear Indian grievances, including the concerns about a frontier war against some Iroquois' allies in western Pennsylvania and western Virginia. Guy was determined to maintain the Iroquois's alliance with the Crown, an alliance that had endured for more than a century.[25]

The Mohawk District Committee of Safety had organized by late May and included Adam Fonda, the son of the prominent trader Jelles Fonda; Frederick Fish and Volkert Veeder, two prominent landholders and traders; and Abraham Yates. Some Patriots from all five district committees of safety convened at Warner Dygert's home in Canajoharie. As "the United Committee," they drafted a June 2 letter to Guy Johnson, because they were concerned about any political decisions he might have made at his May council with the Iroquois. Moderates such as Nicholas Herkimer, Christopher Yates, and Adam Loucks wrote a temperate letter, which explained that the United Committee appreciated Guy's efforts to deal with the anger of the Iroquois. The letter also declared that the Patriots had met peacefully only to protest the unconstitutional acts passed by Parliament. The committee promised to protect Guy in the discharge of his duties as Indian superintendent. But they protested Sheriff Alexander White's dispersal of the peaceful Liberty Pole crowd in early May; the armed force that Guy kept around his manor; and the searching of all people traveling on the King's Highway, which went past Guy's home. It was also in this letter that the moderate position was clearly defined: "We cannot think that as you and your family possess very Large Estates in this County you are unfavorable to American Freedom altho you may differ with us, in the mode in Obtaining a Redress of Grievances."[26]

Nicholas Herkimer and Edward Wall, the Johnstown schoolmaster, took the letter to Guy that same day. Herkimer and two other men decided to wait at Guy Park for the answer and, while they waited, to observe Guy's Indian council. Herkimer personally knew some of the Iroquois attending, because he often traded with them. In fact, his close friend Joseph Brant (Thayendanegea, meaning "bundle of sticks" or "two sticks of wood bound together"), one of the most popular Mohawk leaders, lived only three miles from him. Brant and Herkimer were also fellow Masons in St. Patrick's Masonic Lodge, established in 1766 by Sir William Johnson.[27]

Sir Guy Johnson and his agents were concerned lest the Iroquois ally with the Patriot cause. In December 1774, five months before the Battle of Lexington, Daniel Claus had taken measures in Canada to make sure that the Indian nations there remained allied to the king. Claus advised the British commander in Canada, Gen. Frederick Haldimand, to order councils with the Iroquois held at garrisons such as Fort Niagara, that were far beyond any white settlement. Thus the presence of British troops would impress them, and the Patriots would have difficulty contacting them. Like Claus, Guy Johnson, now in June 1775, began to feel that Indian councils would not serve the Crown's cause, if they were held where the Patriots might intervene. As an example he had only to watch his old friend and fellow Mason Nicholas Herkimer observing his current council. Thus, in the midst of the council, Guy suddenly announced that he was going to German Flats, where he would continue the meeting on the large farm of John Thompson, one of his agents. But after a short council there, during which he spoke against the Patriot cause, he moved to Montreal, taking with him his chief assistants, Daniel Claus and John Butler, as well as all of his agents and interpreters. From now on, royal direction of Indian affairs in the northern colonies would come from Canada.[28]

Tryon Patriots replaced Loyalists in county offices, beginning with the militia. When Guy Johnson fled to Canada, Nicholas Herkimer was appointed in his place as colonel of the militia. Daniel Claus, another militia officer was replaced by Frederick Fisher. Other officers who had followed the Indian Department's superintendent to Canada were also replaced. At Johnson Hall, Sir John Johnson viewed this reorganization with apprehension. Sir John had remained in Tryon to protect his own property and that of his family and friends. For example, he had ordered all of Daniel Claus's cattle except those needed to feed his tenants removed from the riverbank meadows to Claus's isolated farm in the northern part of the Mohawk District, away from the center of Patriot activity. Sir John also supervised the planting of wheat by Claus's tenants.[29] Because he remained in Tryon, Sir John could see that the United Committee was destroying the society that Sir John and his associates had dominated. He became even more alarmed, when the United Committee disarmed all of John Butler's tenants. Sir John wrote to his brother-in-law, Daniel Claus, that "if they make any Attempt here you may expect to hear of some thing being done."[30]

During the fall of 1775 the United Committee was busy rallying support for the Patriot cause and suppressing those who opposed it. The Patriots replaced Sheriff Alexander White with John Frey, a founder of the first committee of correspondence in Tryon County. The United Committee and its subordinate district committees assumed still more power, when they imprisoned men for the "crime" of opposing the "Association" of the Continental Congress. The Association had originally been an oath to uphold the trade embargo declared by the Continental Congress in 1774, but it had evolved into a pledge of allegiance to the Patriot cause, the Continental Congress, and local committees. A Tryon Loyalist was usually given the chance to sign the Association; once he did so, he was left alone, so long as he did not openly espouse the Loyalist cause.[31]

Sir John Johnson was alarmed by the radicalism of the Patriots in Tryon County, for there was even talk of independence. To guard against his own imprisonment by the Patriots, Sir John fortified Johnson Hall, which was already flanked by two blockhouses. He also gathered powder and guns from his neighbors and tenants. On January 11, 1776, his preparations prompted Isaac Paris to warn Maj. Gen. Philip Schuyler in Albany that Sir John had cannons, but the Patriots had none. Schuyler could not tolerate the existence of a Loyalist fort on New York's western flank, so he marched into Tryon County with a small detachment of Continentals. Moderates like Nicholas Herkimer agreed that a show of force was needed. Herkimer, commander of the county militia, thus joined Schuyler (a moderate himself) with a large number of militiamen to intimidate Sir John.[32]

When the American force arrived, the Mohawk River was frozen over, and the ice made a convenient parade ground. In front of Major Jelles Fonda's store, the combined force of well over one thousand men marched in review. The previous September, Sir John had declared that he would not allow the Patriots to disarm his tenants, as they had disarmed John Butler's. But in the face of this combined Patriot force, Sir John quietly surrendered his tenants' guns and returned with General Schuyler to Albany. Sir John was paroled almost immediately, more Tryon citizens signed the Association, and the winter of 1775 to 1776 passed peacefully in Tryon County.[33]

In the Spring of 1776, talk of independence greatly escalated. Because Tryon's inhabitants had no local newspaper, the chairman of the United Committee, Isaac Paris, gathered over sixty-five subscriptions to purchase any New York City newspaper at Albany, to be delivered by express rider.[34]

At Johnson Hall, Sir John's hopes of neutrality vanished, when he learned, sometime during the first two weeks of May, 1776, that the Tryon County Committee of Safety had unanimously instructed Tryon County's delegates to the New York Provincial Congress to vote for independence. Although Sir John could understand, if not agree, with opposition to specific acts of Parliament, he could never accept independence.[35]

Hastily gathering provisions, Sir John assembled 170 of his loyal tenants and fled Johnson Hall on May 13, 1776. Many of his followers took their wives and children with them, but Sir John left his wife Mary at Johnson Hall, because she was four months pregnant. Guided by three Mohawks, the Loyalists trudged north through the wilderness along the path the Iroquois had marked out earlier that spring. A few days after the Loyalists left Johnson Hall, a Mohawk messenger caught up with Sir John and told him that the Patriots had taken Lady Johnson hostage and sent her to Albany. Deeply distressed by this news, Sir John nevertheless led his party on. After seven days, their provisions ran out, and his people were forced to eat roots, leaves, and wild onions. Finally, after nine days, they reached the Mohawk town of Akwesasne (St. Regis), on the St. Lawrence River seventy-five miles west of Montreal.[36]

Military Actions in Tryon County

After the Patriots declared independence, the course of the Revolution in Tryon County was shaped primarily by military events. The British capture of New York City during the summer of 1776 cut off Patriot access to that major port. During the summer of 1777, a three-pronged British campaign attempted to seize control of all New York and to divide New England from the rest of the rebelling states. A major British column under Gen. John Burgoyne moved southward along Lake Champlain toward Albany, while a smaller detachment pushed northward up the Hudson from New York City. Meanwhile, the third component of this British campaign under Col. Barry St. Leger, moved south from Oswego toward the Mohawk Valley and on August 2 besieged Patriot-held Fort Stanwix at the western boundary of Tryon County. About 760 Patriot militia under Nicholas Herkimer, supported by Oneida-Iroquois scouts, attempted to relieve the fort, but on August 6 they were ambushed. The ferocious Battle of Oriskany ended in a draw, but casualties among the British, the Loyalists, and their Iroquois allies, together with the approach of another Patriot relief column, compelled the British to lift the siege of Fort Stanwix.

The Battle of Oriskany was costly to both sides. Among the militia, the usual killed-to-wounded ratio was reversed; about fifty Patriots were wounded and at least two hundred were killed. About thirty Patriots had been taken prisoner, including Maj. John Frey of the important Canajoharie family and Col. Frederick Bellinger, owner of the trading post and tavern at German Flats.[37] Both Frey and Bellinger had been active in the Committee of Safety, and from them the British discovered that a great number of committee members and key Patriot leaders had been killed or severely wounded. Colonel Cox, Major Van Slyck, Samuel Billington, John Dygert, and Jacob Snell were dead. Nicholas Herkimer was mortally wounded, and Isaac Paris, the radical chairman of the county's United Committee, was a prisoner of the Iroquois. Colonel St. Leger wrote to General Burgoyne that "almost all the principal movers of rebellion in that country" were dead.[38] It was no exaggeration. The county's Committee of Safety sent a letter to the Albany committee, which concluded: "Faithful to our country, we remain, your sorrowful brethren, the few members of this committee."[39] On August 17, 1777, eleven days after the battle, Tryon County's most experienced Patriot soldier, Nicholas Herkimer, died of his wounds. Herkimer's death stilled the voice of the county's most powerful moderate Patriot. Although his most vehement critic, Ebenezer Cox, was also dead, other radicals now assumed control of the Patriot cause.[40] Because the Battle of Oriskany had been an extremely bloody encounter, many embittered Patriots came to hate their former neighbors, Loyalist and Mohawk alike, and the intensity of those emotions strengthened the radicals.[41]

The Loyalists, including Sir John's regiment and Butler's Rangers, lost about fifty men, or one-fourth of their number. The Seneca Iroquois lost thirty killed, including a few popular leaders. After the battle, Joseph Brant referred to the decimated ranks of his own warriors as the "poor Mohawks."[42] The results of the Battle of Oriskany deprived General Burgoyne of needed reinforcements from the west and materially contributed to his decision to surrender at Satatoga. The year 1777 was thus the turning point of the Revolution for the Loyalists and pro-British Iroquois warriors.

Radicals in the Committee of Safety led by Dr. Moses Younglove and Isaac Paris now controlled the county. Both men had been captured at the Battle of Oriskany but had managed to return to the county by the end of February 1778. In the following month, Paris was also elected to the State Assembly. The radicals continued to imprison suspected Loyalists and even unsuccessfully demanded the impeachment of moderate state senators Jelles Fonda and Michael Edick.[43] These two were wealthy merchants who publicly opposed the committee's harsh restrictions on suspected Loyalists. Above all, moderates like Fonda deplored the apparently arbitrary and extreme actions that the committee took in the name of "liberty," including the imprisonment of Peter Bellinger and three other Patriots, all with extensive farms, because they refused to sell their wheat to the committee at a price below the market value. Radicals in the committee had also encouraged Oneida Iroquois to attack and burn out suspected Loyalists. The Mohawks, whatever their loyalty, also suffered at the hands of the radicals. White Patriots had already threatened two neutral Mohawk chiefs, Isaac and John, who were also prosperous farmers, and forced them to flee the valley in 1777. Now in 1778, with the tacit approval of the committee, whites robbed and looted the homes of the few neutral or pro-Patriot Mohawks still in Tryon County. General Schuyler finally warned the committee on March 11, 1778, to take steps to stop these crimes, but by that time it was too late. Most neutral and pro-Patriot Mohawks had fled.[44]

Schuyler's letter did not dampen the zeal of the committee against white Loyalists, as the committee continued to advocate strict suppression of suspected Loyalists. When the New York Constitution of 1777 provided for county judges, committee members often became judges, and the committee leaders thereby continued to maintain power. In the spring of 1778, the state legislature abolished all committees of safety in New York in favor of the "Commissioners of Conspiracy" appointed by the governor. There was no longer any justification for the continuation of the Tryon County Committee, but even after all the other committees in New York had dissolved themselves, Tryon County radicals refused to relinquish their power to the state. They feared that state-appointed Commissioners of Conspiracy would be men of wealth and influence, and therefore of moderation. The committee of safety's demise came in May 1778, when it decided to free a debtor from the county jail. The committee organized an armed posse, forcibly released the man from jail, and proceeded to charge the creditor with all of the costs of the case. The state legislature learned of the case and successfully demanded that the committee disband.[45]

To raise money to support the Patriot cause, the Commissioners of Sequestration—Christopher P. Yates, Jacob Klock, Jeremiah Van Rensselaer, and Henry Oathout—sold portions of Loyalist estates. In addition, farms of Loyalists who had fled to Canada were rented out. Personal property, such as bedsteads, chairs, slaves, sheep, and cows were sold from the estates of Sir John Johnson, John Butler, Daniel Claus, and other propertied men. Then, on October 20, 1779, all the lands and homes of these prominent Loyalists were declared forfeit. Sir John's manor, Johnson Hall, and seven hundred acres were sold to James Caldwell from Albany for $30,000 in public securities.[46]

Among the Patriots, Loyalists, and Iroquois, the largest burden of the Revolution fell upon the widows of the men who died at Oriskany or in later battles. Among the Patriots, for example, Elizabeth Irine was left with six children, aged five to thirteen. She petitioned Gov. George Clinton for relief and was granted £7. Loyalist and Iroquois refugee families in Canada received similar compensation.[47]

Of all the settlements in Tryon County, German Flats was the most vulnerable to attack, because it lay on the fringe of the frontier. As a result, by the end of the war, the settlement had been devastated. In 1777 the community lost "a great many of our Sons and Neighbors" at Oriskany.[48] On September 12, 1778, 300 Loyalists, Joseph Brant, and 150 Iroquois struck the settlement at dawn. The pro-British Iroquois were angered not only by the losses at Oriskany, but also by how Patriots had driven neutral and pro-Patriot Mohawk families out of their homes. The inhabitants of German Flats had been warned by scouts and were safely inside two forts, but the Loyalist attackers burned most of the homes, barns, and the freshly harvested wheat. On November 11, 1778, the Iroquois and their Loyalist allies, led by Joseph Brant and Walter Butler, John Butler's son, launched another attack, this time on Cherry Valley to secure winter food supplies for their families. This raid was necessary because supplies the British had promised to the Iroquois had not arrived at Fort Niagara, and the Iroquois were desperate. During the raid on Cherry Valley, some of the Iroquois warriors killed more than 30 civilians.

Although the horrors of war were attributed by each side to everyone on the "other side," terrorist tactics in Tryon County were evidently carried out by only a minority on either side. On both sides, a few lost their self-control and were caught up in the passion of their cause. In Tryon County this process began when *some* Patriot zealots drove neutral Mohawks from their homes and was intensified when *some* Iroquois attacked victims at places like Cherry Valley. Whatever the reasons, the escalation of havoc continued after 1778. The Iroquois raids of 1778 prompted the Patriots to launch an invasion of Iroquois country in 1779, in what became known as the "Sullivan-Clinton Campaign" after its commanders, Gens. John Sullivan and James Clinton. In April the first wave of this assault was launched from Fort Stanwix against the Onondagas. Patriot troops under Col. Goose Van Schaick killed warriors, women, and children— the exact number is not known. Patriot soldiers raped some young Onondaga women and then murdered them.[49]

In August a main Patriot army marched into the country of the Cayugas and Senecas. The Iroquois warriors, knowing what had happened at Onondaga, withdrew the women, children, and old people from their towns. The campaign destroyed Iroquois towns and cornfields but did not knock the Iroquois out of the war. Iroquois warriors retaliated in the following years. The last significant battle fought in Tryon County occurred late in October 1781. Maj. John Ross, Capt. Walter Butler (whom the Patriots detested because of the devastating raid on Cherry Valley), and a force of seven hundred Loyalists, regulars, and Iroquois attacked the Mohawk Valley near Johnstown. About eight hundred militia and

Continental soldiers met Ross's force at Johnstown and fought to a stalemate, after which Ross's force withdrew. As the Patriots pursued the retreating column, an Oneida warrior scouting for the Patriots shot and killed a Loyalist Ranger who turned out to be Walter Butler.[50]

Intermittent raids continued. In June 1782 Loyalists burned the mill serving German Flats, forcing the farmers to cart their grain twenty-two miles to the next mill. Then on July 15, 1782, a month after the mill had been burned, a large force of Iroquois and Loyalists struck German Flats again. All residents were evidently safely inside the forts, but the raiders burned all but seven of the sixty homes, left only five barns standing, and carried off or slaughtered all the cattle.[51]

Revolutionary Warfare Fades to an Uneasy Peace

When the war ended in 1783, pro-British Iroquois warriors and Loyalists felt that they had been betrayed. Under the Treaty of Paris, the new United States claimed jurisdiction over all Iroquois lands. The peace settlement included only a vague provision to compensate Loyalists for property that had been seized by the Patriots. It was a "ruinous peace."[52]

Although the frontier line of white settlements at German Flats never collapsed, the Patriot inhabitants of Tryon County were too few, too exhausted, or too economically depressed to play a major role in the expansion that followed the war. Land speculators from New York City and other eastern cities were soon selling choice lands in German Flats to strangers from Massachusetts and Connecticut. In the late 1790s Adonijah Barnard from Connecticut carved out a farm on the fertile slopes that rose from bog and narrow creek where, in 1777, two hundred Tryon County men had given their lives in the Battle of Oriskany.[53]

After the war, Jelles Fonda reestablished his friendship with Loyalists like John Butler, and they agreed to settle prewar debts. Fonda's tolerant spirit is especially remarkable because pro-British Iroquois warriors under the command of Sir John Johnson had killed his elderly father, Douwe Fonda, during a raid in 1780. Fonda, the moderate Christopher Yates, and the Loyalist Hendrick Frey did their best to persuade, but could not get the state legislature to reimburse Loyalists for their losses. In return, John Butler arranged to have Fonda's slaves, who had been captured and taken to Canada during the war, returned to him.[54] This act of cooperation, however, simultaneously reveals that for most slaves neither Loyalism nor liberty meant freedom.

For more than two centuries after the Revolution, the Mohawk Nation did not reestablish its presence in the Mohawk Valley. Finally, in 1993, the nucleus of a new Mohawk community was established in the valley by Chief Tom Porter (Sakokwenionkwas—"The One Who Wins"). The educational center there encourages the survival of the Mohawk language and Mohawk traditions, and is partially supported by the community's bed and breakfast. The Mohawk and colonial backgrounds of Tryon County's Revolution are evoked by two names visitors encounter there. First, the name of the Mohawk community itself: Kanatsiohareke (Ga-nah-jo-ha-lay-gay), the Mohawk spelling of Canajoharie, meaning "a kettle-shaped hole in the rock" or "the pot that washes itself" because of a rushing stream that seemed to boil over the hole.[55] The second name appears on a metal sign erected by the State of New York that notes that this particular piece of land was once owned by the Patriot Jelles Fonda.[56]

Notes

1. Lester J. Cappon et al., eds., *Atlas of Early American History: The Revolutionary Era* (Princeton, 1976), 4, 21, 79, and 96.

2. The land and legal structures of the Iroquois Confederacy are reviewed in Robert W. Venables, "Some Observations of the Treaty Canandaigua," in G. Peter Jemison and Anna M. Schein, eds., *Treaty of Canandaigua* (Santa Fe, N.M., 2000), 101 and passim; Sherene Baugher and Robert W. Venables, "Indians within New York State: Separate Nations, Not Just Ethnic Minorities," in Thomas A. Hirschl and Tim B. Heaton, eds., *New York State in the 21st Century* (Westport, Conn., 1999), 75–90; and Robert W. Venables, "Iroquois Environments and 'We the People of the United States,'" in Christopher Vecsey and Robert W. Venables, eds., *American Indian Environments: Ecological Issues in Native American History* (Syracuse, 1980), 81–127.

3. A partial list of these Masons is found in the "Will of Sir William Johnson," Jan. 27, 1774, in James Sullivan et al., eds., *The Papers of Sir William Johnson*, 14 vols. (New York, 1921–1965), 12: 1075, 1075 n. 28.

4. Proceedings of the United Committees, June 2, 1775, Tryon County 1774–1794 MSS, New–York Historical Society, New York [hereafter NYHS].

5. Ibid.

6. Frey Papers Catalogue, Introduction, State Library of New York, Albany, N.Y. [hereafter NYSL]; William W. Campbell, *The Border Warfare of New York during the Revolution: or Annals of Tryon County* (New York, 1849), 28; and William Leete Stone, *Life of Joseph Brant (Thayendanega) Including the Border Wars of the American Revolution*, 2 vols. (New York, 1865), 1: 217.

7. Mary Lou Lustig, *Robert Hunter, 1666–1734: New York's Augustan Statesman* (Syracuse, N.Y., 1983), 49–50, 60–98, 126–27, 164–66, and 220; Nelson Greene, ed., *The History of the Mohawk Valley, Gateway to the West, 1614–1925*. 4 vols. (New York, 1925), 1: 654–56; John W. Barber and Henry Howe, *Historical Collections of the State of New York* (New York, 1842), 281; and Campbell, *Border Warfare*, 30.

8. Introduction, Frey Papers Catalogue; deed of Bernard Frey to John Frey, Jan. 23, 1726; and deed of Harme Van Slyck of Schenectady to Hendrick Frey, Oct. 16, 1728;

Frey Papers, NYSL. Campbell, *Border Warfare* (New York, 1849), 28, 32; and Francis Whiting Halsey, *The Old New York Frontier* (New York, 1901), 139.

9. Lois M. Huey and Bonnie Pulis, *Molly Brant: A Legacy of Her Own* (Youngstown, N.Y., 1997), 19.

10. James Thomas Flexner, *Lord of the Mohawks: A Biography of Sir William Johnson* (revised edition; Boston, 1979), 13–16.

11. Ibid., 157–60, 166–67; and Arthur Pound, *Johnson of the Mohawks; A Biography of Sir William Johnson, Irish Immigrant, Mohawk War Chief, American Soldier, Empire Builder* (New York, 1930), 291.

12. Howard Swiggett, *War Out of Niagara: Walter Butler and the Tory Rangers* (New York, 1933), 18; and Pound, *Johnson of the Mohawks*, 430.

13. Barbara Graymont, *The Iroquois in the American Revolution* (Syracuse, N.Y., 1972), 13, 29, 157–59; and Huey and Pulis, *Molly Brant*, 13.

14. Huey and Pulis, *Molly Brant*, 19–23.

15. Isabel Thompson Kelsay, *Joseph Brant, 1743–1807: Man of Two Worlds* (Syracuse, N.Y., 1984), 43.

16. Graymont, *Iroquois in the Revolution*, 30; and H. Pearson Gundy, "Molly Brant—Loyalist" *Ontario History* 45 (1953): 97–108.

17. Grant of permission by Gov. Henry Moore to Johan Jost Herkimer and Henry Bell to collect funds for a church, June 2, 1767; and indenture and grant of land by Han Jost Herkimer to Nicholas Herkimer, July 3, 1771, The Herkimer Family and Battle of Oriskany Portfolio, NYSL [hereafter Herkimer–Oriskany Portfolio]. Greene, ed., *Mohawk Valley,* 1: 650, 670–86. Account of William Hare with Jelles Fonda, 1768 to 1769, MS 250, Abbott Collection, NYSL. Jelles Fonda, Account Book, 1767–1771, MSS 251, 252, NYHS. Indenture and deed by John Cruger et. al. to Jelles Fonda, Nov. 21, 1768, MS 385; Peter Wolleben, Feb. 25, 1769; indenture with Samuel Stringer, Sept. 8, 1769, MS 199; William Hare to Jelles Fonda, Sept. 24, 1769, MS 187; indenture and deed of Hendrick Frey to John Frey, Mar. 5, 1772, MS 246; and indenture and deed of Hendrick Frey to Barent Frey, Mar. 5, 1772, MS 248, Frey Papers, NYSL. Account Book of Jelles Fonda, 1771–1772, MS-3–35, Fort Johnson, New York; and William Wane to Jelles Fonda, Mar. 8, 1766, MS 925, Fort Johnson.

18. Flexner, *Lord of the Mohawks*, 347.

19. Perhaps three times as many Mohawks lived in the St. Lawrence Valley. They had once been allies of the French, but in 1763, during ceremonies held by both the Iroquois Confederacy and the Mohawk Nation, these Mohawks allied themselves with their Mohawk Valley relatives, politically reuniting these St. Lawrence Mohawks with both the Mohawk Nation and the whole Iroquois Confederacy. Sir John Johnson to Daniel Claus, Jan. 20, 1777, Claus Papers, Microfilm, 4 vols., Public Archives of Canada, Ottawa [hereafter Archives Ottawa], C-1478, 1: 232–33; Huey and Pulis, *Molly Brant*, 15; "An Indian Congress," Sept. 1–18, 1763, in Sullivan et al., eds., *Papers of William Johnson*,

10: 839–43, 852; and Sir William Johnson, "Present State of the Northern Indians," Nov. 18, 1763, in E.B. O'Callaghan, ed., *Documents Relative to the Colonial History of the State of New-York*, 15 vols. (New York, 1856–1861) 7: 582.

20. Committee of Correspondence, May 18, 1775, draft of the Committee of Correspondence; two Declarations, May 18, 1775, Tryon County 1774–1794, NYHS. Three Declarations of opposition to the recent statement of the Grand Jury, May 15, 1775, NYHS. Also see Report of United Committee, Aug. 1775, endorsed by the Committee on Aug. 29, 1775, in Sullivan et al., eds., *Papers of William Johnson*, 8: 1204–1206.

21. Proceedings of the United Meeting of the Committees of Palatine, Canajoharie, Kingsland, and German Flats, May 24, 1775, Tryon County 1774–1794, NYHS.

22. Ibid.

23. Ibid. Ebenezer Cox to Nicholas Herkimer, July 16, 1774; and Writ for the arrest of [Julian] Cox, June 15, 1767, Herkimer–Oriskany Portfolio, NYSL.

24. Proceedings of the United Meeting of the Committees of Palatine, Canajoharie, Kingsland, and German Flats, May 24, 1775, Tryon County 1774–1794, NYHS; and Greene, ed., *Mohawk Valley*, 1: 695.

25. Halsey, *Old New York Frontier*, 149–50.

26. Proceedings of the United Committees, June 2, 1775, Tryon County 1774–1794, NYHS.

27. Proceedings of the United Committees, June 3, 1775, Tryon County 1774–1794, NYHS; Daniel Claus to Gen. Haldimand, Dec. 2, 1774, Claus Papers, Archives Ottawa, C-1478, 1: 176–78; Joshua Chew to Henry Hughes and Henry Holland, Mar. 3, 1775, Frey Papers, NYSL; Kelsay, *Joseph Brant*, 43; and Greene, ed., *Mohawk Valley*, 1: 641.

28. "A Speech from the People of the German flats to the Oneidas & Tuscaroras—28 June 1775," Tryon County 1775, NYHS; Halsey, *Old New York Frontier*, 150.

29. Ibid.

30. Sir John Johnson, Sept. 10, 1775, to Daniel Claus, Claus Papers, Archives Ottawa, C-1478, 1: 206.

31. Declaration of Crownridge Rinkeu, John Collens, and Marte J. Van Alstyne, Sept. 7, 1775, Tryon County 1774–1794, NYHS; Lewis Clement, Sept. 6, 1775, to Tryon County Committee of Safety, Tryon County 1774–1794, NYHS; Memorial of Alexander White to Gov. Haldimand, Sept. 15, 1783, Haldimand B.215, 59; Campbell, *Border Warfare*, 74; and Proceedings of the Tryon County Committee of Safety, Dec. 27, 1775, Tryon County 1774–1794, NYHS.

32. Isaac Paris, Chairman, Tryon County Committee of Safety, to Maj. Gen. Philip Schuyler, Jan. 11, 1776, Tryon County 1775, 1776, 1776 [sic], NYHS; Campbell, *Border Warfare*, 78.

33. Sir John Johnson to Daniel Claus, Sept. 10, 1775, Claus Papers, Archives Ottawa, C-1478, 1: 206; Mabel G. Walker, "Sir John Johnson, Loyalist," *The Mississippi Valley Historical Review* 3 (Dec., 1961): 318–46; Barber and Howe, *Historical Collections*, 170. Oaths of allegiance by five men, Jan. 22, 1776; Oaths of neutrality by six men, Jan. 23, 1776, Tryon County 1775, NYHS. Also see Indenture and deed of Bernard Frey to John Frey, Jan. 23, 1776, MS 249, and Memorandum of [Jelles Fonda] at Caughnawaga, Apr. 20, 1776, MS 91, Frey Papers, NYSL; copy of the Record of the New York Provincial Congress, Feb. 15, 1776, Tryon County 1775, NYHS.

34. Subscription agreements, April 24, May 11, 1776, Tryon County 1775, NYHS.

35. Thomas Spencer [Oneida chief] to unknown person, April 14, 1776; Frederick Fisher to Samson Sammons, Mar. 2, 1776, Tryon County 1775, NYHS. Campbell, *Border Warfare*, 80.

36. Sir John Johnson, to Daniel Claus, Jan. 20, 1777; Guy Johnson, [to Daniel Claus], Aug. 9, 1776, James [Blackburn?] in London to Daniel Claus, Aug. 28, 1776, Claus Papers, Archives Ottawa C-1478, 1: 232, 216, 226. Memorial of Sir John Johnson to Commissioners of Parliament, [1780s], Upper Canada Village Restoration, Ontario, Canada.

37. "Juvinus," *"General Harkemer's Battle: A New Song to the Tune of the British Boys,"* Dec. 5, 1777, New York, Willett Collection, NYHS. "Juvinus" was undoubtedly Marinus Willett, second-in-command at Fort Stanwix. This fascinating manuscript, dedicated to the officers of the 3rd New York, contains twenty-two verses of poor poetry but valuable information that has not come down through other sources. Also see Christopher Ward, *The War of the Revolution*, ed. John Richard Alden, 2 vols. (New York, 1952), 2: 491; Campbell, *Border Warfare*, 102.

38. *Gentleman's Magazine*, XLVII, 1777 (London, 1777), 241.

39. Sir John Johnson, *Orderly Book*, ed. William Leete Stone (New York, 1882), 111n.; Stone, *Brant*, 1: 242, 249; Campbell, *Border Warfare*, 105, 107; and Oneida Historical Society, *Memorial of the Centennial Celebration of the Battle of Oriskany* (Utica, New York, 1878), 79, 128.

40. William M. Willett, *A Narrative of the Military Actions of Colonel Marinus Willett, Taken Chiefly from His Own Manuscript* (New York, 1831), 53; Stone, *Brant*, 1: 246; Barber and Howe, *Historical Collections*, 193; Oneida Historical Society, *Memorial*, 88; Campbell, *Border Warfare*, 104; and Henry R. Schoolcraft, *Historical Considerations on the Siege and Defense of Fort Stanwix in 1777* (New York, 1846), 104.

41. List of officials, Palatine District, Feb. 7, 1778, Tryon County 1774–1794, NYHS; Milo Nellis, *The Mohawk Dutch and the Palatines* (St. Johnsville, N.Y., 1951), 84–85.

42. William Colbrath, Aug. 6, 1777, Journal Written at Fort Schuyler (Fort Stanwix) Apr. 17–Aug. 24, 1777, Photostat, New York Public Library, New York; Marinus Willett, Aug. 6, 1777, Diary, Aug. 2–Aug. 6, 1777, photostat, NYHS; Willett, *Narrative*, 313;

Ward, *War of the Revolution*, 2: 491; Stone, *Brant*, 1: 243–44; and Campbell, *Border Warfare*, 105.

43. List of officials, Palatine District, Feb. 7, 1778, Tryon County 1774–1794, NYHS; Poll list for [Palatine District?] Tryon County in accordance with an act of the state legislature on Mar. 27, 1778, MS204, Frey Papers, NYSL; and Declaration of the Committee of Safety of Tryon County, Mar. 10, 1778, Tryon County 1774–1794, NYHS.

44. Nicholas Rosecrantz, Matthew Wermot, George Ekar Jr., and Peter Bellinger, to the Tryon County Committee of Safety, Mar. 22, 1778, Tryon County 1774–1794, NYHS; Daniel Claus to Sir John Johnson, Oct. 15, 1781, Claus Papers, Archives Ottawa, Microfilm C-1478, 3: 51–52; and Philip Schuyler to the Tryon County Committee of Safety, Mar. 11, 1778, MS 12, Philip Schuyler Papers, NYSL.

45. Matthew Visscher and [John?] Rensselaer, May 17, 1778, to the Tryon County Committee of Safety, Tryon County 1774–1794, NYHS.

46. William Barent Wemple, "Wemple Family Genealogy" (handwritten, Fonda, N.Y., 1898), courtesy of the family of W. Barent Wemple, Fonda, N.Y.; Pound, *Johnson of the Mohawks*, 366; and Nellis, *Mohawk Dutch and the Palatines*, 85. Also see Hendrick Frey, Frederick Young, Adam Loucks, and Peter Ehl to the Chairman and the Tryon County Committee of Safety, Oct. 3, 1777, Tryon County 1775, NYHS; receipt of John Deygert to Richard Loucks, July 28, 1779, Upper Canada Village Restoration.

47. Petition of Elizabeth Hiller, Catherine Remar, Elizabeth Irine, Catherine Ringle, Gertrude Steinwax, Elizabeth Bowen, and Elizabeth Brown, widows of German Town, Kingsland District, after [Aug. 2, 1779], to Gov. George Clinton, including "A Return of the Within Families" indicating allowances granted, Tryon County 1774–1794, NYHS; Peter S. Dygert, Mar. 1782–Sept. 1783, Account of the Commissioners of Sequestration at Caughnawaga, MS 200, Abbott Collection, NYSL. Rachel Hansen to Peter Hansen, Feb. 27, 1780; Jelles Fonda to Peter Mansen, Mar. 4, 1780; R. Mathews to Daniel Claus, Mar. 16, 1780; and Guy Carleton to Daniel Claus, Mar. 1780, Claus Papers, Archives Ottawa, C-1478, 2: 181, 182, 191–92;195.

48. Petition of the Inhabitants of German Flats to the State Legislature, Feb. 15, 1783, Miscellaneous Papers of Tryon County, NYHS.

49. Tioguanda [Tiahogwando], Onondaga leader, speech to Maclean, Dec. 11, 1782, Haldimand B.102, 250; Col. Bolton to Guy Carleton, Jan. 13, 1778, Haldimand B.100, 11; Daniel Claus to James Blackburn in London, June 18, 1781, Claus Papers, C-1478, 3: 29; Col. Bolton to Gov. Haldimand, Oct. 12, 1778, Haldimand B.100, 58; and Graymont, *Iroquois in the Revolution*, 192. Also see Frederick Cook, ed., *Journals of the Military Expedition of Major General John Sullivan Against the Six Nations of Indians in 1779 with Records of Centennial Celebrations* (Auburn, N.Y., 1887) and Joseph R. Fischer, *A Well-Executed Failure: The Sullivan Campaign against the Iroquois, July–September 1779* (Colombia, S.C., 1997).

50. Swiggett, *War Out of Niagara*, 238–45; Ward, *War of the Revolution*, 2: 651–52; and Gov. Haldimand to Brig. Gen. H. Watson Powell, Nov. 16, 1781, Haldimand B.104, 289.

51. Two Petitions of the Inhabitants of German Flats to the State Legislature, July 24, 1782, and Feb. 15, 1783, Miscellaneous Papers of Tryon County, NYHS; and Ward, *War of the Revolution*, 2: 633.

52. Daniel Claus to James Blackburn in London, June 14, 1783, Claus Papers, Archives Ottawa, C-1478, 3: 223–24.

53. Greene, ed., *Mohawk Valley*, 1: 656; Minnie E. Barnard to the Rome Historical Society, Oct. 28, 1957, Fort Stanwix Museum, Rome, N.Y.

54. Jelles Fonda to John Butler, June 10, 1783, MS263; Jelles Fonda to John Butler, Mar. 22, 1784, MS265; and Jelles Fonda to John Butler, July 7, 1786, MS269, Abbott Collection, NYSL. Jelles Fonda to (Dr. Davi?) at Niagara, Feb. 25, 1786, MS 191, Frey Papers, NYSL. Swiggett, *War Out of Niagara*, 214.

55. William M. Beauchamp, *Aboriginal Place Names of New York*, Bulletin 108 (May 1907) *Archaeology* 12 (Albany, N.Y., 1907), 120–21; and George R. Stewart, *American Place-Names* (New York, 1970), 74.

56. Kanatsiohareke, on four hundred acres, is located at 4934 State Highway 5, Fonda, N.Y.

9

Charlotte County

Paul R. Huey

Colonial Charlotte County was created on March 12, 1772, out of northern Albany County. In 1786, without what is now Vermont, it had a population of 4,456 persons. The story of this county is one of constant hostility among a few people in a large region. The new county included all of Lakes George and Champlain, the eastern Adirondack Mountains, the headwaters of the Hudson River, and what is now western Vermont. After the Revolution, the part that remained in New York State included most of present-day Washington, Warren, and Franklin Counties and all of Essex and Clinton Counties.

Throughout the colonial period, the territory that became Charlotte County included the Hudson River-Lake George-Lake Champlain corridor, which was economically crucial and the major trade route between Albany and Canada. From 1690 to 1815, this corridor was the scene of nearly continuous military conflict and civil unrest. Following Britain's victory in the French and Indian War (1754–1763), an explosive mixture of people—Anglican and Congregational New Englanders, immigrants (including Scottish and North Irish Presbyterians and British veterans), New Yorkers, and New Jersey Presbyterians—inundated the region to acquire farms, exploit its natural resources, and develop its economy. Many settlers had arrived carrying land titles that conflicted with those held by other residents and settlers.

In the Revolution, as in earlier wars in the northern colonies, much of Charlotte became a "Seat of War." Nonetheless, to this multiethnic population the military events taking place here, although some of the most consequential in the state, were secondary to the bitter land disputes that plagued them. Thus, Charlotte was really a series of frontier settlements, whose residents were more concerned with wresting a living or a fortune from the land than with debating

199

or resisting British imperial policy. This essay will demonstrate that allegiances during the Revolution were, in part, the results of colonial conflicts, as many prewar friends and allies remained so in wartime, and many prewar antagonists remained so after 1775. The Revolution inadvertently helped to force the settlement of old grievances throughout the region.[1]

1.

Disputes over land titles, many of which turned violent, were fundamental in shaping Charlotte County throughout the colonial and Revolutionary periods.[2] The eighteenth-century struggle for empire between Britain and France palpably influenced the pace of settlement and the ensuing conflicts in Charlotte County. King George's War (1740–1748) and the French and Indian War halted settlement along the upper Hudson River. However, during the interwar period, the thirst for land provoked discord. In November 1749 Gov. Benning Wentworth of New Hampshire notified New York's royal governor, George Clinton, of his intention to issue land grants in western New Hampshire. He asserted that his colony's southern boundary line, when extended westward, met the Hudson at its junction with the Mohawk River. Clinton replied that New York and Connecticut had agreed in 1684 to set the latter's western boundary, which was finally surveyed in 1725, at about twenty miles east of the Hudson, but that north of Connecticut, New York's eastern boundary remained the Connecticut River. In 1751 Wentworth intrepidly issued the Bennington grant, in present Vermont, which conflicted with New York grants in the same area. In March 1751 he unilaterally "extended the Western Boundary of New Hampshire as far West as the Massachusetts have done theirs, that is, within twenty miles of Hudsons River." During the French and Indian War, Wentworth issued New Hampshire land grants in the area west from the Connecticut River (the present western boundary of New Hampshire) to twenty miles east of the Hudson.[3]

During the war, the British constructed new bastions at Fort Edward, Lake George (Fort George), Ticonderoga, and Crown Point. Nearby communities that had been abandoned at the war's outset could now be reoccupied, and new settlements established. Because New York claimed this region from the upper Hudson through Lake Champlain as part of northern Albany County, it distributed several grants in the area. In 1761 John Henry Lydius, who had earlier settled at Fort Edward, sought a land grant to establish a community of New Englanders on the east side of the upper Hudson. In May 1762 New York's acting governor, Cadwallader Colden, gave Irish-born James Bradshaw and twenty-two associates, mostly from southwestern Connecticut, a grant for the town of Kingsbury, just north of Fort Edward.[4] In 1759 Maj. Philip Skene (a retired British army officer, who had been wounded in the war) had petitioned

Maj. Gen. Jeffery Amherst, the British commander-in-chief, for land at the southern edge of Lake Champlain, where he had already settled a "number of poor families" in what would become Skenesborough in 1765. Meanwhile, Irish-born William Gilliland in 1763 petitioned New York for land on the west side of Lake Champlain, north of Crown Point. All of the patents were in areas claimed by New Hampshire.[5]

Settlers were not far behind. Many Connecticut families traveled up the Housatonic River and headed west along the Batten Kill, the southern boundary of what would become Charlotte County. Former British soldiers were applying for land from New York pursuant to the British Proclamation of 1763, which provided for land grants to veterans of the French and Indian War. New Yorkers were consequently alarmed that New Hampshire continued to complicate land titles by pushing its claim westward to Lake Champlain and by granting new townships there. New Hampshire considered its boundary to be twenty miles east of the Hudson, even though at this latitude the river was many miles west of Lake Champlain. In 1764 the Board of Trade decided the dispute in New York's favor, by declaring that the boundary between the two colonies was the Connecticut River. New Hampshire ceased issuing grants. But violence erupted almost immediately in the area, between the Connecticut and Hudson Rivers, where New York and New Hampshire had been issuing conflicting land patents, because settlers with New Hampshire patents refused to acknowledge that the Green Mountain region belonged to New York.[6] Meanwhile, settlement occurred rapidly in the region twenty miles east of the Hudson and north of the Batten Kill, where in 1764 Lt. Gov. Cadwallader Colden issued several patents: the Argyle Patent of 47,450 acres to a group of Scottish immigrants; the Provincials Patent of 26,000 acres; the Artillery Patent of 24,000 acres; a grant of 10,200 acres to John Tabor Kempe, John Morin Scott, and others; and another patent of 25,000 acres to Alexander Turner and a group of investors from Massachusetts and New Hampshire. In 1765 Turner sold part of his patent to Rev. Thomas Clark (a Scottish-born Presbyterian minister, physician, and financier) and his congregation from northern Ireland. They named the settlement New Perth. Settlers from New England bought another part of the same patent and called their community White Creek. Along the Batten Kill, Baptists from Rhode Island also began settling in 1764.[7]

Conflict occurred almost immediately between Yorkers and Yankees and between previous and recent New York grantees. In the spring of 1765, on the Argyle Patent, several new allottees under New York patents found their land occupied by a person claiming title under an earlier New York patent. Violence ensued, and the original settler was arrested. Other newcomers faced land title conflicts in the Lake Champlain region, because parts of the area had already been granted as seigniories to French owners. Some New York patentees, such as Philip Skene and William Gilliland, were angry with Colden and his son Alexander, the surveyor general, for not promptly settling patent conflicts. Trouble developed, too, in Gilliland's Willsborough settlement on the west side of Lake Champlain, north of Crown Point. Between February and June 1766 at least eight disgruntled tenants left the patent with some of his property. Soldiers from Crown Point were called out to subdue them. Interestingly, this event coincided with the violent tenant riots in Dutchess and Albany counties and the Stamp Act disturbances in the cities of New York and Albany. Clearly many Charlotte County residents were more concerned about local disputes than imperial relations.[8]

Increasing numbers of New Englanders settled on the east side of the lake. On May 20, 1766, Capt. John Montresor, a British officer, reported: "They declare that possession is Eleven points in the Law and that they will take advantage of these [Stamp Act] Disturbances and as no law prevails at present will support themselves . . . as new England men." Subsequently, a number of settlers owning land or living at Willsborough, Crown Point, Ticonderoga, Skenesborough, but especially at Kingsbury (because of its strong Connecticut ties) supported the New Hampshire grants. Another alarming development was the rapid and very visible decay of the recently built British forts at Ticonderoga and Crown Point by 1765. Who would defend the new settlers from Indians or from rival claimants?[9]

Despite these problems, the economic potential of the Lake Champlain region impressed many people. English- and Irish-born veterans continued to arrive in Skenesborough and elsewhere in 1767 and 1768, while Connecticut settlers flocked to Kingsbury.[10] More settlers, many from Scotland, Ireland, and England, arrived between 1770 and 1774. Groups from southeastern and western Massachusetts settled in Skenesborough and nearby Granville. Connecticut, too, contributed settlers: from Killingly in the eastern part of the colony; from Hebron and Lebanon in the central part; and from Colchester, Woodbury, Wallingford, and New Haven in the west. In addition, members of a Presbyterian congregation in Morris County, New Jersey, moved to Willsborough.[11]

The growing population inevitably caused more conflict over land titles. On June 11, 1771, Robert Cochran and a band of fourteen armed men, who supported the New Hampshire grantees, violently dispossessed a patentee of his 350 acres in Argyle Patent, attacked some of his neighbors, and burned their homes. Gov. William Tryon of New York warned the British ministry that unless the problem of conflicting land titles was resolved, "the daring insults of these people will in a short time lead to serious consequences." On December 9, Tryon offered a reward for the arrest of Cochran, Ethan Allen, Remember Baker, and Seth Warner, the leaders of the "New Hampshire Rioters." In February 1772 these men responded with a defiant proclamation offering rewards for the apprehension of New York attorneys, James Duane and John Tabor Kempe, because they had purchased from New York authorities lands that New Hampshire grantees claimed.[12]

Despite the unrest, Governor Tryon issued still more grants early in 1771, including over one thousand acres at Crown Point to Adolphus Benzel and his wife. Northwest from Crown Point, Tryon granted Philip Skene three thousand acres that included a valuable iron ore bed. Skene began to mine the ore and transport it to Skenesborough. He built a large new home, Skenesborough House, a barn of limestone, a bloomery to produce iron from his mines, and vessels to navigate Lake Champlain between Skenesborough and Canada. In one of the first statements made in this region about the impending imperial conflict, he had declared in 1770 that as a British officer he would have stoutly opposed the mob at the Boston Massacre, and that Americans were attempting rapid change a century too soon.[13]

Despite their distance from population centers, some aspiring households developed considerable refinement. A visitor to Adolphus Benzel's Crown Point home later recalled "seeing silver plate upon the table, with other appliances of wealth and luxury in the village." A letter promoting Gilliland's Willsborough settlement mentioned "the men in good circumstances, and remarkable for industry and activity." English-born William Duer arrived in New York in 1768, purchased timberland, established large sawmills along the Hudson River in the Fort Miller area, and built an elegant frame house having "an air of baronial splendor." An observer considered it the "first regular country-house" south of Canada and wondered how this "magnificent" house, which "could be called a small castle," existed "in this wilderness." At Fort Edward Irish-born Patrick Smyth, who acquired land from Duer in 1772, also built a stylish, two-story frame house.[14]

In the early 1770s land speculators continued to obtain large tracts. In July 1772, four months after New York had established Charlotte County, the Mohawk and Oneida Indians conveyed about nine hundred thousand acres to Thomas Palmer's syndicate and to Joseph Totten and Stephen Crossfield of New York City. Because these large tracts involved direct private purchases and were contrary to the Proclamation of 1763, the British government sharply scolded Gov. William Tryon. Nevertheless, Totten ultimately became a Loyalist. In late 1772 Edward and Ebenezer Jessup of Connecticut and some Dutch investors from the Mohawk Valley obtained forty thousand acres from New York in the rugged mountain area of the upper Hudson, where they established the township of Hyde.[15]

Violence soon came. On the morning of April 21, 1773, a fire broke out at Crown Point in a barracks chimney. The fire spread, and the magazine bastion exploded. "New England People" allegedly started the fire and plundered the burning fort. They were further antagonized when New York and Massachusetts resolved their boundary dispute by extending the New York-Connecticut boundary line northward to the Green Mountain region claimed by New Hampshire. Ethan Allen and the "New Hampshire Rioters" soon embarked on a campaign to drive out settlers having New York land grants between the Connecticut River and Lake Champlain. The renewed violence led William Gilliland to request that New York protect the fifty families he had settled near Lake Champlain and also persuaded other patentees to abandon plans to settle the nearby Beekman patent with Highland Scots.[16]

With New Englanders now building their own blockhouses east of Lake Champlain, New York hoped to rebuild Crown Point, but the British instead built a solid redoubt at Point au Fer at the north end of Lake Champlain. In desperation, the New York Council sought from Gen. Thomas Gage, the army commander-in-chief and governor of Massachusetts, two hundred troops to reestablish control over the region the "New Hampshire Rioters" were terrorizing. Gage instead wrote the ministry for instructions, and in November 1774 he received orders to repair the forts at Crown Point and Ticonderoga. Soon thereafter, in June 1775, when Philip Skene arrived in Philadelphia from England, where he had been lobbying to be named lieutenant governor of Crown Point and Ticonderoga, the Americans arrested him. The Revolution had begun. The British never rebuilt Crown Point.[17]

2.

The situation in Charlotte was so confused at the outbreak of the Revolution that people's allegiances are difficult to explain. Many picked a side and remained firm in their loyalty throughout the war. Some residents (and patentees) switched from the American to the British side; others did the opposite. Too often, the reasons are unknown and can only be conjectured. Robert Cochran, for example, one of the "Green Mountain Boys," whom New York once considered an outlaw, became an officer in the New York Continental Line in 1776. Inexplicably, several inhabitants became spies, even double agents. Perhaps long years of self-interested conflicts over land had led some Charlotte residents to look upon the Revolution as but a way to advance their own ends.[18]

Understanding how the Revolution affected the allegiances of people in specific towns is also complicated. Although some communities had an ethnically or religiously mixed population, many people lived in patent-based, closely knit communities with distinctive cultural origins. The latter often agreed to support one side in the Revolution. This was especially true in places where Presbyterian and Baptist congregations had been established, for these churches tended to control their settlements and to uphold a cohesive moral discipline. In June 1775, for example, the Rhode Island Baptist congregation along the Batten Kill began recording their meetings and documenting their rigid discipline.[19] Members of the congregation supported the Patriot cause.

If the outbreak of war bound many communities more closely together, it created or sharpened divisions in others. Typically, a community that was divided against itself before the Revolution split over the Revolution. Argyle, for example, had three hostile groups of inhabitants: Scottish immigrants, to whom New York had granted patents in 1764; earlier settlers, who claimed title under the old New York Lydius patent; and defenders of the New Hampshire titles. Argyle predictably had its mixture of Patriots and Loyalists. Skenesborough and Kingsbury also split into Loyalist and Patriot factions. Skenesborough had been settled not only by people from Massachusetts and eastern Connecticut but also by settlers recruited by Philip Skene. Kingsbury was populated by settlers from both eastern and western Connecticut. Included were Anglicans, who tended to become Loyalists. Thomas Sherwood of this town joined the British, and his brother Justus Sherwood of Vermont became a British agent, while their cousin, Seth Sherwood, became an American militia captain.[20]

These three settlements suggest that one's place of origin helped determine the side one took in the Revolution. In general, the New Englanders, who populated the area of colonial Charlotte that became part of New York, were from Connecticut, Massachusetts, and New Hampshire. Interestingly, most Massachusetts settlers became Patriots. Settlers from Connecticut as well as from the vicinity of Pelham, Hampshire County, in western Massachusetts were attracted to White Creek; many became Patriots. Those from Westfield, Hampshire County, in southwestern Massachusetts went chiefly to Skenesborough and also included Patriots.[21]

Connecticut presents a complicated picture, but a pattern emerges. How Connecticut people living in Charlotte split over the Revolution reflected what was happening in Connecticut itself. With a few notable exceptions, if a line is drawn on a map of that state connecting Saybrook, Middletown, Farmington, and Simsbury, it appears that settlers from west of that line tended to become Patriots, and that those from the east leaned toward Loyalism. Many Patriot settlers who came from the vicinity of Woodbury, Litchfield County, in western Connecticut, settled at Crown Point/Ticonderoga, Granville, Black Creek, New Perth/White Creek, Argyle, Kingsbury, and the township of Hyde. For example, Seth Warner, a Green Mountain Boy who eventually became a Patriot militia captain, came from Woodbury. Remember Baker, another Green Mountain Boy, and his aunt, who was Ethan Allen's mother, also came from Woodbury. Ethan himself was born in Litchfield County.[22]

The relatively few people of this region who came from western Connecticut and became Loyalists included Kingsbury's Benjamin and Ebenezer Seelye (of New Milford and Litchfield), Thomas Sherwood (of Stratford), James Bradshaw (of New Milford), and the Jessup brothers (of Stamford). Ebenezer Jessup was an Anglican, and most of Connecticut's Loyalists were also Anglicans, people who lived concentrated "in the southwestern Fairfield County towns of Newtown, Redding, Ridgefield, Stratford, Stamford, and Norwalk, extending as far north as Woodbury, Litchfield, and Waterbury and east as far as New Haven." Hence, it may well be that the Charlotte Patriots who had migrated from western Connecticut were anti-Anglicans who left because of old conflicts with their predominantly Anglican neighbors in that part of Connecticut.[23]

Eastern Connecticut had "the reputation of being more radical than the western part of the colony." Hence, settlers who left this area for Charlotte before the Revolution and who later became Loyalists may have done so to escape their more radical neighbors. Eastern Connecticut, which was more densely settled than the western area of the colony, also suffered from an acute land shortage. The area around Killingly in northeastern Connecticut furnished numerous future Loyalists in Willsborough, Kingsbury, Skenesborough, and Granville, but especially in the latter two.

In 1775 the Charlotte Patriot militia was organized in the county's southeastern region and was commanded by English-born Col. John Williams, of the White Creek-New Perth area. Called the Dorset Regiment, it was composed of companies from White Creek, Kingsbury, Argyle, Black Creek, Skenesborough, and Granville. Interestingly, Dr. Thomas Clark's son, Ebenezer, and two militia officers, Capt. John Barnes and the Scottish-born Alexander Webster (who won election to the New York Provincial Congress in 1776), challenged Williams's leadership in 1778. The three complained to New York Gov. George Clinton about the harsh treatment and unreasonable fines that Williams had imposed on "a great many of our poor Distrest Inhabitants for Different reasons." Webster also accused Williams of "taking the New England's peoples part, who are Determined to root out the old Country people if they Can." Williams threatened to resign his commission as colonel, unless he (and not Webster) was appointed judge of the Charlotte County Court of Common Pleas. However, on June 25, 1778, Williams was dismissed from the militia for using false payrolls to defraud the Continental Pay Office, and he was also removed as a judge of that court. On April 13, 1779, Webster presided as judge over the Court of Common Pleas, which was held, ironically, "at the house of Dr. John Williams in New Perth."[24]

The intensifying military struggle in 1775 soon sharpened divisions among Charlotte residents. In May the British reinforced Ticonderoga with a small detachment of fifty troops from Canada. On May 10, Benedict Arnold, Ethan Allen, and the Green Mountain Boys captured Ticonderoga. The next day Seth Warner and another body of about one hundred Green Mountain Boys captured Crown Point.[25] The same month, the Charlotte County townships elected Dr. John Williams and William Marsh as the county's two delegates to the New York Provincial Convention. By June more than one hundred residents signed an Association in support of the Continental Congress. The first signer was William

Duer. Among the others were the brothers, Patrick and George Smyth, from Fort Edward, both of whom would eventually become Loyalists. Not to be outdone, ardent Loyalists soon began to unite in open opposition to the Association. An anti-Patriot "mob" of Charlotte County residents, who were "mostly debtors," joined by some men from Albany County, marched on the County Court with the "evil design" of closing the court and putting "a period to common law." However, the mob dispersed when Connecticut militia stationed at the fort, assisted by Remember Baker and Robert Cochran, two Green Mountain Boys, prepared to intercept them. In January 1776, Ebenezer Jessup, an Anglican, began raising Loyalist troops, while his brother Edward quickly sold lots in the mountainous township of Hyde to a Loyalist Anglican investor. The Jessups then successfully led a party of Loyalists to Canada, thanks to intelligence provided by Patrick and George Smyth.[26]

In the summer of 1776, as the American army that had been defeated in Canada retreated into the Lake Champlain region, tensions increased within Charlotte. At Crown Point, demoralized American troops clashed with the inhabitants of the nearby village, many of whom were Loyalists. In July most of the army withdrew southwards. In October British troops from Canada occupied Crown Point, but when they returned to Canada in November, most Crown Point residents and many other county Loyalists fled with them. The American Patriots soon arrested William Gilliland and some of his tenants who had remained in the town for allegedly aiding the British.[27]

In 1777 a British army under Lt. Gen. John Burgoyne invaded New York by advancing southward through the Champlain Valley. They captured Crown Point, Ticonderoga, Skenesborough, and then pushed on to Fort Edward, turning Charlotte into a battlefield. State authorities arrested Patrick Smyth of Fort Edward for Loyalism and took him to Albany. However, many other local Loyalists fled to Burgoyne. Adding to the confusion, the Indians who were aiding Burgoyne occasionally failed to distinguish Loyalist from Patriot. On July 26, in a bloody surprise attack, they raided the Argyle farm of John Allen, a Loyalist sympathizer, and brutally killed him, his wife, their two small children and baby, his sister-in-law, and two slaves. Their house afterward "presented a horrid spectacle." The next day, near Fort Edward, Indians captured, killed, and scalped a young woman named Jane McCrea, who was betrothed to a Loyalist officer serving under Burgoyne. This event "caused quite an uproar in the army," and Burgoyne severely reprimanded the Indians. News of both events spread terror throughout the region. The story of Jane McCrea later became romanticized, and she was transformed into a virtuous beauty—albeit a Loyalist. She became symbolic of the chaos of Burgoyne's campaign; the Allen family tragedy, on the other hand, has largely been forgotten.[28]

Burgoyne's army continued south, and on August 14 he made his headquarters across from Fort Miller at the palatial home of William Duer, now a delegate to the Continental Congress. However, Burgoyne soon learned that Lt. Col. Friedrich Baum, whom he had sent on a foraging expedition toward the southeast, had been defeated near Bennington. Within a month, the Americans had also attacked Burgoyne's overextended supply line from Canada, hitting the British at Ticonderoga and other places. At Ticonderoga, the Americans captured 200 bateaus, 17 gunboats, an armed sloop, and 293 prisoners, and they freed the more than 100 British-held prisoners. The Americans then sailed southward on Lake George but failed to take Diamond Island on September 24. Burgoyne was in trouble; help from Canada was not forthcoming, the British failure to pass Oriskany stopped help coming from the west along the Mohawk Valley, and aid from Sir Henry Clinton in the lower Hudson Valley never materialized. Outnumbered, Burgoyne was defeated at the Battle of Saratoga in October 1777.[29]

A number of Loyalists remained in the county after the battle, quietly worked on their farms, and hoped to escape retribution; others actually purchased farms or additional land in 1778. A few who quietly accepted the new state government remained after the war. But other more militant Loyalists instigated fear among residents by spreading rumors of another allegedly imminent British attack or of Loyalist terrorism. An anonymous letter found in Albany in late February 1778 stated that "the plan is to burn your City, all your Stores and all your Mills, as soon as the River opens; great many negroes are enlisted, Regular Soldiers, Tories." Such reports led frantic Patriots to ask Gov. George Clinton to send soldiers to Skenesborough, Fort George, and Jessup's Patent. Lacking available troops, Clinton could do nothing.[30]

A year after Burgoyne's defeat, the route along the Hudson, northward from Stillwater in Albany County to past Fort Edward, was still "marked with Devastation, and of the many pleasant habitations . . . , some were burnt, others torn to Pieces and rendered unfit for Use, and but a few of the meanest occupied: the Inhabitants in general having been forced to leave their once peaceful Dwellings to escape the Rage of War. Thus this once agreeable and delightful Part of the Country now displayed a most shocking Picture of Havock and wild Desolation." Reconstruction would be a slow, complicated process. It required that aid be given to the inhabitants, that the New Hampshire land title controversy be settled, and that militant Loyalists be driven out and their property confiscated. The task would not be easy. The old controversy over New Hampshire land titles flared again in 1778, probably because Ethan Allen, who had been a British prisoner since his capture at Montreal, was released. In May, Allen ominously threatened "that Vermont at present was contented with moderate Bounds: but, if these could not be enjoyed in peace, they should extend them by right of Conquest!" He and his supporters harassed Charlotte residents who held New York land titles and forced them to "acknowledge themselves subjects of the pretended State of Vermont." The New York Legislature finally decided on

October 21, 1779, to submit the matter to the Continental Congress for resolution. However, the Continental Congress failed to reach a decision until August 20, 1781, when it declared that if it ever recognized Vermont, that state would be required to accept a western boundary beginning at the northwest corner of Massachusetts and running northward twenty miles east of the Hudson.[31]

On October 22, 1779, the New York legislature passed an Act of Attainder, under which the estates of "Persons who have adhered to the Enemies of this State" could be forfeited and sold. The law ipso facto forfeited the property of fifty-nine individuals, including some who owned land in Charlotte: Robert Leake of Albany County (a partner in Palmer's Purchase [1772]), Peter Dubois of Ulster County (a partner in the Provincials Patent [1764]), Edward and Ebenezer Jessup of Albany County, John Tabor Kempe, Philip Skene, and his son Andrew. The law also stated that if the Continental Congress decided in New York's favor in the land grants dispute, the 1779 Act of Attainder could be used against anyone who owned land in that area and had assisted the enemies of the state.[32]

As late as 1780, Charlotte County still remained vulnerable to British attack. Destitute families were leaving for Canada, claiming to be Loyalists. Spies abounded. Dr. George Smyth of Fort Edward, whom the Americans still trusted, was sending valuable information to the British in Canada under the code name "Hudibras." In part, because of this information, in May 1780 the ardent Loyalist Sir John Johnson, son of Sir William and owner of thousands of acres in the Mohawk Valley, led an expedition of more than fifty men against that valley. He started at Crown Point and moved down and across the southern Adirondacks to ravage his home area.[33]

The charismatic Ethan Allen was at the heart of the Vermont problems. His activities aroused suspicion among Patriots at the time, and they remain an enigma to historians today. In July 1780 George Washington's spy, "Amicus Republicae," reported that Allen had arrived in New York City on July 2 for negotiations with the British. He had "entered this City in disguise & was introduced by a Mr. Griffis, [a noted British partisan] to the Commandant by whom he was most graciously received, & had a long Conference with his Honor, after which he retired with the most profound Secrecy, & was to take his departure from hence for Bennington, the Same Night." Undercover New York City Patriots reportedly believed "that he came with Propositions from the Green Mountain Boys in Consequence of Congress refusing to acknowledge Vermont a Seperate State." These same Patriots "farther imagined, that he with a large Body of his valiant Countrymen, will join [Joseph] Brant & [Walter] Butler, raise the Savages & make Sad Havoc on your frontiers, or by a Conjunction will divert Genl. Washington, while Genl. Clinton attempts the Reduction of the grand Fort at West Point. The Preparations that are making a Movement indicate its Probability." They could learn nothing further about this "plan of operations." However, by the time of Allen's visit to New York City, British power in Charlotte was already in decline for several reasons. First, the British were losing some of their intelligence-gathering capability; spies were being detected and forced either to flee or to be arrested. For example, Dr. George Smyth of Fort Edward had been discovered, arrested, and released on bail on good behavior, although he evidently continued to send some information to Canada through his son, Terence. Second, many Charlotte Loyalists had already fled to Canada.[34]

Washington's appointment of the traitorous Benedict Arnold to command West Point, on August 2, 1780, further complicated the Vermont problem. Leaving Canada only a day or so after the American detection of Arnold's plot to surrender West Point, British troops under Maj. Christopher Carleton attempted another attack. They captured both Fort Anne and Fort George. To aid the invasion Loyalists destroyed much property for a distance of fourteen miles below Fort Edward. However, doubtless upon hearing of Arnold's capture, Carleton and his forces retreated to Ticonderoga. When news of this retreat reached Albany, Dr. George Smyth requested permission "to go With his Family to Canada." Because Smyth reportedly remained an "agent for [the British] secret service," the request was rejected. The doctor nonetheless made "his escape to Bennington in Vermont, thinking himself safe there," but the governor of Vermont turned him over to New York authorities, who restricted him to a farm outside Albany. Smyth nonetheless continued preparing detailed spy reports for Gen. Frederick Haldimand, the British governor of Quebec, who was secretly negotiating with Vermont. Unfortunately for Smyth, one of these reports was intercepted on May 27, 1781. The New York Commissioners for Detecting and Defeating Conspiracies immediately tried to arrest him and his son, Terence. The son ("Young Hudibras") was caught, but his father escaped to Canada early in June.[35]

On October 26, 1780, the British forces under Carleton that were leaving Ticonderoga for Canada received orders to remain on Lake Champlain to facilitate negotiations with Vermont. Two days later Capt. Justus Sherwood, a Vermont Loyalist, began a series of private meetings with Ethan Allen. Officially, Sherwood was only to negotiate a truce for the exchange of prisoners. However, he proposed that because of their land disputes with New York and the Continental Congress's mistreatment of them, Vermonters should "resume their former Allegiance to the King." Protesting that he would be part of "no Damd Arnold Plan to sell his Country and his own honour by Betraying the trust reposd in him," Allen scoffed at Sherwood's suggestion. He insisted that the British could assist Vermont to be independent. As a result, Sherwood not only agreed to a prisoner exchange, but recognized Vermont's jurisdiction as far west as the Hudson. In effect, the British were now recognizing that river as Vermont's western boundary, if Vermont remained aloof from New York.[36]

The crisis over Vermont rapidly worsened. Unaware of the details of Sherwood's truce and fearful of fresh British incursions, Gov. George Clinton notified Washington of "the very extraordinary Conduct of Colo. Allen." The general ordered a further investigation and directed that Allen be apprehended, if that proved advisable. In January 1781, British military officials in Canada, detecting the arrival of rebel troops in Albany, concluded that the Americans were organizing an expedition "for the Reduction of Vermont." In February Vermont declared that its jurisdiction extended from the Connecticut River westward over all the land north of the Massachusetts border and east of the Hudson River. Just below Lake George the Hudson River veers northwest; its headwaters are in the Adirondacks significantly west of Lake Champlain. By expanding its western boundaries north from that river's headwaters to the Canadian border, Vermont was claiming much of northern New York. This placed the southwest corner of Vermont opposite the junction of the Mohawk and Hudson Rivers (near present-day Troy, New York), giving Vermont access to the Hudson and providing the state with its own tidewater port at New City (present day Lansingburgh). To counter this threat, New York State tried to gain the support of some of its enemies by leniently treating Charlotte residents suspected of Loyalism. This was done over the objections of Governor Clinton and Col. Alexander Webster, who apparently in protest resigned from the Charlotte County militia.[37]

Vermont next announced that a convention would be held on May 9, 1781, in Cambridge (Albany County) to decide upon a proper defense of its frontiers, the quota of Vermont troops to be raised, and the "Articles of Union" with the area of Charlotte that Vermont now claimed.[38] Fortunately for the American cause, spies soon uncovered details of the relationship between Vermont and British officials in Canada. They discovered that the British planned to issue a proclamation, declaring that the Continental Congress had no authority over Vermont and that Vermont troops would garrison Fort Edward and Skenesborough once the "Articles of Union" were signed. Gen. Philip Schuyler, whose property at Saratoga was in danger of being annexed to Vermont as a result of these developments, was incredulous that people in that area, "chiefly emigrants from the eastern states," could be so misled by their leaders and could defect "from the common cause" because of their disputes over land with New York. "I confess my faith in the political virtue of these people is . . . staggered."[39]

The convention at Cambridge lasted from May 9 to 15, 1781. The resulting "Articles of Union" affirmed Vermont's newly claimed western and southern boundaries and avowed that Vermont military forces would defend these borders, "especially against the Common Enemy." The Articles declared further that Vermont would in due course apply to the Continental Congress for admission to the United States and proposed terms of reconciliation. The convention set May 22 as the date for a meeting of the various districts in Charlotte to vote on the Articles.[40]

Emboldened by the "Articles of Union" and eager to reinforce Vermont's claim to the territory from Lake Champlain westward to the headwaters of the Hudson (an area that included much of the Adirondacks), dozens of individuals petitioned the Vermont Legislature between May and July for land grants in this area. At the end of June 1781, striving for control of the region, Washington appointed Gen. John Stark of New Hampshire to command the area north of Albany because of his "knowledge of, and influence amongst the Inhabitants of the Country." Washington ordered Stark to march to Saratoga with four hundred Massachusetts militiamen from Berkshire and Hampshire Counties to replace other regiments that Washington began withdrawing. New Yorkers justifiably had misgivings about Stark. However, as mentioned above, on August 20, 1781, the Continental Congress resolved that if it ever recognized Vermont, that state would be required to accept a western boundary beginning at the northwest corner of Massachusetts and running northward twenty miles east of the Hudson to Lake Champlain.[41]

This decision did not please Vermont leaders, so they continued to negotiate with the British. By October 1, 1781, the British had decided to issue a proclamation confirming and granting the territorial claims that Vermont desired. Meanwhile, British troops advanced southward from Canada toward Ticonderoga. Fearful rumors of this new invasion spread rapidly. On October 14, Washington ordered New Hampshire and Massachusetts regiments, with artillery, to advance from the Highlands of the Hudson Valley, near West Point, to Albany, where, according to the American Gen. William Heath "matters wore a more serious aspect." But military developments elsewhere intervened. The American siege of Yorktown had begun on October 1, 1781, and within two weeks the British position there was crumbling. By October 15 it was clear that Britain was losing the battle and the war. Britain therefore delayed further action in regard to Vermont.[42] By coincidence, on the evening of October 14, a sharp skirmish occurred in New City (present day Lansingburgh) between American militia and some Loyalists commanded by Col. Samuel Fairbanks, who held a Vermont commission. The clash resulted in a military impasse between New York and Vermont that lasted for several months and that nearly caused a civil war in the region. In November, despite Yorktown and the defeat of a Loyalist raid from Niagara into the Mohawk Valley, Vermont rejected the boundary the Continental Congress had proposed and declared that it would resist by force any claim New York State made to the entire jurisdiction it claimed.[43]

The situation in Charlotte remained confused and tense. Ongoing communications between the British in Canada and their spies in upper New York State as late as February 1782 strongly suggest that the British had not yet abandoned their efforts to keep Vermont loyal to the Crown. Nevertheless, on February 22, the Vermont Assembly reconsidered its demands and accepted the boundary set by the Continental Congress, twenty miles east of the Hudson, extending north from the northwest corner of Massachusetts to Lake Champlain. Although this decision dissolved the "Articles of Union," Ethan Allen wrote Haldimand on June 16, 1782: "I Shall do Every thing in my Power to render this

State a British province." One of Washington's agents warned in July 1782 that the British also persisted in "there intention to Execute rigorus measures against the opposers of Vermont." New York State halfheartedly intensified its policy and arrested some county residents who had been loyal to Vermont, even though it forgave others.[44]

That summer, the Americans in northern New York dreaded fresh British assaults from Canada, and the British feared an American and French attack. To defend their position the British assured Ira Allen, Ethan's brother, that the British would recognize Vermont's "Articles of Union" despite the defeat at Yorktown. Nonetheless, in a coded letter General Haldimand in Canada wrote Sir Henry Clinton, the British commander-in-chief in New York, that further negotiations with Vermont were pointless and that it would be necessary to reduce Vermont by force. Ira Allen, for his part, concluded that further communications on certain topics with Capt. Justus Sherwood, who was now assisted by Dr. George Smyth, were simply too dangerous to continue. Nonetheless both sides continued negotiating prisoner exchanges, including one for the return of the American-held Terence Smith, "Young Hudibras." Even after hostilities between the United States and Britain had ceased, the situation in Charlotte remained fraught with peril. Dr. George Smyth, Ethan Allen, and Ira Allen were still attempting to negotiate "a Mutual Intercourse, and Free Trade" between Vermont and Canada, and British officials ominously maintained a military presence on Lake Champlain.[45]

American officials were apprehensive. On July 12, 1783, Washington sent Baron von Steuben to Canada to meet with Haldimand and to arrange for the transfer to the United States of all posts that remained under British control and that were situated on American territory. When Von Steuben and Haldimand met in August, the British general was entirely uncooperative, refusing even to negotiate the surrender of the military posts until a final treaty was signed. Old land disputes and the grudges that resulted from them also continued to poison the atmosphere in Charlotte. At Crown Point, for example, a land investor with a New York patent, Robert Cochran was embroiled in a bitter, violent dispute over New York land he claimed there. On September 3, 1784, at least four men attacked him, his family, and an associate. Years of controversy finally led Cochran in 1787 to advertise his "Valuable Farm" of seven hundred acres at Crown Point for lease and to move elsewhere.[46]

3.

Even though for some people the war dragged on past the proclamation of the end of hostilities early in 1783, Charlotte did begin the process of renewing itself. Symbolically, the county's name was changed to Washington County. As most observers could doubtless have predicted, land sales and speculation now abounded. For example, in 1784, through the purchase of military warrants, Zephaniah Platt of Dutchess County and thirty-two associates acquired almost thirty-five thousand acres on the west side of Lake Champlain. The next year, the group purchased Skene's old ore bed tract of three thousand acres. They commenced building mills and began preparing to mine iron ore. William Gilliland, who had suffered heavy financial losses during the war, began selling some of his lands in the county. When he was unable to pay damages to an ex-slave who had successfully sued him, he was imprisoned for debt in 1786 and remained in jail until 1791. New York State forced other landholders to defend their prewar titles against appropriation. In 1785 the proprietors of the huge Totten and Crossfield Purchase, many of whom were Loyalists or had strong ties to prominent Loyalists, petitioned the state to protect their land claims in the Adirondacks. In the end, however, the townships of the patent were redistributed in 1786.[47]

It is probably impossible to ascertain the total amount of land that New York State confiscated from Charlotte Loyalists. A "Book of Forfeitures" for Washington County, which was apparently begun in 1784, listed three hundred fifty lots or parcels of Loyalist property seized and sold. Of these lots, 45 percent were in Skenesborough, 42 percent in New Perth-White Creek, and 5 percent in the Artillery Patent. Some Loyalists, however, managed to keep their property and make remarkable financial recoveries.The lucky ones were usually people who had been passive or nonbelligerent and had made no significant enemies during the war. Some even returned from Canada to start over. Noteworthy is the case of William Sherriff, who had received in 1765 a two thousand-acre grant for land northeast of the Argyle Patent. In March 1766 he wed Margaret Bayard, the cousin of Margaret Kemble, the wife of Gen. Thomas Gage, then the British commander-in-chief. Gage soon secured for Sherriff a promotion in the army and the post of deputy quarter master general. He served very profitably (and corruptly) in that position during the Revolution in Boston and New York City. Sherriff returned to England in 1779, a rich man. Because he was British, and not a Loyalist, William Sherriff of the "Kingdom of Great Britain" was able to keep possession of his two-thousand-acre patent, which he sold in parcels between 1790 and 1792.[48]

Most individuals and groups adjusted as best they could to the changed world in which they now lived. The Baptist congregation that was located on the Batten Kill at the southern edge of Charlotte County gambled on peace and voted in November 1782 to build a new meetinghouse. Dr. Thomas Clark and his New Perth congregation had endured the hard years of war to find themselves pulled in different directions afterwards. A few members of his flock went to Abbeville, South Carolina, where he joined them as their minister in 1786. The conflict over naming the town "New Perth" or "White Creek" was resolved in 1787, when residents agreed to call the town "Salem."[49]

That area of colonial Charlotte that eventually became part of Vermont had a longer, harsher road to travel before finding peace. Vermont remained independent of the United States through the 1780s, and unrest continued in the area for the entire period. Finally, in October 1790, a joint commission, whose members were appointed by New York and Vermont, decided that the western boundary of Vermont would begin at the northwest corner of Massachusetts and extend northward to Lake Champlain and through the middle of that lake to Canada. Vermont agreed to pay New York thirty thousand dollars for land claims. The way was thus clear for Vermont to enter the union as the fourteenth state on March 4, 1791. At last, the key land title dispute that had caused Charlotte so much conflict during the late colonial and Revolutionary periods had come to an end. The people who lived in what had been Charlotte could now face the future with hope. Even though most Charlotte residents had been more concerned at the outset of the Revolution with their land disputes than they had been with the imperial crisis, the Revolution did fortuitously help settle many outstanding claims and thus promote peace throughout the region.[50]

Notes

1. Thomas Kitchin's map "Part of the Counties of Charlotte and Albany in the Province of New York; being the Seat of War between the King's Forces under Lieut. General Burgoyne and the Rebel Army," *The London Magazine, or Gentleman's Monthly Intelligencer*, Feb. 1778, 51; Joel Munsell, *The Annals of Albany*, vol. 1 (Albany, 1869), 95.

2. Examples of conflicts that emerged in Charlotte County before, during, and after the Revolution are the well-known New Hampshire grants controversy (1750s-1770s), the quarrel over John Henry Lydius's claims to lands lying within twenty miles of the upper Hudson, where he wanted to create settlements for New Englanders in the 1760s, fights over the boundaries of Philip Skene's and William Gilliland's patents, and the controversial purchases of lands in the Adirondacks from Iroquois Indians (July 1772).

3. E. B. O'Callaghan, ed., *The Documentary History of the State of New-York*, 4 vols. (Albany, 1849–1851), 4: 531–35, 538–41, 544, 547, 549, hereafter cited as *DHNY*; and Mary Greene Nye, ed., *State Papers of Vermont*, vol. 7, *New York Land Patents, 1688–1786, Covering Land Now Included in the State of Vermont* (Montpelier, 1947), 3–4.

4. *DHNY*, 4: 556–57. E. B. O'Callaghan, ed., *Documents Relative to the Colonial History of the State of New York*, 11 vols. (Albany, 1853–1861), 7: 456, hereafter cited as *DCHNY*. Chrisfield Johnson, *History of Washington Co., New York* (Interlaken, N.Y., 1991), 421; and Fred Q. Bowman, *Landholders of Northeastern New York, 1739–1802* (Baltimore, 1987), 6.

5. Jennie M. Patten, *The Argyle Patent and Accompanying Documents* (Baltimore, 1979), 9–11; and Fuller Allen and David Kendall Martin, trans. and ed., *The Journal of*

William Gilliland, 18th Century Pioneer of the Champlain Valley (Plattsburgh, N.Y., 1997), x; E. B. O'Callaghan, comp., *Calendar of New York Colonial Manuscripts: Indorsed Land Papers* (Harrison, N.Y., 1987), 290–93, 299–300, 314–22; Berthold Fernow, comp., *Calendar of Council Minutes, 1668–1783* (Harrison, N.Y., 1987), 401; Doris Begor Morton, *Philip Skene of Skenesborough* (Granville, N.Y., 1959), 19, 22, 31; John Pell, "Philip Skene of Skenesborough," *The Quarterly Journal of the New York State Historical Association* 9 (1928): 29; Alexander Fraser, *Second Report of the Bureau of Archives for the Province of Ontario* (Toronto, 1905), 1266; Nye, *Land Patents,* 4; and Johnson, *History,* 35.

6. Paul R. Huey and Ralph D. Phillips, "The Migration of a Connecticut Family in Eastern New York in the Eighteenth Century," *The Connecticut Nutmegger,* 13 (1980): 390; Fred Anderson, *Crucible of War* (New York, 2000), 568; *DHNY,* 4: 558; and Nye, *Land Patents,* 4–6. For a discussion of the conflict from New York's point of view, see Cadwallader Colden to Board of Trade, January 20, 1764, *DCHNY,* 7: 595–98.

7. *DCHNY,* 7: 630; *The Letters and Papers of Cadwallader Colden,* 8 vols., The New-York Historical Society, *Collections,* vols. 50–56, 67 (New York, 1917–1923, 1937), 6: 367; and Johnson, *History,* 121–23, 230–31, 337.

8. Patten, *Argyle Patent,* 21–35, 56, 65–66; Bowman, *Landholders,* 6; Bernard Bailyn, *Voyagers to the West* (New York, 1987), 613; Elisha P. Thurston, *History of the Town of Greenwich, From the Earliest Settlement, to the Centennial of our National Independence* (Salem, N.Y., 1876), 13–14; Colden, *Letters and Papers,* 6: 286; 9: 207–10; *DHNY,* 1: 537, 539–40, 585–86; O'Callaghan, *Land Papers,* 342, 344–45; Allen and Martin, *Journal of Gilliland,* xii–xv; Morton, *Philip Skene,* 23, 25, 33; and Pell, "Philip Skene," 29.

9. Allen and Martin, *Journal of Gilliland,* 18–20, 23–24; Sung Bok Kim, *Landlord and Tenant in Colonial New York Manorial Society, 1664–1775* (Chapel Hill, N.C., 1978), 385–91; *DHNY,* 1: 548; 4: 820; G. D. Scull, ed., *The Montresor Journals,* New-York Historical Society, *Collections* (New York, 1882), 367; Albert Stillman Batchellor, ed., *The New Hampshire Grants, Being Transcripts of the Charters of Townships* (Concord, 1895), 592–609; Ralph Izard, *An Account of a Journey to Niagara, Montreal and Quebec, in 1765* (New York, 1846), 28; and Clarence Edwin Carter, ed., *The Correspondence of General Thomas Gage,* 2 vols. (New Haven, 1931–1933), 1: 178–79, 2: 322.

10. Johnson, *History,* 131; Kenneth A. Perry, comp., *The Fitch Gazetteer: An Annotated Index to the Manuscript History of Washington County, New York,* vol. 1 (Baltimore, 1999), 76; and Fraser, *Second Report,* 1013, 1027, 1089, 1107, 1265. In 1768 Adolphus Benzel, a distinguished Swedish-born soldier, surveyor, and engineer, at Crown Point proposed construction of a large town there "to encourage the settlements" along the lake. Although the Board of Trade had issued strict orders not to grant new patents in conflict with earlier French grants, Cadwallader Colden did so in 1769 and 1770 on the northwest portion of the lake and in the eastern Adirondack Mountains. The Map Division of the Library of Congress has a copy of Benzel's plan of the proposed town, and it is reproduced in the booklet *18th Century Crown Point Maps* published by the Crown Point Foundation, New York, N.Y. (n.d.), 11. *DCHNY,* 8: 139–40;

O'Callaghan, *Land Papers*, 466, 449, 466, 655, 472, 474, 482; and E. Eugene Barker, ed., "Memorial Address by Adolphus Benzel to King George, 1761–1769," *The Bulletin of the Fort Ticonderoga Museum* 9 (1954), 304. *Third Annual Report of the State Historian of the State of New York, 1897* (New York and Albany, 1898), 889; *The Papers of Sir William Johnson*, 14 vols. (Albany, 1921–1965), 7: 191; Bowman, *Landholders*, 12; Philip L. White, *Beekmantown, New York: Forest Frontier to Farm Community* (Austin and London, 1979), 3–9; *DHNY*, 1: 553; Fernow, *Calendar*, 551; Allen and Martin, *Journal of Gilliland*, 72, 74; and Gustave Anjou, *Ulster County, N.Y., Probate Records*, vol. 2 (New York, 1906), 20–22.

11. Fraser, *Second Report*, 329, 347–48, 365, 377, 398, 400, 433, 1020, 1053, 1013, 1090, 1265; and William Ogden Wheeler and Edmund D. Halsey, trans., Presbyterian Church Records of Hanover, Morris Co., N.J., typescript, 1893.

12. *DHNY*, 4:720; "New York and the N. H. Grants," New-York Historical Society, *Collections* (New York, 1870), 303–304; John Pell, *Ethan Allen* (Boston and New York, 1929), 39–40, 42; K. G. Davies, ed., *Documents of the American Revolution: 1770–1783*, vol. 3 (Shannon, Ireland, 1973), 205; and E. B. O'Callaghan, ed., *Calendar of Historical Manuscripts, in the Office of the Secretary of State, Albany, N.Y.*, Part 2 (Albany, 1866), 800.

13. Bowman, *Landholders*, 9, 11; Nye, *Land Patents*, 204–208; O'Callaghan, *Land Papers*, 514, 523, 536–38; *The Struggle and The Glory: A Special Bicentennial Exhibition* (Dearborn, Mich., 1976); Pell, "Philip Skene," 31–32; and Morton, *Philip Skene*, 26, 29.

14. Winslow C. Watson, *Pioneer History of the Champlain Valley* (Albany, 1863), 14n.; Allen and Martin, *Journal of Gilliland*, xvi, xxxi; Bowman, *Landholders*, 61; Robert F. Jones, "William Duer and the Business of Government in the Era of the American Revolution," *William and Mary Quarterly*, 3rd ser., 32 (1975): 395, 413; Deed from Henry Cuyler to William Duer, December 28, 1771, Albany County Deeds, Albany County Hall of Records, Albany, N.Y., 9: 290; Winston Adler, ed., *Their Own Voices: Oral Accounts of Early Settlers in Washington County, New York Collected by Dr. Asa Fitch, 1847–1878* (Interlaken, N.Y., 1983), 125; Ray W. Pettengill, trans., *Letters From America, 1776–1779* (Boston and New York, 1924), 87; Helga Doblin, trans., and Mary C. Lynn, ed., *An Eyewitness Account of the Revolution and New England Life* (New York, 1990), 68; and Fraser, *Second Report*, 347–48, 378. The Patrick Smyth house at Fort Edward is now a museum.

15. *The Papers of Sir William Johnson*, 8: 413; Johnson, *History*, 38; O'Callaghan, *Land Papers*, 575, 582; Fernow, *Calendar*, 494, 567, 569; *DCHNY*, 8: 308–309; Alfred L. Donaldson, *A History of the Adirondacks*, vol. 1 (Harrison, N.Y., 1977), 51, 54–57; Paul David Nelson, *William Tryon and the Course of Empire* (Chapel Hill, N.C., and London, 1990), 110–12; and Bowman, *Landholders*, 10.

16. Gregory Furness, ed., "Proceedings of a Garrison Court of Enquiry Regarding the Destruction of His Majesty's Fort of Crown Point on Lake Champlain," typescript, Crown Point State Historic Site, Crown Point, N.Y., 1978; "New York and the N.H. Grants," 324–25; *DHNY*, 4: 842–55; Allan S. Everest, *Point au Fer on Lake Champlain*

(Plattsburgh, N.Y., 1992), 13; and White, *Beekmantown*, 11–13. The Washington County Archives in the Washington County Clerk's Office, Fort Edward, N.Y., has the original Court of Common Pleas record book beginning October 19, 1773. This information is courtesy of Gregory Furness.

17. Allen French, *The Taking of Ticonderoga in 1775: The British Story* (Cambridge, Mass., 1928), 7, 11–14; *DHNY*, 4: 873–86, 888–89; Carter, *Gage Correspondence*, 1: 354, 368, 2: 158, 177; Everest, *Point au Fer*, 12–14; and Morton, *Philip Skene*, 38–39.

18. Fraser, *Second Report*, 1025; Berthold Fernow, *New York in the Revolution* (Cottonport, La., 1972), 186, 322; Bowman, *Landholders*, 10; and Willis T. Hanson, *A History of Schenectady during the Revolution* (Privately Printed, 1916), 269–70.

19. Fraser, *Second Report*, 152–53, 351, 363, 433, 934, 1081; Colden, *Letters and Papers*, 7: 302–303; and Thurston, *History of Greenwich*, 26–27.

20. Fernow, *New York*, 275–76, 322, 455; Fraser, *Second Report*, 1012–13, 1025, 1089–91; Bowman, *Landholders*, 6, 10; Hanson, *History of Schenectady*, 269–70; and Sharon Dubeau, *New Bruswick Loyalists* (Agincourt, Ont., 1983), 128.

21. "White Creek" was the name used by New Englanders from Massachusetts and western Connecticut who had settled in Turner's Patent. Dr. Thomas Clark's Scotch-Irish congregation, with whom they shared the town and frequently quarreled, called it "New Perth."

22. Bruce C. Daniels, *The Connecticut Town: Growth and Development, 1635–1790* (Middletown, Ct., 1979), 58–63; Robert A. East, *Connecticut's Loyalists* (Chester, Ct., 1974), 6.

23. James Bradshaw and Edward Jessup were the principal grantees of Kingsbury and of the township of Hyde. East, *Connecticut's Loyalists*, 6, 14–15, 50n.; and Kevin Phillips, *The Cousins' Wars: Religion, Politics, and the Triumph of Anglo-America* (New York, 1999), 198.

24. Williams maintained his base of support, for he subsequently had an outstanding political career. Peter Force, comp., *American Archives*, 4th Ser., 6 vols. (Washington, D.C., 1837–1846), 3: 758–59, 5: 1190; Perry, *Fitch Gazetteer*, 99, 527, 540–41; Clinton, George, *Public Papers of George Clinton, First Governor of New York, 1777–1795, 1801–1804*, 8 vols. (Albany, 1899–1914), 3: 320, 329–32; and Fernow, *New York*, 276. The Washington County Archives, in the Washington County Clerk's Office, Fort Edward, N.Y., has the original record books of Minutes of the Court of Common Pleas from 1779 to 1786 and of Minutes of the Court of General Sessions from 1779 to 1786. This information is courtesy of Gregory Furness.

25. Allen and Martin, *Journal of Gilliland*, 94–95; French, *Taking of Ticonderoga*, 19, 21, 42, 51, 77; James Thomas Flexner, *The Traitor and the Spy* (New York, 1953), 42–45; Brooke Hindle, ed., *The Narrative of Colonel Ethan Allen* (New York, 1961), 9–10; and Paul L. Stevens, *A King's Colonel at Niagara, 1774–1776* (Youngstown, N.Y., 1987), 31.

26. Force, *American Archives*, 4th Ser., 2: 833, 1124–25; 3: 618–19; Perry, *Fitch Gazetteer*, 541; *DHNY*, 4: 872; Fraser, *Second Report*, 378, 1051–52; Talman, *Loyalist Narratives*, 389; Deed from Edward Jessup to John Thurman Jr., Jan. 25, 1776, Albany County Deeds, Albany County Hall of Records, Albany, N.Y., 10:181; Fernow, *New York*, 275–76, 527–28; and Force, *American Archives*, 4th Ser., 5: 286, 1190–91; 6: 1322.

27. Stefan Bielinski, ed., *A Guide to the Revolutionary War Manuscripts in the New York State Library* (Albany, 1976), #994.

28. Fraser, *Second Report*, 329–30, 347, 351, 398, 433, 1013, 1025–27, 1063, 1081, 1089, 1265; Horatio Rogers, ed., *Hadden's Journal and Orderly Books* (Boston, 1972), 71n.; Benson J. Lossing, *The Pictorial Field-Book of the Revolution*, vol. 1 (New York, 1855), 96–101; Doblin and Lynn, *Eyewitness Account*, 66; Adler, *Their Own Voices*, 51–60; S. Sydney Bradford, ed., "Lord Francis Napier's Journal of the Burgoyne Campaign," *Maryland Historical Magazine*, 57 (1962): 306–307; Perry, *Fitch Gazetteer*, 8–13; Gerald Howson, *Burgoyne of Saratoga: A Biography* (New York, 1979), 178–79, 320n.; and June Namias, *White Captives: Gender and Ethnicity on the American Frontier* (Chapel Hill, N.C., 1993), 117–44.

29. Rogers, *Hadden's Journal*, 111–17; Peter Nelson, "The Battle of Diamond Island," *The Quarterly Journal of the New York State Historical Association*, 3 (1922): 42–43, 45–51; "Col. John Brown's Attack of September, 1777, on Fort Ticonderoga," *The Bulletin of the Fort Ticonderoga Museum*, 11 (1964): 206–13; and Howson, *Burgoyne of Saratoga*, 214–15.

30. Fraser, *Second Report*, 398–400, 433, 1036, 1044, 1063, 1091, 1107; Louis Fiske Hyde, *History of Glens Falls, New York, and Its Settlement* (Glens Falls, 1936), 137; and Hastings, *George Clinton Papers*, 2: 849, 851, 3: 206–207, 209–11, 330–331, 384–387, 604, 5: 260, 384, 411–12.

31. Talman, *Loyalist Narratives*, 48, Richard B. Morris, ed., *John Jay: The Making of a Revolutionary*, vol. 1 (New York, 1975), 493–94; *DHNY*, 4: 956–57; Hastings, *George Clinton Papers*, 4: 859–60; Charles Z. Lincoln, ed., *Messages From the Governors*, vol. 2 (Albany, 1909), 102–105; and Ira Allen, *The Natural and Political History of the State of Vermont* (Rutland, Vt., 1971), 113.

32. *Laws of the State of New-York, Comprising the Constitution, and the Acts of the Legislature, Since the Revolution, from the First to the Twentieth Session, Inclusive*, vol. 1 (New York, 1798), 26.

33. Adler, *Their Own Voices*, 91–93; Hastings, *George Clinton Papers*, 5: 680–81; Hyde, *History of Glens Falls*, 157–58; Paltsits, *Minutes*, 435; and Ernest A. Cruikshank, *The King's Royal Regiment of New York* (Toronto, 1984), 38–39, 41–42, 67.

34. American Intelligence to George Washington from Amicus Republicae, July 4, 6, 1780, and Washington to John Mercereau, July 12, 1780, Series 4 (General Correspondence) and Series 3b (Varick Transcripts, Letterbook 12), George Washington Papers, Library of Congress, Washington, D.C.; Pell, *Ethan Allen*, 190–91; Cruikshank,

The King's Royal Regiment, 44; Paltsits, *Minutes*, 477, 479, 483, 503, 508, 596; Hastings, *George Clinton Papers*, 6: 269–70; and Huey and Phillips, "Migration," 391.

35. Flexner, *Traitor and Spy*, 317, 366; Cruikshank, *King's Royal Regiment*, 55, 67; Hastings, *George Clinton Papers*, 6: 287–88, 339–40, 631; 7: 320; Elizabeth Cometti, ed., *The American Journals of Lt. John Enys* (Syracuse, 1976), 44–46; Fernow, *New York*, 545; Adler, *Their Own Voices*, 97–103; Paltsits, *Minutes*, 488, 545–46, 549–50, 561, 579–80, 611–12, 675, 683, 720–21, 726, 728, 730–31; Fraser, *Second Report*, 365; "Revolutionary Relics," *The Zodiac: Devoted to Science, Literature and the Arts*, 1 (1836): 118–19; Allen, *History*, 96; Mary Beacock Fryer, *John Walden Meyers: Loyalist Spy* (Toronto and Charlottetown, Prince Edward Island, 1984), 132–33; and Washington to Benjamin Hicks, June 4, 1781, Series 3b (Varick Transcripts, Letterbook 13), Washington Papers, Library of Congress.

36. Cometti, *American Journals of Lt. John Enys*, 49–51; Justus Sherwood, "Journal," *Vermont History*, New Ser., 24 (1956): 102–106; Henry Hall, *Ethan Allen: The Robin Hood of Vermont* (New York, 1892), 174–75; and Allen, *History*, 95–96.

37. Hastings, *George Clinton Papers*, 6: 374–75; Washington to George Clinton and to James Clinton, Nov. 6, 1780, Series 3b and 3c (Varick Transcripts, Letterbooks 12 and 4), Washington Papers, Library of Congress; Cruikshank, *King's Royal Regiment*, 65; and Allen, *History*, 98; Paltsits, *Minutes*, 631–33; Charles Z. Lincoln, ed., *Messages from the Governors*, vol. 2 (Albany, 1909), 128; and Fernow, *New York*, 276.

38. Hastings, *Public Papers of George Clinton*, 6: 760–61.

39. Ibid., 771–72, 787–88, 840–41, 843–45.

40. *DHNY*, 4:1004–1005; and Hastings, *George Clinton Papers*, 6: 865–67, 885.

41. Nye, *Petitions*, 248–52, 256–60, 262–70, 272–74, 276–80, 282–83, 287–89, 316n.; Washington to James Clinton and to John Stark, June 25, 1781, Series 3b (Varick Transcripts, Letterbook 14), Washington Papers, Library of Congress; Allen, *History*, 113.

42. Allen, *History*, 115, 118–19; and Hastings, *George Clinton Papers*, 7: 300–302, 320–21, 356; A. J. H. Richardson, "Chief Justice William Smith and the Haldimand Negotiations," *Proceedings of the Vermont Historical Society*, New Ser., 9 (1941): 97–98; and Rufus Rockwell Wilson, ed., *Heath's Memoirs of the American War* (Freeport, N.Y., 1970), 329.

43. Hastings, *George Clinton Papers*, 7: 402–403, 407, 512, 611–18; Caleb Stark, *Memoir and Official Correspondence of Gen. John Stark* (Concord, N.H., 1860), 301, 304–305; and Allen, *History*, 121–22.

44. Azariah Pritchard to Thomas Johnson, February 1782, Azariah Pritchard to George Smyth and Thomas Johnson, Feb. 16, 1782, and Thomas Johnson to Washington, May 30, 1782, with Narrative, and July 30, 1782, Series 4 (General Correspondence), Washington Papers, Library of Congress; John J. Duffy, ed., *Ethan Allen and His Kin: Correspondence, 1772–1819* (Hanover, N.H., and London, 1998), 128–31; Allen,

History, 123–24, 130–31; Hastings, *George Clinton Papers*, 7: 611–18; Nye, *Petitions*, 316n.; Ann Eliza Bleecker, *The Posthumous Works of Ann Eliza Bleecker, in Prose and Verse* (New York, 1793), 151–54, 156–57; and *DHNY*, 4: 1006, 1009.

45. Richardson, "Chief Justice William Smith," 103, 105, 107; Everest, *Point au Fer*, 28; Wilson, *Heath's Memoirs*, 349, 364; Duffy, *Ethan Allen*, 127, 141–142; Paltsits, *Minutes*, 675, 683, 720–21, 726, 728, 730–31; "Revolutionary Relics," *The Zodiac: Devoted to Science, Literature and the Arts*, 1 (1836): 118–19; Cruikshank, *King's Royal Regiment*, 67; Allen, *History*, 96; Fryer, *John Walden Meyers*, 132–33; Washington to Benjamin Hicks, June 4, 1781, Series 3b (Varick Transcripts, Letterbook 13), Washington Papers, Library of Congress; David J. Fowler, *Guide to the Sol Feinstone Collection of The David Library of the American Revolution* (Washington Crossing, Pa., 1994), 247; *Votes and Proceedings of the Senate of the State of New-York, Beginning with the Fifth Session*, vol. 2 (Poughkeepsie, 1782), 83; Bruce E. Burgoyne, trans., *Georg Pausch's Journal and Reports of the Campaign in America* (Bowie, Md., 1996), 132; and William Sumner Jones, ed., "Vermont Legislative Records, Miscellaneous Papers, 1761–1772," *Records of the States of the United States of America: Vermont*, Microfilm Reel A1 (Washington, D.C., 1949), Unit 2, 258:69.

46. *Fine Printed and Manuscript Americana*, Sotheby's auction catalogue for May 22, 1990 (New York, 1990), #123; Hastings, *George Clinton Papers*, 8: 249; O'Callaghan, *Land Papers*, 652–53; and Indictments, 1784, microfilm roll #690, Washington County Archives, Washington County Clerk's Office, Fort Edward, N.Y. (This information is courtesy of Gregory Furness.) Robert Cochran to Zephaniah Platt, Mar. 4, 1785, No. 9828–182, Zephaniah Platt Papers, New York State Library, Albany, N.Y., hereafter cited as NYSL; Patten, *Argyle Patent*, 66–68; Johnson, *History*, 137; and *The Albany Gazette*, Aug. 2, 1787.

47. O'Callaghan, *Land Papers*, 654, 693; Peter S. Palmer, *History of Lake Champlain* (New York, n.d.), 143; J. H. Mather and L. P. Brockett, *A Geographical History of the State of New York* (Utica, 1848), 217; and Zephaniah Platt to George Clinton, July 12, 1785, No. 9828–172, Zephaniah Platt Papers, NYSL; Allen and Martin, *Gilliland Journal*, xxviii–xxx, 87; O'Callaghan, *Land Papers*, 658, 669–70; and Donaldson, *Adirondacks*, 58–59.

48. Thomas J. Lynch, transcr., "Book of Forfeitures, Washington Co., NY, 1784," from the original in the The Washington County Archives in the Washington County Clerk's Office, Fort Edward, N.Y., and on-line at <http:/bfn.org/~ae487/forfeit.html>; O'Callaghan, *Land Papers*, 349, 382; Bowman, *Landholders*, 7, 167; "Records of Trinity Church Parish, New York City," *The New York Genealogical and Biographical Record* 70 (1939): 272; Carter, *Gage Correspondence*, 2: 467, 610, 688; Mark Mayo Boatner, III, *Encyclopedia of the American Revolution* (New York, 1976), 572; *Report on American Manuscripts in the Royal Institution of Great Britain*, vol. 2 (Dublin, 1906), 231; R. Arthur Bowler, *Logistics and the Failure of the British Army in America, 1775–1783* (Princeton, N.J., 1975), 22–23, 184, 186n.; James Thomas Flexner, *States Dyckman: American Loyalist* (Boston and Toronto, 1980), 74, 93, 180–81; 225; and Perry, *Fitch Gazetteer*, 196, 336, 451.

49. Thurston, *History of Greenwich*, 32; Patten, *Argyle Patent*, 66–68; Johnson, *History*, 137.

50. Marius Péladeau, "The Letters of Royall Tyler: A Checklist," *Vermont History* 40 (1972): 296; George Richards Minot, *The History of the Insurrections in Massachusetts* (Freeport, N.Y., 1970), 156–59; *DHNY*, 4: 1023; and Everest, *Point au Fer*, 42.

Conclusion

The Other New York, the people of the rural counties examined in this book, endured wartime experiences and conditions that were significantly different from those of the metropolis. Some of these counties survived similar ordeals, such as their occupation by the British army from 1776 to 1783. Others had different experiences; for example, the British army never occupied the mid-Hudson Valley counties.

Outside of New York County, the province and state was overwhelmingly agricultural. The urban interests of the port city in the years following the Seven Years' War were different from those of the many communities in the hinterland, whether these were situated close by New York City or remotely distant from it in the north and west. The only other major urban center in the province was the city of Albany. Its residents had formed committees as early as the Stamp Act, but had difficulty getting such bodies established elsewhere in its county. The manors, estates, and small farms that surrounded that city limited Albany County's consciousness of imperial and continental issues. Hence, *The Other New York* experienced a significantly different American Revolution than did the city and county of New York.

The Other New York comprised several distinct regions. The port area, composed of those counties that were near the metropolis, included Richmond County (Staten Island); Kings, Queens, and Suffolk Counties on Long Island; and Westchester County. Their proximity to New York City, their contact with royal officials, the presence of the British navy, and their wartime occupation by the British army made the experiences of the people who lived here similar in many ways. To mention but one, Loyalism was stronger in the port area than elsewhere in the province and was probably strongest in Richmond County, which had no active protestors. The exception was Suffolk County, which still had strong ties to New England. The people of the mid-Hudson Valley—Dutchess, Orange, and Ulster counties—endured their own experience, albeit with variations caused by their economic and social differences. Orange and

223

Ulster lacked the landlord-tenant disputes that plagued Dutchess and Westchester counties. Further north, Albany had a somewhat different experience because of its urban center, although its rural regions survived the war in ways similar to the mid-Hudson Valley. Finally, the frontier region to the north— Charlotte County—and to the west—Tryon County—although different ethnically and economically, were both involved in the invasions of 1777 and suffered several raids from Canada and Niagara.

The chapters of *The Other New York* discuss allegiance and suggest that several factors influenced how and why people took sides in the Revolution. One element was the presence of British power. The greatest fleet in the world shadowed Long Island and helped to suppress the Patriot cause. In Queens, a sizable minority supported the king, until the severity of the British occupation finally impelled most residents into the Patriot camp. In Suffolk, Patriotism was suppressed early in the British occupation, but as the severity of that control became onerous, Whig sentiment reemerged, as it had done in Queens. On Long Island's Kings County, Loyalist tendencies were related to Dutch antipathy to non-Dutch neighbors; the British offered support against these non-Dutch colonists, who threatened to relegate the Dutch to a minor significance. As an island, Richmond was at the mercy of the British fleet. One need only look at a map of the port area to note why Britain poured men and equipment into Richmond. To control New York City, it had to control Richmond and Kings, two counties that throttled the entrance to New York's massive harbor at The Narrows. Richmond was, from the beginning of the imperial crisis, overwhelmingly loyal, and the presence of British troops in the county did little more than reinforce this support. The British presence also clearly swayed sentiment in Westchester. The threat posed by British forces in Canada had an important influence on political developments in Charlotte and Tryon counties. However, in Albany and the mid-Hudson counties, where New Yorkers were isolated from direct British military threat, Loyalism was weakest in the state.

Local circumstances and conflicts also influenced how people sided in the Revolution. In Suffolk County, as already noted, the American cause found its greatest support among the descendants of New England. In western Queens, Patriotism was strongest among Presbyterians, who resented Anglican hegemonic pretensions. The Dutch in Kings County linked British power to their cultural survival and to their ownership of slaves. In Richmond, no ethnic or cultural motives clearly explain the county's Loyalism. However, the county's small population may have led its people to feel isolated and thus dependent on royal power in a time of trial. Also the two key families that dominated the county's political and economic life were ardent Loyalists, carrying with them many dependent people. Another possible cause of Richmond's overwhelming loyal political allegiance may have been its isolation from the rest of New York. In Westchester, residency was an important determinant of allegiance; in early 1775 the Whig cause was most popular in the southern and eastern portions of the county. Later in the war, however, civil strife, guerilla conflicts and banditry blurred these allegiances, and people appear to have taken sides in response to which brigands had molested them.

The local situation also played a role elsewhere in New York. In Dutchess County, unpopular landlords drove their tenants into the opposite camp, but land-lords who were perceived as benefactors won the allegiance of their retinue. The same may well have occurred in Tryon County, where the powerful, land-rich Johnson family, appears to have been the touchstone of allegiance. The family's members, tenants, and friends became Loyalists; its prewar enemies became revolutionaries. In Orange and Ulster Counties, which had few powerful Loyalists, British and Dutch settlers tended to join the Whig cause.

The situation in nearby Albany County was much more complicated because of its multiethnic population. The Whigs, many of whom were descen-dants of the original Dutch settlers, dominated the city and surrounding Rensselaerwyck, an area where few Britons lived. In Watervliet, the pacifist Shakers sought to stay neutral in a multiethnic district that had many Loyalists. The Connecticut immigrants, who had settled in nearby Kings District became ardently pro-American. Northern Albany County and Charlotte County, how-ever, were inhabited by many discharged British soldiers who had fought in the Seven Years' War to defend and expand the empire. Along with other recent British immigrants and Anglican settlers from eastern Connecticut, these vet-erans constituted the zealous core of Loyalism on the northern frontier, south of Canada.

Throughout the northern part of the province, where many British veter-ans settled after the Seven Years' War, Loyalism and neutrality were strong. These settlers lacked the American experience to appreciate the colonists' fears, arguments, and frames of reference. These newcomers consequently did not per-ceive the British policies of the 1760s and 1770s as detrimental. They became a threat to the success of the Revolution. Of course, some of these veterans, including revolutionary generals Richard Montgomery and Horatio Gates, were exceptions to the Loyalist tendency of these people.

Although the British army was headquartered in New York City, the area north of southern Westchester remained under American political control. The British initiated raids northward up the Hudson River, but their forces were never strong enough to risk an invasion; because redcoats were needed to occupy Manhattan, Long, and Staten Islands. In 1777, during Gen. John Burgoyne's campaign from Canada, Gen. Sir Henry Clinton sent a raiding party up the river. It burned Kingston and reached Livingston Manor. However, following Burgoyne's surrender at Saratoga, Clinton's forces retreated to the city and never again menaced the heart of the state. North of Westchester the American forts and iron chain across the Hudson helped to maintain the boundary.

Warfare and violence nonetheless permeated the state. Probably Orange and Ulster Counties suffered least, but they were victims of British raids. In the north and west, Charlotte and Tryon counties were the sites of destructive raids throughout the war. Albany was not attacked after 1777; but Loyalist raiders, prisoners brought in from the frontiers, and the constant ebb and flow of troops disrupted the normal patterns of everyday life. Dutchess County was vexed by the hard feelings that had characterized the landlord-tenant fights. Westchester endured horrific violence; brigandage and vigilante activities destroyed the semblance of civilian government. Queens, Kings, Suffolk, and Richmond were occupied by British troops and suffered from the violence engendered by autocratic martial law. The rancor over military occupation was doubtless greater in the port area than in areas the American army held, because Loyalism was strongest in that region. The people who had identified the most with the mother country before 1776 were now horrified at and alienated by being treated as if they were foreigners. Ironically, if the presence of the British navy helped secure New York to the empire before the Battle of Long Island, the British military's subsequent occupation of the port area helped to seal the empire's demise in New York.

By the end of the conflict, New York was a changed place. In 1771 the colony's total population had been 168,000, of which 11 percent were African Americans. On the eve of the Revolution, Albany was by far the most populous county with over 42,000 people. It had nearly twice the population of the next most populous county, Dutchess. As a region, the mid-Hudson Valley counties (Ulster, Dutchess, and Orange) had over 46,000 people, slightly more than Albany by itself. The lower counties (Westchester, Richmond, and those on Long Island) had 52,000 residents. New York County had 21,800. Thus the part of the colony that straddled the Hudson north of Westchester had almost 89,000 people, over half the colony's population. New York City may have been the colony's capital and a major port region for the Middle Colonies, but it did not have the majority of the province's population. Albany, the most populous county, also had the largest African-American population. However, blacks constituted a larger percentage of the population of Kings County (over 30 percent) than they did in any other county.

By 1786, despite war and its destruction, the population of New York State had grown by over 70,000 people, an increase of over 42 percent. The county with the largest growth was Albany, which increased by 69 percent. The remarkable expansion occurred, even though Tryon (postwar Montgomery County) and Charlotte (postwar Washington County) were carved from it, and the Green Mountain area was lost to Vermont. The mid-Hudson Valley counties increased by almost 50 percent. The Long Island counties and Richmond increased by approximately 11 percent. Westchester lost almost 6 percent of its population, probably because people had fled from the almost constant guerilla warfare con-

Table 3
Total Population of Counties: 1771 and 1786

COUNTY	1771	1786	INCREASE	%
Albany	42,706	72,360	29,654	69%
Charlotte	included in			
(Washington)	Albany	4,456	—	—
Dutchess	22,404	32,636	10,232	45%
Kings	3,623	3,986	363	10%
New York	21,863	23,614	1,751	8%
Orange	10,092	14,062	3,970	39%
Queens	10,980	13,084	2,104	19%
Richmond	2,847	3,152	305	11%
Suffolk	13,128	13,793	665	5%
Tryon	included in	15,057	—	—
(Montgomery)	Albany			
Ulster	13,950	22,143	8,193	58%
Westchester	21,745	20,554	-1,191	-5%
TOTALS	168,007	238,897	70,890	42%

From Evarts B. Greene and Virginia D. Harrington,
American Population Before the Federal Census of 1790
(New York: Columbia University Press, 1932), 102–104.

ducted there during the war. The data are less clear for African Americans, but their numbers probably increased from over 19,000 in 1770, to approximately 21,000 in 1780, and over 25,000 in 1790 (21,193 of whom were slaves).

With this tremendous rise in population came dynamic social and economic change: Native Americans forcefully pushed westward; a more heterogeneous population of Europeans; new settlements founded; more land cultivated; the development of new markets; and increased production of foods, raw materials, and semifinished products, including flour and lumber dressed for use. This period also witnessed the relative decline of traditional Protestant religions, including Anglican/Episcopal and Presbyterian, and the relative increase in importance of such Protestant denominations as the Baptists and Methodists. The Dutch churches slowly atrophied, as use of the Dutch language declined, and these people became more culturally American.

The Revolution also opened political opportunities to a broader segment of the state's population. From the outset the Patriots had needed manpower to defend the state, to fill the ranks of the militia and state regiments, and to assume local and state offices. Even before the first state elections were held in 1777, the many district, town, and county committees had already become de facto local governments, and the Provincial Congresses the effective provincial authority. The old colonial elite was manifestly incapable of satisfying this need for new civil and military officeholders; not only was the group too small, but some had become Loyalists. Thus, with a myriad of new offices to fill, Patriots had to recruit new people, people who had never before enjoyed political power. Ambitious middle-class men seized the opportunity by serving in the officer corps, running for office, or accepting appointive positions. The increased popular participation in government understandably created political and social tensions in the state, for the old gentry was forced to share and sometimes to surrender political power. The change was irreversible.[1]

Although property qualifications for voting and office holding remained, the tendency was for a widened distribution of property among white male New Yorkers and thus an expanded electorate.[2] After the Treaty of Fort Stanwix (1784), New York State opened to white settlers frontier territory in Tryon County that had belonged to the generally pro-British Iroquois nations. As Native Americans moved into Canada, the state encouraged the westward movement of white settlement toward Niagara.[3] In addition, some confiscated or forfeited Loyalist properties also passed into the hands of small farmers and lower-class Americans, especially in Dutchess and Westchester Counties. New York State generally gave the tenants on confiscated Loyalist estates the opportunity to buy the property they had farmed before the war. However, because the state government desperately needed money for the war effort and postwar reconstruction, Loyalist property throughout the state tended to be purchased by Patriots who could pay for it. For example, in Suffolk County, seven men— John Lloyd II, Benjamin Floyd, Benjamin Tallmadge, Joseph Brewster, Caleb Brewster, Mills Philips, and Nathaniel Norton—purchased the property that the state had confiscated from four county Loyalists.[4]

White males shared in this democratization of power, but not women or African Americans. The war did give many women a chance to participate in the struggle. Their participation in the boycotts opposing parliamentary legislation was noteworthy. They also used their social and economic power to resist price gouging in the marketplace. They demonstrated and participated in riots to stop some profiteering Patriot merchants from driving up prices during shortages. However, after the peace treaty, these activists typically returned to their homes and did not remain an active political force.

The Revolution did bring about a gradual end to slavery in the state, even though the institution had been widespread and economically significant in colonial New York. Not only did many African Americans take advantage of the wartime situation to gain their freedom, but the ideological and intellectual underpinnings of the Revolution also led many European Americans to conclude that abolition was necessary. Manumission became common among whites in many parts of the state but especially among the small-scale farmers of Long Island. Nonetheless, farmers in the mid-Hudson Valley consistently resisted the passage of legislation designed to end slavery gradually in New York State. Although the reasons for the difference between Long Island and the mid-

Hudson Valley are not clear, it is already possible to see in the latter area the beginning of what later became a common tendency. Leaders in the fight for increased white suffrage, white landholding, and white political participation tended to oppose the manumission of slaves, civil rights for free blacks, and expanded rights for women. Advocates for these reforms were often influential persons, new aristocrats, gentry, or intellectuals, including Gov. George Clinton, John Jay, and Alexander Hamilton.

Thus did the Revolution seriously affect *The Other New York*. At the outset, many Americans in the rural counties had interpreted the Revolution in terms of their own local perspectives and interests. In consequence, the imperial issues that divided the British Empire were, for many New Yorkers, intimately connected to issues (and conflicts) within their own towns, cities, and counties. To put it another way, between 1774 and 1776, many residents perceived imperial problems as local problems, writ large. Nonetheless, by 1790, the Revolution had already changed New Yorkers in a number of ways that made them more alike. For example, new political leaders, from different social classes, had emerged to govern New York; religious freedom had been extended; new economic enterprises had been started; and the institution of slavery had been put on the road toward legal extinction. Hence, although New Yorkers from the various regions had initially understood the Revolution in different ways because their perspectives had been shaped by their particular circumstances, the event itself was a unifying force that led them to create a new state that was more open, free, and republican than colonial New York had been. There was not as much freedom and liberty as the Declaration of Independence had promised, but a solid start had been made.

Notes

1. Thomas Jones dismissed the Albany County Whig Committee that was harassing Sir John Johnson as "a set of common fellows . . . , a pack as much below him, as they were themselves superior to the wolves that prowled the woods." Thomas Jones, *History of New York in the Revolutionary War and of the Leading Events in the Other Colonies at that Period*, ed. Edward Floyd De Lancey, 2 vols. (New York, 1879), 2: 74.

2. The Constitution of 1777 gave the vote for the governorship and the State Senate to adult freemen who had property worth at least £100 and for the Assembly to those who had the right of freemanship in New York City or Albany, owned a freehold valued at £20 or more, or had a leasehold with a yearly rent of at least £40 shillings; see Joseph S. Tiedemann, *Reluctant Revolutionaries: New York City and the Road to Independence* (Ithaca, 1997), 252.

3. Wilcomb E. Washburn, *The Indian in America* (New York, 1975), 158–159; Colin G. Calloway, *The American Revolution in Indian Country: Crisis and Diversity in Native American Communities* (Cambridge, Eng., 1995), 282–283.

4. For the situation in Queens County, see Joseph S. Tiedemann, "Response to Revolution: Queens County during the Era of the American Revolution" (Ph.D. diss., City University of New York, 1977), 215. Also see Harry B. Yoshpe, *Disposition of Loyalist Estates in the Southern District of the State of New York* (New York, 1939).

Contributors

Stefan Bielenski, Project Director, *Colonial Albany Social History Project*, New York State Education Department, has authored *Abraham Yates, Jr. and the New Political Order in Revolutionary New York* (1975); *A Loyalist Odyssey: The Ordeal of Frederick Philipse* (1976); *Government by the People: The Story of the Dongan Charter and the Birth of Participatory Democracy in the City of Albany* (1986); and *The People of Colonial Albany: A Community History Project* (annual edition, 1984-present).

Edwin G. Burrows is Distinguished Professor of History at Brooklyn College, City University of New York. He is the coauthor of *Gotham: A History of New York City to 1898* (Oxford), winner of the Pulitzer Prize for History in 1999. He is currently writing a book about prisoners of war in New York during the American Revolution.

Eugene R. Fingerhut, Professor Emeritus of History, California State University, Los Angeles, has authored *Survivor: Cadwallader Colden II in Revolutionary America* (1983); "Uses and Abuses of the American Loyalists' Claims: A Critique of Quantitative Analyses," *The William and Mary Quarterly*, 3rd series, 25: 245–58; "Loyalists" in Richard L. Blanco, ed. *The American Revolution, 1775–1783: An Encyclopedia* (New York, 1993), 1: 963–72.

Paul R. Huey earned his Ph.D. in American Civilization from the University of Pennsylvania. He is currently employed as a scientist (archeology) with the Bureau of Historic Sites, New York State Office of Parks, Recreation & Historic Preservation, Peebles Island. He has published numerous articles on Charlotte County, New York.

Jacob Judd, Professor Emeritus of History, Herbert H. Lehman College and The Graduate School and University Center of The City University of New York, is the author of *Colonial America: A Basic History* (1998) and the editor of *The Van Cortlandt Family of Cortlandt Manor*, 4 vols. (1976–1986). He has authored numerous articles on early New York history.

Phillip Papas, a native Staten Islander, received his B.A. and M.A. from Hunter College, and his Ph.D. from The Graduate School and University Center of The City University of New York. He teaches History at Union County College in Cranford, New Jersey.

John G. Staudt teaches at Hofstra University and Kellenberg Memorial High School in Uniondale, New York. Before his teaching career, he served as a paratrooper in the United States Army. He has published numerous articles and reviews, and has lectured extensively on topics relating to Long Island history and the American Revolution. He is completing a social history of Suffolk County, Long Island, 1640–1800.

Joseph S. Tiedemann, Professor of History at Loyola Marymount University in Los Angeles, is the author of *Reluctant Revolutionaries: New York City and the Road to Independence, 1763–1776* (1997). His articles on New York history have appeared in the *Historical Magazine of the Protestant Episcopal Church*, *Journal of American History*, *Journal of Social History*, *New York History*, and *William and Mary Quarterly*.

Robert W. Venables (Ph.D. American History, Vanderbilt University, 1967) teaches two large lecture courses in the Department of Landscape Architecture, Cornell University: "The Symbols of New York State's Cultural Landscape" and "American Indian Environments." He coedited *American Indian Environments* (1980). His other publications include chapters in *Exiled in the Land of the Free* (1992); *New York in the 21st Century* (1999); and *The Treaty of Canandaigua* (2000).

Thomas S. Wermuth, Associate Professor of History at Marist College, is the author of *Rip Van Wink's Neighbors: The Transformation of Rural Society in the Hudson River Valley, 1720–1850* (2000). His articles have appeared in *Business and Economic History, Hudson Valley Regional Review*, and *Journal of Social History*.

Index

A.B.C., 7
Act for the Gradual Abolition of Slavery
  (N.Y.), 75
Act of Attainder of 1779 (N.Y.). *See*
  Forfeiture Act of 1779
Adgate, Matthew, 162
Adirondack Mountains, 134, 156, 211,
  214; eastern, 199; southern, 209
African Americans, 83, 96, 128, 144,
  165; Albany Co., 156, 165; central
  Hudson Valley, 143; Loyalists, 93;
  New York State, 12, 226, 227, 228;
  Westchester Co., 108
Akwesasne, N.Y. (or St. Regis), 187
Albany County, N.Y., 155–68, 202,
  207–12 passim; allegiance in, 159–63
  passim; eastern, 162; northern, 162,
  199, 200, 225; population, 10; and
  Revolution, 10, 11, 223, 224, 225,
  226; rural districts, 159, 163;
  southern, 163
Albany Gazette, 157
Albany, N.Y. (city), 55; and central
  Hudson Valley, 134, 139; and
  Charlotte Co., 199, 202, 210, 212,
  223; in Revolution, 4, 7, 9, 10; in
  Revolutionnary Albany County,
  165–68; and Tryon Co., 179, 182–89
  passim; and Westchester Co., 108,
  110, 116
Alexander, William. *See* Stirling, Lord
Allen family, 9
Allen, Ethan, 9; in Charlotte Co., 202–13
  passim
Allen, Ira, 213
Alsop, John, 113

Amberman, Paul, 51, 52
American Board of Customs at Boston
  (Britain), 8
Amherst, Jeffery, 201
Amicus Republicae, 209
André, John, 107, 120, 135
Anglican Church, 224, 225, 227; Albany
  Co., 163; American bishop, 112;
  Bishop of London, 112; Queens Co.,
  44, 45; Richmond Co., 84; Suffolk
  Co., 71; Westchester Co., 108, 111
Anglicans, 199, 205, 206, 207;
  Richmond Co., 84, 85; Queens Co., 9,
  44, 45, 49; Westchester Co., 111, 112
anti-Tory legislation (N.Y.), 55, 56, 72,
  96, 112, 122
Appalachian Mountains, 5
Arbuthnot, Marriot, 70
Argyle Patent, N.Y., 201, 202, 205, 214
Arnold, Benedict, 107, 120, 121, 135,
  206, 210
Arthur Kill (or creek), 83
Articles of Union (Vt.), 211–13 passim
Artillery Patent, N.Y., 201, 214
Asia (British warship), 48, 49, 87
Association (Ulster Co.), 137
Austin, John W., 117
Avery, Ephraim, 112
Axtell, William, 23, 27, 31, 33, 34

Baker, Remember, 202, 205, 207
Ballstown, N.Y., 156, 160, 166
Bancker, Adrian, 88, 92
Bancker, Evert, 88
Bancker family, 96
Baptist Church, 204, 214

233

Charleston, S.C., 25, 89, 93
Charlotte County, N.Y., 199–215, 226,
    227; allegiance in, 200, 204, 205, 206;
    mentioned, 9, 87, 155, 179
Charlton, Richard, 86
Chatfield, John, 70
Chatterton's Hill, N.Y., 117
Cherry Valley, N.Y., 181, 190
Church of England. *See* Anglican
    Church
Clark, Ebenezer, 206
Clark, Thomas, 201, 206, 214
Clarkson, David, 27
Claus, Daniel, 182, 185, 186, 189
Clinton County, N.Y., 199, 208
Clinton, George (Britain), 200
Clinton, George (N.Y.), 4; Albany (city),
    163; central Hudson Valley, 128,
    132–34 passim, 144, 148; Elizabeth
    Irvine, 190; John Williams, 206;
    Queens Co., 56, 57; slavery, 229;
    Vermont, 210, 211; Westchester Co.,
    115, 122–24
Clinton, Henry, 28, 53, 93; André, 120,
    121; Battle of Long Island, 25, 28–32
    passim; British navy, 70; Burgoyne
    campaign, 134, 135, 225; and
    Vermont, 209, 213
Clinton, James, 190
Cochran, Robert, 202, 204, 207, 213
Coercive Acts. *See* Intolerable Acts
Colchester, Conn., 202
Colden, Alexander, 201
Colden, Cadwallader, 132; Charlotte
    Co., 200, 201; Queens Co., 48
Colden, Cadwallader, Jr., 132
Colden, David, 48
Colden family, 131
Committee of Sixty (N.Y.C.), 85, 86
Committees of Correspondence: Albany
    Co., 157–65 passim, 188;
    Brookhaven, N.Y., 66; Flushing, N.Y.,
    46; Jamaica, N.Y., 46; New York City,
    46 113; Newtown, N.Y., 46; Queens
    Co., 48; Suffolk Co., 65; Tryon Co.,
    183–89 passim

Committees of Observation (N.J.):
    Elizabethtown, 86, 89; Woodbridge,
    86
Committees of Safety: Albany Co., 158;
    Brookhaven, N.Y., 66; central Hudson
    Valley, 135, 136, 137, 138, 148;
    Dutchess Co., 138; Huntington, N.Y.,
    66, 67; Kinderhook, N.Y., 160;
    Kingston, N.Y., 129, 136, 137, 140;
    Mohawk District, 184; New Windsor,
    N.Y., 132, 138, 139; New York City,
    87, 88; New York State, 115, 118,
    189; Poughkeepsie, N.Y., 139;
    Richmond Co., 88, 89, 91, 95;
    Schenectady, N.Y., 158; Suffolk Co.,
    67, 73; Ulster Co., 131, 132, 137, 138,
    146; Westchester Co., 115, 118
Common Council (Albany), 163
Common Sense, 123
Coney Island, N.Y., 34
Confiscation Act of 1784 (N.Y.), 123
Confiscation of Loyalist property, 228;
    Albany Co., 160, 164; central Hudson
    Valley, 130, 141; Dutchess Co., 143,
    148; Charlotte Co., 208, 209, 214;
    Kings Co., 33, 34; Queens Co., 55,
    56; Richmond Co., 96; Suffolk Co.,
    69, 72; Westchester, 122
Congregational Church: Westchester Co.,
    108
Congregationalists, 199; Suffolk Co., 74
Connecticut, 90, 91, 145; and Albany
    Co., 161; and Charlotte Co., 200–207
    passim; eastern, 205, 206, 225; and
    Kings Co., 25, 27, 31, 33;
    northeastern, 206; southwestern, 200,
    206; and Suffolk Co., 63–73 passim;
    and Tryon Co., 181, 191; and
    Westchester Co., 108, 109, 118, 121;
    western, 205, 206; western boundary,
    203
Connecticut Assembly, 69
Connecticut Valley, 9
Conner, Richard, 86, 89
Continental Association, 8; central
    Hudson Valley, 137; Charlotte Co.,